Cycling France

Cycling France

The Best Bike Tours in All of Gaul

_____ Jerry H. Simpson, Jr.

Bicycle Books – San Francisco

copyright © 1992, Jerry H. Simpson, Jr.

First printing, 1992
Printed in the United States of America

Published by Bicycle Books, Inc., PO Box 2038, Mill Valley, CA
94942 (USA)

Distributed to the book trade by:
USA: National Book Network, Lanham, MD
Canada: Raincoast Book Distr. Vancouver, BC
UK: Chris Lloyd Sales and Services, Poole, Dorset

Cover design: Kent Lytle, Lytle Design
Cover photo: The Image Bank

Maps: Meridian Mapping, Oakland, CA

All photographs by the author, except where credited otherwise

Publisher's Cataloging in Publication Data:
Simpson, Jerry H, Jr., date
Cycling France, The Best Bike Tours in All of Gaul
Series Title: The Active Travel Series
Bibliography: p.
Includes index
1. Travel, guidebooks and manuals
2. France, guidebooks and manuals
3. Bicycles and Cycling, guidebooks and manuals
4. Authorship
I. Title
Library of Congress Catalog Card No. 91-77705
ISBN 0-933201-47-8 Paperback original

Dedicated to Janie,
but for whom neither this book
nor Bike Tour France would exist.

Jerry H. Simpson, Jr. is the founder and director of Bike Tour France, an organization that specializes in designing and arranging bicycle tours in France for Americans. A former professional soldier, he later became a writer for newspapers and magazines. This took him back to France to live (for the third time) in 1972, a sojourn that culminated in his first bicycle tour, a 720-mile trip from Mirebeau southward across the Pyrénées to Spain and back—on a single-speed bicycle.

Nearly three years of research (checking out roads, restaurants, and hotels) preceded his first full-blown 'commercial' tour. Since then, he has led nearly 40 tours and cycled solo on road-research trips for a total of more than 20,000 miles. In addition, he has designed dozens of self-guided tours for individual clients.

For four years, he taught a college-level wine appreciation course, a subject in which he became interested while living in France. In the off-season, he works as a translator of books, stories, and articles.

His wife Janie works as an advertising copywriter and is also a cyclist who has accompanied him on three tours, including that first one across the Pyrénées.

Both Simpsons are collectors of paintings. They live amongst a clutter of books, bicycles, and assorted art objects, along with a cat named after the notorious French gangster Jacques Mesrine.

They may have been nine or ten years old, the two boys who were taking turns coasting down Lyndhurst Hill on the blue bicycle. Although it wasn't hot yet, the slow drone of cicadas confirmed the presence of summer. It was June 1932; I was six. I didn't know these boys. I sat on the curb with my elbows on my knees, my chin in my hands, and watched them roll down the half-mile hill and disappear into the curve.

After they had taken several turns apiece, coasting down, pedaling part of the way back but finally walking when the slope got too steep, one of them asked me, "Would you like to try it?"

I nodded and stood up. It was a beautiful bicycle. The frame was the color of a robin's egg. The wheels had wooden rims, probably made of ash, sanded smooth and varnished. The handlebar grips were wooden, too, and rounded at the ends. It did not have balloon tires: those would come later. But these tires had white sidewalls and looked elegant indeed.

One of the boys held the bike up while the other showed me how to get on it. When I sat on the saddle, my toes barely reached the rubber pedals.

"When you want to slow down and stop, push backward on the pedal," one of the boys said. I wasn't sure what he meant.

They gave me a little shove to get me started, and down I went. I seemed to be flying, but I wasn't frightened. I felt a sense of transcendent elation, of exaltation. I had never before felt such overwhelming joy. It was to be many years before I would experience it again.

In 1972, I was working in France, living in a small town called Mirebeau, 30 km north of Poitiers and 46 km south of the Loire. I had lived in France twice before, but this was my wife's first time there. Six weeks before our scheduled return to the States, Janie said she wished she could see more of the country.

A reasonable suggestion. "Shall we take a train trip?" I asked.

"No, that's too fast. You can't see anything," she said.

"Do you want to rent a car again?" We'd done that when we'd first arrived. I rented a car in Paris and we drove to Bordeaux and the Médoc; I wanted her to taste wine in the *chais* of the great *châteaux*.

"That's such a hassle," she said. "Driving through narrow streets, trying to find a place to park...."

True, but I couldn't think of much else.

"Do you want to hike?" I asked.

"We woudn't see much that way," she said.

"Well, what do you suggest?"

"Why don't we buy some bicycles and ride them down to Spain and back?" she said.

I was 46 at the time; I had not been on a bicycle since I was 14. But I remembered that distances had never daunted me then; her idea sounded perfectly plausible. Why not? As the crow flies, the Spanish frontier was about 300 miles south of us. I'd never crossed a mountain on a bicycle before, but surely it couldn't be terribly difficult....

We took a bus to Poitiers and shopped around for bicycles. I knew nothing about 'ten-speeds.' Besides, they looked too fragile and complicated. I wanted something like I'd had as a child. We finally found them: upright frames, plastic saddles, rubber pedals and handlebar grips, oversize tires, and bells one pushed with the thumb.

A village nestled in the Pyrénées.

We also bought lightweight sleeping bags. We planned to camp out to make it more of an adventure. We didn't know about bungee cords and water bottles. We lashed the sleeping bags to the luggage racks with nylon cord, and stopped at every wayside tavern for an Orangina on our 30-km ride back to Mirebeau.

We made a list of items to take; Sir John Hunt's list for the 1953 assault on Mount Everest could hardly have been longer. We didn't know about panniers either; we stuffed the gear into duffle bags, then the sleeping bags on top of that, all of it lashed to the rack with nylon cord.

We left Mirebeau on Thursday, 17 August, 1972. At 6:20 p.m. Friday, 25 August, after riding overloaded one-speed bikes for 382 miles, we reached the Roncevalles Pass in Spain. From Arneguy on the border, we had climbed 13.25 miles in rain and fog on poorly paved switchback roads, but we had made it. We got off the bikes and inhaled the cold, damp mountain air. My legs ached, my lungs were burning, but I had made it. For a moment, I felt like Sir Edmund Hillary.

No … that wasn't it. I felt like the child I once was, forty years before—exuberant, free, coasting down Lyndhurst Hill. Joy welled up in my throat. At that moment, I knew this was what I wanted to do for the rest of my life: ride a bicycle in France.

That was twenty years ago. I've learned a lot about cycling since then, but that's how it started: in 1932 on Lyndhurst Hill; in 1972 on the Pyrénées Mountains in France and Spain.

Apart from Janie herself, who suggested it, cycling has been the most wonderful thing in my life. I hope this book may help make it like that for others.

Table of Contents

Part I – General Information

CHAPTER 1

Why France?

Compared with Canada, China, Australia, Brazil, Russia, or the United States, France is a very small country. It is only four-fifths the size of Texas. Yet it has four major mountain ranges: the Alps, the Pyrénées, the Vosges, and the Jura; seven major rivers: the Loire, the Rhône, the Seine, the Marne, the Dordogne, the Garonne, and the Vienne; a vast forest: the Landes, and a vast marshland: the Camargue.

It has water on the north (the English Channel), the west (the Bay of Biscay), and the south (the Mediterranean Sea). It shares borders with seven countries: Belgium, Luxembourg, Germany, Switzerland, Italy, Spain, and the principality of Monaco.

Although the entire country is more northerly than New York City (Paris is closer to the North Pole than Montreal, Canada), the climate is so mild that palm and citrus trees

Chinon's castle dates back to the early Middle Ages.

flourish. French is the national language, of course, but four other distinct languages are spoken on mainland France: Breton (akin to Gaelic), Alsatian (akin to German), Provençal (akin to French), and Basque, which is kin to no other language on earth.

It produces ten distinct types of wine (several of which rank as the best in the world), more than 350 kinds of cheese including the incomparable Roquefort and Brie, and is unequaled for its culinary excellence. Its Renaissance châteaux are without rival for their architectural splendor, and its Gothic cathedrals are awesomely inspiring. No other country in Europe — or elsewhere — can approach France for sheer variety or superlatives. But it is yet another distinction that attracts thousands of cyclists to France each year: 450,000 miles of secondary roads unmatched for their sublime scenery and tranquility.

During the 1930's, when the Great Depression caused unemployment worldwide, France initiated a program of road building to link farms to villages and villages to towns. These small ribbons of pavement wound their way through vineyards, meadows, forests and farms. Many of them were so narrow that two cars could not pass. No matter: there were few cars in the Thirties and those few were concentrated in cities. World War II and German occupation, plus a shortage of fuel, severely restricted traffic for five years. After the war, the liberated French clamored for new highways. Main roads were improved and a system of *autoroutes* (comparable to US Interstates) was constructed.

Consequently, the incredible network of country lanes built during the thirties was spared the sort of usage that results in broken pavement, potholes, billboards, and service stations — the ugliness and distractions that make cycling unpleasant in much of America. As a result, these lovely little roads are ideal for cycling.

Another appealing fact is the courtesy of French motorists, even the drivers of semi tractor-trailer rigs, toward bicyclists. In France, cycling is a major sport — the annual three-week Tour de France is the greatest single sports event in the world — but it is also a major form of daily transportation. Elderly farm wives pedal their forty-pound soft-tired antique bikes to the villages every day to do their shopping. Businessmen with briefcases pedal to work in urban traffic. Millions of children ride their bikes to school each day. Consequently, motorists are accustomed to sharing the road with cyclists.

Moreover, the French national traffic laws (there is only one set of laws for the entire country rather than fifty different sets as in the United States) specify the rights and obligations of cyclists. Every motorist in France must know these laws in order to obtain a license. Cyclists are not licensed, but they grow up knowing these laws. Thus the cyclist knows what to expect of the motorist; the motorist knows what to expect of the cyclist; and the two forms of conveyance share the city streets and country roads with no antagonism or harassment.

Further, cycling is a recreational activity on a much larger scale than it is in the United States. Almost every city and town in France has a cycling club; Blois, a typical city with a population of slightly more than 50,000, has two such clubs, each with more than a hundred members. The Pyrénées bike club has more than 3,000 members. These clubs sponsor dozens of regional races throughout France every Sunday from late spring through early autumn, and club members, in matching outfits, go on outings two or three times a month. Children learn to ride a tiny bicycle as soon as they learn to walk, and men in their mid-eighties ride their bikes every day as a matter of course. Cycling in France is as normal as drinking wine or breathing air.

French good humor brightens the café atmosphere.

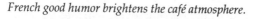

All of these factors together — geography, scenery, safety and serenity — plus a multiplicity of attractions such as castles, abbeys and cathedrals, not to mention vineyards, forests, and secluded villages with their convivial cafés, make France far and away the best country in the world for cycling.

But there is yet another attraction: the friendliness of the French people. Many Americans have heard horror stories of French rudeness, especially toward Americans. To the extent that these stories have some basis in fact, the rudeness is in reaction to a minority of American tourists who behave abominably abroad. They flaunt their wealth, they drink too much, they talk too loud, they complain about everything, and are, in every way possible, obnoxious.

If the foreign visitor approaches the French with courtesy and friendliness, he will not find anywhere a warmer and more generous reception than in France. The French are a naturally convivial people. That's why they have so many cafés and spend so much of their time in them. That's why strangers share tables in restaurants — something never done in the United States. To the civilized visitor, the French are the most hospitable hosts one can find anywhere.

If you go to France with a positive attitude, prepared to like the people, their culture, their customs, they will sense this and reciprocate. This, in turn, will make you like them all the more. They will sense this, too, and become even warmer in their hospitality. Soon, it's a mutual love affair.

Because of the varied geography, the cyclist has a wide choice of terrains. Some areas of France are more suitable to cycling than others. Some are ideal for the easy-going rider or for families with young children. Others are challenging even to the strongest and most experienced cyclist. All of these are easily accessible by train. (The French railway system is one more superlative: the best in the world.)

The climate, though never precisely predictable, varies with both the region and the season. Cycling is feasible in France from early April through late October. Geography and climate will be discussed in detail in a separate chapter. The point I wish to make here is that the vacationing cyclist has an incredibly wide range of choices as to terrain and time of year.

All of this taken together helps explain why thousands of American cyclists find France the best country in the world for biking — and not only Americans: You'll find bike touring enthusiasts there from all over the world.

CHAPTER 2

Preparation: Selecting the Area and the Time

Selecting the area of France in which to cycle should be governed by several considerations:

☐ What are your interests? Do you want to see great cathedrals — or some particular cathedral? Do you want to see the splendor of the Renaissance châteaux? Are you interested in sampling French cuisine and wines? Are you a history buff? Do you want to immerse yourself in the slow rhythms of daily life in rural France?

☐ What kind of cyclist are you? Do you want rides that are challenging for their demands on your physical stamina and cycling skills, or do you prefer to take it easy and simply enjoy the scenery? Scenery, by the way, can be lovely in the flat areas, but is more spectacular in the high-hill country and in the mountains.

Taking a break, two cyclists enjoy the spectacular view.

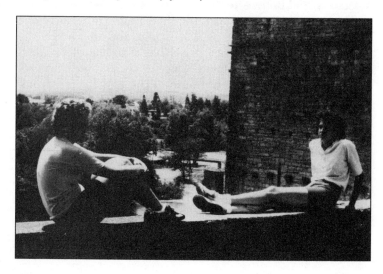

☐ When do you want to go? Take into consideration not only the seasonal differences, but also summer vacations and religious holidays.

In the spring, you can see vast fields covered with bright yellow. These are fields of mustard plants. You'll also see meadows covered with crimson poppies. These are not opium poppies, of course. They are the poppies portrayed in Impressionist paintings. It is also the time of year when the vineyards flower.

In the autumn, the chestnuts ripen and fall (France has edible chestnuts); the leaves are turning red and gold; meadows are awash in wild flowers; and depending on how the summer has been—hot and dry or rainy and cool—late September and most of October are the wine-harvest season. This is a particularly happy time to be in a country where wine is a part of daily life and integral to religion as well. It is a familiar creature, but has about it a mystical aura also. Wine graces every peasant's table at every meal—even including breakfast. It is also, however, an essential part of the most solemn of religious sacraments.

Summertime is the least desirable time to be in France simply because it is so crowded with tourists. August is the worst month of all because this is French national vacation month when approximately 75% of the population is on vacation. It is almost impossible to find a room in the small, desirable hotels; people are elbow to elbow in the châteaux and museums; and in the afternoons, the roads are dangerous.

On vacation, the French indulge in wine and other alcoholic beverages more than they usually would, and after lunch, the normally cautious and courteous driver is transformed into a racer competing at Le Mans. The police know this and patrol the national routes and autoroutes. (The penalty for drunk driving in France is severe.) But the drivers know the police know this, so they take to the secondary roads to test their racing skills. The police can't be everywhere, so the back roads become especially dangerous during the afternoons of August.

Account must also be taken of religious holidays. France is, nominally at least, a Catholic country, and shuts down for many religious days that go by unnoticed in the United States, such as Ascension Day, Pentecost, etc. Banks and stores close, and restaurants are jammed.

In selecting a geographical area, a knowledge of the terrain and the weather conditions is important. Provence is beautiful because it is hilly and, in some parts, mountainous. The underlying stone there is granite, which is hard to cut. This makes road building expensive, so there is not the plethora of secondary roads from which to select a route you will find in other parts of France. This means riding in traffic, often quite heavy.

Because of its scenic beauty, Provence has long been popular with wealthy persons from all over the world. They have their villas there, summer homes or 'second' homes, or they go there on vacation. Thus, prices at hotels and restaurants are apt to be higher there than in other areas of France.

Northeast France, the area known as Picardy, is largely industrial. Consequently, it lacks the charm of some of the other areas. Eastern France is wine country, but very hilly and, in some parts, mountainous. It is the region in which are found the vineyards of Chablis (very hilly), Champagne (hilly), Alsace (mountainous), Arbois (hilly-to-mountainous), Burgundy (hilly), Beaujolais (hilly), and Côtes du Rhône (very hilly).

The backroads of Burgundy and the Beaujolais are attractive and are within the abilities of any good cyclist. The same is true of Champagne—the area around Reims and Épernay. The town of Beaune is especially colorful; the cathedral of

A vinyard in the Jura mountains. Photo courtesy Henri Maire.

Reims is one of the six greatest in France (which has 140 cathedrals). The area is easily accessible by trains to Reims, to Dijon, and to Lyon.

The Auvergne is high-hill country. It is also one of the poorest regions of France—with the result that hotels and restaurants here are bargains. The villages have a sad drabness about them, but, on the other hand, provide a glimpse of authentic antiquity. There hasn't been much 'fixing up.' The region is famous for its folk songs which have a wistful, haunting quality. The region is accessible by trains to Clermont-Ferrand.

Southern France, which includes Orange, Avignon, Pont du Gard, Arles, and Nîmes, is extremely hilly around these famous old cities that date back to Roman times, but just to the south is the vast marshland called the Camargue, which is bounded roughly by Montpellier on the west, Arles on the north and Marseilles on the east. This area is pancake-flat and includes the colorful Mediterranean Sea resort town of Les Saintes-Maries-de-la-Mer. It is accessible by trains to Avignon, Nîmes, and Montpellier.

Normandy is famous for its apple orchards and dairy cattle. It produces vast quantities of apple cider, much of which is 'sparkling' and most of which is alcoholic. From cider is made the apple brandy called Calvados, known in bars as 'calva.' Cheap 'calva' is a fiery potion. A fine old Calvados long aged in oak barrels is as smooth as velvet and is often more expensive than the finest Cognacs. The cuisine of the region derives from its production of butter and cream (anything served with the appendage *Normande* or *à la Normande* means with a thick sauce made with heavy cream and calvados) and is very rich in fat, calories, and cholesterol. Consequently, it is delicious. (Almost everything that's 'bad for you' tastes wonderful.)

Among the attractions are Rouen, of whose cathedral Claude Monet made two dozen paintings to show the subtle changes of light at various times of day, and Deauville, once the most fashionable beach resort in France and immortalized in the writings of Marcel Proust and the paintings of various Impressionists including Monet.

The disadvantages of Normandy are that it is wet, windy, and often cold. This is why the beverage here is apple cider instead of wine: grapes require warm weather and sunshine. Apples will flourish in cool, rainy weather (Washington State in the United States produces apples for the same reason). It is also hilly. It is accessible by trains to Caen, Deauville and Rouen. (Rouen was the capital of the ancient Duchy of Normandy.)

Brittany juts out into the Atlantic and is the western-most part of France. The Bretons are of Celtic origin and have a language of their own, akin to the Gaelic of Ireland and Wales. From time to time, the Bretons try to secede from France, and a Breton 'patriot' blew up part of Versailles not too long ago. Its climate is even wetter, colder, and windier than that of Normandy. It is also quite hilly.

Le Mont St. Michel is the principal tourist attraction and is on the north coast of Brittany. However, the best cycling is on the southern coast. Brittany produces enormous quantities of seafood, and its fishing towns and villages are quite colorful, even in the rain. Its culture and heritage set it apart from the rest of France; its architecture reflects this as well. But the differences in architectural styles derive also from the hardness of the stone found in Brittany. It is accessible by trains to Brest, Quimper, and Vannes. Anyone planning to cycle there should take the train to the far western end, then ride back eastward in order to take advantage of the prevailing winds.

Western France includes two areas that are totally flat: the Marais Poitevin that fans out eastward from La Rochelle, and the Landes south of Bordeaux. The Marais was once mostly under water. Dutch engineers were brought to France by Henri IV to supervise construction of canals to drain the area. This feat of engineering produced an incredible network of canals which in turn gave rise to a different way of life, one of isolation rather than clusters of villages, and the use of flat-bottomed punts for transportation. Cattle are raised on the rectangular tree-shaded islands formed by the canals and are tranported in these same flat-bottomed boats which are poled along rather than rowed.

The coast includes the colorful harbor of La Rochelle and the seaside resort of Les Sables d'Olonne. Nearby are the towns of Marennes, the source of one of France's most famous breed of oysters; Saintes, with its ancient Roman arena; and Niort, a castle and cathedral town (Eleanor of Aquitaine often resided in the castle here; it is now a museum of history) with an attractive museum of fine art. Niort is the insurance capital of France and is a city of spacious parks and beautiful buildings. The area is accessible by trains to Poitiers, Niort, and La Rochelle.

Southwestern France includes the Landes, the other coastal area that is flat, and every other sort of terrain as well. The 'corridor' southwestward from Poitiers embraces the regions that produce Cognac and Armagnac; the Bordeaux wine areas such as Pomerol, St. Emilion, the Médoc, Graves, Barsac, and Sauternes; the Arcachon oyster beds; the resort of Biarritz; part of the Dordogne, the area that produces the famous Bayonne cured hams; the French Basque country, and the Pyrénées that form the natural frontier between France and Spain.

The Landes is an enormous flat pine forest that extends south from Bordeaux to Bayonne and Biarritz. The roads are so straight for so far that when the occasional car passes you, you eventually lose sight of it because it diminishes to an invisible speck. Riding these roads can be hypnotically beautiful or unbearably boring, depending on your perceptions and personality. On the coast of the Landes (much of which is a national park) are seaside resorts such as Vieux Boucau.

The weather in this area is completely unpredictable. Any given summer month can be showery and warm, rainy and frigid, or dry and hot. The region is accessible by trains to Poitiers, Angoulême, Liborne, Bordeaux, Mont-de-Marsan, Dax, Bayonne-Biarritz, and also to Tarbes and Lourdes—depending on one's interests.

The Loire Valley—which includes the tributaries of that famous river, such as the Loir (without the final 'e'), the Cher, the Indre, and the Vienne—offers the greatest selection of secondary roads of any region in France and also some of the finest scenery. It has the mildest climate of any inland region, and is the area in which the kings of France resided when they had a choice. For this reason, it is the 'château country' of France. Here are all the famous names: Chambord, Beaugency, Cheverny, Amboise, Chenonceaux, Azay-le-Rideau, Blois, Ussé, Loches, Chaumont, Langeais, Villandry, Saumur, Angers, and a host of others.

It is also wine country, producing the white wines of Vouvray and Saumur, the red wines of Chinon, Bourgeuil and Champigny, along with many other *appellations contrôlées*.

Although the Loire itself is the longest river in France—626 miles—and makes a great arc across central France from the eastern mountains to the Atlantic Ocean, the area called the Loire Valley can be roughly defined as a trapezoid with the castle town of Châteaudun on the Loir, in the northern corner; the cathedral town of Orléans in the eastern corner; Poitiers, a cathedral town on the Clain River and ancient seat of the Dukes of Aquitaine in the southern corner; and with Angers, the ancient capital of Anjou whence came the Plantagenet Dynasty of kings of England, in the western corner. The city of Tours is the largest city in the Loire Valley, with its fine cathedral, ancient abbey, and variety of museums—including a museum of master craftsmanship that is unique in France—and a university that attracts students from all over the world to its famous school of music.

'The Valley' also includes the castle town of Chinon on the Vienne, where Joan of Arc first met the Dauphin who would be crowned Charles VII of France after Joan led his faltering armies to victory over the English and raised the seige of Orléans. It also includes Vendôme, a charming town filled with flowers and built on islands in the Loir.

The principal stone in this area is limestone that is so soft you can scratch it with your thumbnail. This made road construction easy and inexpensive, which accounts for the amazing web of small country lanes that go everywhere and are ideal for cycling. This also has determined the architecture of the region: houses, castles, barns, walls enclosing fields, everything is made of this soft, peaches-and-cream-colored stone, much of it quarried from the escarpments that border the rivers.

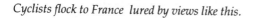

Cyclists flock to France lured by views like this.

Of all the areas of France, none is better suited to cycling than the Loire Valley. However, because of its multiplicity of châteaux, splendid cities, ancient towns, wine districts, and fine restaurants, it is popular with tourists and is crowded from early May through the end of September. This means hotel reservations must be made many months in advance. The area is accessible by trains to Orléans, Châteaudun, Vendôme, Blois, Tours, Chinon, Saumur, Angers, and Poitiers.

Finally, we come to the Île de France. This is the region around Paris, and in feudal times was the king's personal domain: the rest of the country was in the hands of dukes (the duchies of Burgundy, Aquitaine, Normandy, and Brittany, for example) and counts (the counties of Anjou, Vendôme, Blois, etc.).

The region is hilly, and is the most heavily populated area of France. More than 12% of France's total population of 56 million lives here. Although Paris itself is small in size (it covers only 26,044 acres, which is less than a seventh the size of Charlotte, North Carolina, but has a population that is 5½ times greater) the agglomeration of townships surrounding Paris make it a megapolis that sprawls for miles in all directions.

It includes, however, some beautiful forests, notably those near Fontainebleau and St. Germain-en-Laye, the royal châteaux of Fontainebleau and Versailles (the latter is the largest palace in the world and was the seat of the French monarchial government for more than a century), and such attractions as the Chevreuse Valley, the town of Pontoise, and Chartres Cathedral.

The weather is generally mild throughout the spring, summer, and fall. Precipitation is frequent but usually takes the form of showers that last a few hours, then give way to sunshine. This part of France was especially popular with the Impressionist painters, especially Argenteuil, Pontoise, and Marly-le-Roi. Every part of the Île de France is accessible by frequent trains that run all day long and most of the night.

In conclusion, a word about the cathedrals of France. As mentioned earlier, there are 140 cathedrals in France, plus many other churches so impressive that they are often mistaken for cathedrals. The greatest of these are the Gothic cathedrals that were built during the High Middle Ages—the 12th to 14th centuries.

Notre Dame de Paris has the most beautiful flying buttresses and three of the most beautiful rose windows. Reims has the most awesome façade and west portals. All the cathedrals point like arrows in the general direction of Jerusalem. This is why the 'front doors' are always facing west, with a great rose window over them that is illuminated by the afternoon sun. However, the latitude of France is such that the sun is more to the southwest than the west during the afternoons, so the rose window in the south transept shares this illumination.

The largest Gothic cathedral in France is that of Amiens. The highest is that of Beauvais. The cathedral of Beauvais consists of choir and transept only. After the nave fell in a second time, killing more than 200 persons, it was not rebuilt.

The cathedral of Bourges is one of the most harmonious. Other cathedrals worth visiting are those of Senlis, Noyon, Rouen, Tours, and Bazas in southwestern France.

The cathedral of St. Gatien in Tours.

Chartres is, of course, the greatest of the great, noted for its spires, its incomparable windows, and the medieval sculpture around its portals.

The Basilica of St. Denis just to the north of Paris proper was the first great Gothic edifice, built during the middle of the 12th Century by Bishop Suger, tutor and advisor to Louis VII, the first husband of Eleanor of Aquitaine. St. Denis is the traditional burial place of the kings of France.

The Holy Trinity Abbey 'chapel-church' at Vendôme is the finest example in France of what is called *flamboyant* Gothic architecture. The adjective derives from the intricacy of the stone carving, the interstices of which resemble tongues of flame.

Here too are found the best examples in France of *miseri cords*, which are cartoons in wood. The carvers were itinerant members of a guild who went from town to town where cathedrals and other churches were being built to ply their curious trade. These small wooden sculptures are sometimes humorous, sometimes grim, sometimes simply scenes of daily life, such as a huntsman warming his hands before the fire or a farmer preparing to butcher a hog. Under the choir seats of the abbey near Burgos in Spain, there are even 'pornographic' carvings.

To decide what area is right for you, consider the terrain, the weather, the scenery and attractions, and your own special interests. You might want to make a list of various possibilities, then evaluate the advantages and disadvantages of each. Avoid the mistake of trying to see too many areas in too brief a time. It's far more satisfying to select one area that appeals to you, and explore it as thoroughly as your vacation time allows.

CHAPTER 3

Getting a Bike in France

To get a bicycle for your cycling tour of France, you have three choices:

☐ Take your own bike to France;

☐ Rent one while you are there;

☐ Buy one there, then sell it or take it home.

In this chapter, we will consider the advantages and disadvantages of each option.

Taking Your Own Bike With You

The advantages are that you are accustomed to how it feels, to how the shifters work (that is, the feel of the 'throw' unless they are click-stop), and to the braking characteristics. If you have a custom-built bike, then it fits you perfectly—or should. At any rate, you're used to it. You're comfortable on the saddle.

Claude Leblond (with his back to the camera) adjusting bikes to fit the riders.

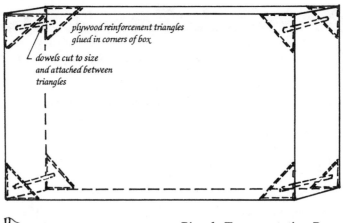

plywood reinforcement triangles glued in corners of box

dowels cut to size and attached between triangles

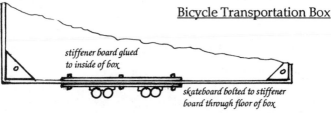

Bicycle Transportation Box

stiffener board glued to inside of box

skateboard bolted to stiffener board through floor of box

The disadvantages are that it's cumbersome; it delays your travel; it could get damaged; it could get stolen. To protect the bike, it must be carefully crated. If you put it into a bicycle box—the sort of packing case the manufacturer used to ship it to the bike shop—you must partially disassemble the bike. This means you must take with you the tools needed for reassembly. You will have to remove one or both wheels, remove or reverse the pedals (which are threaded peculiarly), lower or remove the saddle, and either remove or turn the handlebars sideways.

Baggage handlers are not the least concerned with the fragility of the contents of the box. They handle thousands of pieces of baggage every day. A large cardboard carton will not be deliberately damaged, but neither will it be given special care.

If you want to take your own and take it in a carton, select the sturdiest carton available. The strongest ones I know of are those in which Panasonics are shipped from Japan to the United States. This box is also one of the most compact and requires the greatest amount of disassembling and reassembling.

No matter how strong the box is, you may want to reinforce it. Do this by cutting out eight isosceles right-angle triangles of plywood about ten inches long along the hypotenuse. Using a strong wood glue, glue one in each of the carton's eight corners. After they are dried in place, measure carefully between two opposite triangles, then cut four dowels the proper length from an old broom or mop handle. Brace these dowels between the triangles and glue them in place. It doesn't hurt to nail them as well.

To make it easier to move the box, cut a two-foot piece of a board no wider than the inside of the box. Drill four ¼-inch holes, two of them three inches from each end and all of them two inches from their respective sides.

Buy a cheap skateboard with a plywood top. Center the board on the skateboard and mark the drilled holes. Drill holes in the skateboard at the marked spots.

Now turn the box upside down, center the board on the bottom of the box, and mark the location of the holes. Using an awl or a barbecue skewer, punch these holes in the box.

Turn the box back right-side up and glue the board to the inside bottom of the box, making sure the holes line up exactly. Insert bolts with washers through the holes and fasten them with washers and nuts to the skateboard (apply glue to the top of the skateboard for firmer adhesion).

A properly fitted bicycle adds to the pleasure of a tour.

Now you have a carton on wheels. The procedure may sound like a lot of trouble, but it's nothing compared with trying to carry or drag a carton this size through airports and train stations, while carrying your panniers and handlebar bag as well.

As an added precaution, when I took my bikes back and forth to France, I painted the sides of the box with a cathedral on one side and flowers on the other. Why? Because I reasoned that while baggage handlers may be blasé about their work, something in their subconscious will tend to make them a little more careful with what looks vaguely artistic. They won't slam it around quite so hard. It seems to work: my bike was never damaged.

Once the bike is inside, fill the box with styrofoam 'peanuts' and pack them down as tightly as you can. When the box is filled, lay a folded plastic 33-gallon trash bag on top of the packing material. Also, pack in a partially used roll of heavy-duty 2-inch packing tape. The bag is to hold the styrofoam peanuts when you remove the bike. The tape is for resealing the box for the return trip.

Seal the box securely along all edges and be sure your name and address and phone number at home and at your first stop in France—if you know it—are displayed on the box and taped over with clear packing tape.

You can, if you wish, buy a heavy-duty bike transport case. It is made of material like fiberglass, has a handle, and has built-in rollers. Like the box, it requires considerable disassembly of the bike. It also contains a tool compartment. These cases weigh as much as a good bike and are just as cumbersome as a box. Their only advantage is that they are virtually uncrushable—no reinforcement or styrofoam is needed.

Also on the market is a canvas bike bag. This occupies the least space and can be carried with a shoulder strap. But it requires almost complete disassembly of the bike and offers no protection against crushing.

What do you do with the box or case once you get to France and want to start cycling? The most practical thing to do is to plan your itinerary so that you spend your first and last nights in the same hotel, so that you can leave the carton there, or start and end your cycling in the same city or town, so that you can leave the carton in the train station's baggage *consigne*.

An alternative is to take the bike in the carton to where you want to start cycling, remove the bike and reseal the box, then send the box by train to the city or town where you want to stop cycling. It will be waiting for you when you get there. But be sure to hang on to your receipt.

The last take-it-with-you choice requires more bravery than I possess, but I've seen it done: Take the bike loose (but with the handebars turned sideways and the pedals removed) to the check-in counter and say, "Here. I want to check this, please."

I knew a couple from White Plains, New York, who did that on a TWA flight from J. F. Kennedy Airport to Paris-Charles de Gaulle. Their (very expensive) bikes arrived without a scratch. Their reasoning was that the baggage handlers will be more careful with something obviously fragile than with something in a crate. For them it worked, but I wouldn't have the nerve to try it. Also, many airlines will not accept loose bikes as checked luggage.

Renting a Bike in France

Major train stations in France have rental bikes. These are sturdy 40-pound monsters (mostly, Lejeunes) with thick tires and no toe cages. For trips of any distance, they are eminently impractical — but they are available, and many vacationers who want to make a two- or three-day jaunt seem not to mind the weight and the restricted choice of sizes.

Most—but not all—cities have bike shops that rent bikes of varying quality. These are usually second-hand and second-rate bikes, but they're better than those obtainable at train stations. Some of them are reasonably decent Gitanes, Peugeots, or Motobécanes. To find out whether any given town has a bike rental shop, write to the town's *Syndicat d'Initiative*. This is an office the sole purpose of which is to encourage tourism in the town and surrounding area. You do not need the street address: just address it to the *Syndicat d'Initiative*, then postal code followed by the name of the city. (An appendix at the back of this book contains the five-digit postal code of every town and city named in this book, plus some, but not all, villages. Please note that the code precedes the name of the town, instead of coming afterward.) In some towns the S. I., as it is called for short, is more appropriately named the *Office de Tourisme*. Use that name if you prefer. Either way, your inquiry will reach the right office.

Your Full Name   *Your Street Address*
                                    Your Town, State & Zip
                                    U.S.A.

Syndicat d'Initiative
01234 French Town
FRANCE

Monsieur,

Voudriez-vous bien m'envoyer le nom et l'adresse d'une maison, boutique ou atelier òu on peut louer une vélo par jour où par semaine? Je m'interesse de visiter votre region et je voudrais me conduire au vélo.

Je vous remercie d'avance de votre gentillesse et je vous prie d'agréer, Monsieur, l'expression de mes salutations distinguées.

Your Name and Signature

Do not hold your breath while awaiting an answer. Air mail one way takes up to eight days, and the clerk who receives your letter may reflect upon it a few days before answering. Allow three weeks to a month for a reply to your inquiry. The personnel in these offices speak and read English, but it is more polite to write in French. See the sample letter above.

It is a further courtesy to enclose a couple of International Postal Coupons and a self-addressed envelope. Be sure to mark the words *Par Avion* to the enclosed envelope; otherwise, the reply may come back by surface mail, which takes about six months. And affix adequate airmail postage to your own envelope. This increases year to year, as the overseas service gets slower and slower.

Once you receive a reply, write to the source of rental bikes and ask to reserve one (or as many you and those with you will need) and specify, in centimeters, the frame size and style. In French, 'frame' is *cadre*. Your style choices are *demicourse* for a diamond-frame (man's) bike, and *mixte* for a modified-frame (women's) bike. Some shops now rent mountain bikes, called in French, *tout-terrain*.

The French determination of frame size is the length of the seat tube from the center of the tube to the center of the bottom bracket, that is, to the center of the axis on which the crank

---

Monsieur,

Le Syndicat d'Initiative m'a donné votre nom et l'adresse, dont je suis bien reconnaissant.

Je voudrais réserver un vélo demi-course [or mixte] cadre 58 [or whatever] cms, à partir du 3 juin pour deux semaines, s'il vous plaît. [Or whatever date for whatever duration].

Si cela vous convient, voudriez-vous me faire le savoir par poste aérienne, avec le prix par jour—ou par semaine—et la caution aussi.

---

arms turn. If you measure this in inches, then multiply by 2.54 to convert to centimeters.

If you do not know the correct frame size, you can obtain it this way: Wearing the shoes in which you will be cycling, place your feet ten inches apart. Now measure—or have someone measure for you — the distance straight down to the floor from the top of your crotch. Multiply this number by 0.68 (sixty-eight hundredths) to get your proper frame size in.

Using the same sort of heading and closing as the letter on page 30, write the letter shown above. What you have said is: "The Syndicat d'Initiative has given me your name and address, for which I am most grateful. I wish to reserve a man's

The Cyclamen shop in Poitiers is popular with cycle tourists heading for southwest France.

[or women's] bike with a 23-inch frame, for two weeks starting June 3rd, please.

"If this is possible, please let me know by airmail, and inform me of the rental fee by day or week, as well as the deposit." [*Caution* is the French word for deposit.]

Situations change, but at the time this book was written, bikes could be obtained on a buy-back basis from Francis Kelsall in Paris. His address is:

M. Francis Kelsall
La Maison de Vélo
8, rue de Belzunce
75010 Paris
FRANCE

The telephone number (by direct dial from the US) is: (011 33) 1 42 81 24 72. The first three digits connect you with the overseas system. The next two, 33, are the code for France. The 1 is for Paris. The remaining eight are his number. His shop is near the Gare du Nord. Kelsall speaks perfect English as well as perfect French. At one time he rented bikes, but so many Americans abused them or stole them that he switched to the buy-back plan. You pay the full retail price for the bike. If you return it in good condition, then he buys it back from you, deducting what would be the normal rental charge. But if you lose it or abuse it, you are out the full purchase price. He will not buy back a damaged bike.

A shop named Cyclamen in the rue Arsène Orillard, 86000 Poitiers (that address will suffice) rents bikes of indifferent quality. Some of them are adequate; some of them leave much to be desired. Reasonably good bikes are available from:

Maison de Vélo Motobécane
Faubourg Chartrain
41100 Vendôme
FRANCE

The best source of rental bikes I've found in France is Claude Leblond, the proprietor of Cycles Leblond, at:

M. Claude Leblond
44, Levée des Tuileries
41000 Blois
FRANCE

His telephone number (from the US) is (011 33) 54 74 30 13. He speaks only French.

Leblond is a former professional racing cyclist and is a third-generation bike builder. Some of his rental bikes bear his name; others are Raleighs, Merciers, Gitanes, and so forth. All of them are of excellent quality. On request, he will put flat handlebars on men's bikes or dropped handlebars on the 'mixte' bikes. For a small labor charge, he will re-equip a bike with whatever chain rings and sprockets you request. That is to say, he can provide whatever gearing ration you want—within reason, of course. The lowest ratio is a 1 : 1—the same number of teeth on the small chainring as on the largest sprocket (referred to as a 27-inch gear in the English-speaking world). He does not provide reverse-ratio gearing.

The highest gear ratio is 1 : 4.15 (a 112-inch gear). That is, for every time you turn the cranks one complete revolution, the rear wheel turns 4⅙ revolutions. This gear is useful for racing down steep hills. Leblond's bikes come equipped with what is considered standard gearing for the Loire Valley terrain.

Buying a Bike in France

This is not to be confused with the Kelsall buy-back plan. This is an option for someone who wants to buy a good bike in Europe and bring it home—or re-sell it for just slightly under the original retail cost.

Many brands of bikes are made in France—Peugeot, Mercier, Gitane, Motobécane, Lyjack, and Leblond—and even a town of 9,000 total population is apt to have two or three excellent bike shops. No matter where you start your trip, if it has a train station, it has one or more bike shops.

The great shops are in the large cities, of course. Paris has innumerable shops, the greatest of them collected on the Avenue de la Grande Armée just west of the Arc de Triomphe. But if you buy a bike in Paris, then you have the hassle of getting it through Paris traffic to the train station and then to wherever you are starting your trip. (Because of the population density around Paris, and the truly awesome traffic, it is unwise to start a bike trip from downtown Paris.)

In Versailles, 12 miles southwest of Paris and gateway to the southwest, including Chartres, Châteaudun, Vendôme, Blois, etc., the shop called Cycles Raymond offers a full range of Peugeots, plus a choice of every component and accessory you can possibly think of. To get there, take the commuter train from the Gare St. Lazare. When you reach Versailles, go out the front of the station which is on the rue du Marechal Foch.

Turn left (south) and walk four blocks to the rue Carnot. Turn right and walk four blocks and you will see the shop across the street from you on the corner of rue Madeleine and rue Carnot.

The same is true of the Peugeot shop on the rue Nationale near the Woodrow Wilson Bridge in Tours. This is another enormous and fully stocked shop. It even has such esoteric items as a 47-tooth chainring. It is, however, high priced. Repair work there is, in my opinion, exorbitantly priced. You can find more reasonably priced bikes at the Motobécane shop on the Avenue Grammont. Trains leave the Gare d'Austerlitz in Paris for Tours almost at hourly intervals. If you take the high-speed TGV, the trip takes about 58 minutes and you must get off at St. Pierre-des-Corps then take the (free) 10-minute shuttle train into downtown Tours. If you go via Orléans and Blois, the trip takes about 150 minutes but you see a lot of pretty little towns and countryside.

The question of whether to buy a bike in France depends largely on the dollar-franc exchange rate. If the dollar is 'weak,' then buying a bike in France doesn't make sense. (The dollar, if left alone, has a tendency to be strong against foreign currencies. But the Administration manipulates the value artificially in an effort to keep the economy ever expanding, regardless of inflation. The Federal Reserve Board, independent of the Administration, once appointed, usually wants to curb inflation and does so by raising interest rates. This makes foreign investments and holdings all the more profitable, and thus the value of the dollar all the higher. In the summer of 1980, the dollar would buy slightly less than four francs. The franc was worth 26 cents. In 1984, the dollar would buy almost 10 francs, and almost eight in 1985. Then the Reagan and Bush administrations kowtowed to American manufacturers and artificially lowered the value of the dollar to the point that it would buy just barely more than five francs. So the decision about buying a bike in France should depend on the strength of the dollar.) The *Wall Street Journal* and most big-city newspapers publish the exchange rates daily.

In 1984, I sent my torso, leg, and arm measurements to Claude Leblond along with component specifications—everything I wanted on the bike—and asked him what it would cost to build the bike for me and equip it. He replied with a price that was then the equivalent of $378. At the same time, I sent the same specifications to an American builder of custom bikes and asked for a price. It was $1,800. The American price was unreasonably inflated. Americans seem to accept being gouged. French bike builders are, I think, far more honest and far less greedy. The bike I bought for $378 would only cost $616 in mid-1991 francs. The American builder can say that import duties and shipping costs to the USA would increase that cost. True. But only by about $100 altogether, not by a thousand.

If you buy an ordinary bike, or even a good bike, in France, you won't save much money by the time you ship it home. But if you buy a custom-built bike, you can get it for about one-third to one-half of what you would pay in the States.

Unless something cataclysmic happens, Leblond will be in business at least through the 1990's and probably the decade after that as well. If you want to buy a custom-built bike, use the bike nomenclature glossary in Chapter 10.

Monsieur Leblond's wife, Annie, was also a professional racer. She is now a registered nurse working at a clinic. She is barely five feet tall. When she was a racer, her specialty was sprinting up mountains.

So you have the choice of taking your own bike to France, renting one there, or buying one to re-sell (to some other foreign cyclist) or take home. Taking your own involves so much inconvenience that it's hardly worth the trouble. It

The roofs of a small French town. View of Ribeauvillé

seems to be done only by masochists (who take weary pleasure in the hardship and suffering) and egotists (those who want to show off the quality of their bikes), but of course this is not always the case. I've known some very nice and mentally normal people who took their bikes to France simply because they wanted to ride their own bikes there. For them, the inconvenience is outweighed by riding a comfortable and familiar bike. Nevertheless, I cannot help but ask myself: Is it really worth all that trouble?

Buying a bike in France is fine if the exchange rate is favorable and you buy a custom-built bike. Otherwise, it's hardly worthwhile. Apart from La Maison de Vélo in Paris, bike shops rarely buy back a bike from a customer. In most instances where you find a place that does this, the difference between the purchase price and the buy-back offer is one third to one half of the original cost, depending on how long you use the bike.

You can possibly sell the bike to another tourist. The best way to do this is to make the arrangement beforehand. For example, you are going to France in June for three weeks; a friend is going in July. You buy the bike, ride it, and when you are ready to leave, you put it in the *consigne* at some agreed-upon railway station, then give your friend the receipt.

An alternative is to go to the American Express in the rue Scribe in Paris, and talk with the American students and vagabonds you will find there. Some of them may be about to begin a cycling trip and in the market for a good used bike.

But if you are going to France to cycle there from one week to three or even four weeks, renting a bike is by far the best option. It obviates the unavoidable hassles involved in taking your own bike to France; it saves you a potentially enormous outlay of money. Bike rental in France averages from $5 to $8 a day. If you are on a two-week vacation, you will use the bike maybe a total of 10 days. Thus you will be spending $50 to $70. This is about 25 cents per hour, plus or minus a few cents, depending on the exchange rate.

Weigh the choices carefully, then choose the option that seems best for you. The extent to which you enjoy the trip may depend to a large degree on what you decide.

CHAPTER 4

Personal Gear

It should be axiomatic that cycling lightly encumbered is more enjoyable than struggling to pedal a bike loaded with tons of extraneous junk. Nevertheless, many cycle tourists go to France for two weeks of cycling with enough gear to outfit a six-month expedition to the South Pole. I met an American cyclist in Chartres who bragged about how light his bike was. Indeed, it was so light it practically floated off into space unless someone held it down. But he nullified this advantage by loading it with front and rear panniers the total weight of which was more than sixty pounds. This is madness.

I confess, on my first cycling trip in France in 1972, my wife and I carried tons of stuff we didn't need. I would like to attribute this to inexperience rather than stupidity. At any rate, we both have learned to pack lightly. When my wife accompanied me on a three-week Loire Valley trip in 1980, her total luggage consisted of one small rear-rack pack and a very small handlebar bag. The combined weight was 7¼ pounds. Not to be outdone, in 1982, I made one trip with a total luggage weight of 5¾ pounds. That, however, is going to extremes.

Janie Simpson with her loaded bike—all 7¼ lbs of luggage. What you see on the bike is all she took for a three-week tour.

One should be comfortable and have at hand whatever is needed. But *needed* is the important word. At least half of what the average traveler packs to France is wholly unnecessary. Also, it seems to be overlooked that France is a civilized country with stores and shops of every sort. If you get there and discover you do need something you neglected to bring along, you simply go to the store and buy it.

In the spring of 1981, I cycled with a group of five friends across the Pyrénées to Spain and back. I was appalled by the weight of the gear they were carrying. By the time we got into the hills of southwestern France and had a free day in a town called St. Sever, every single one of them mailed cardboard boxes of unneeded gear back to our final hotel rather than pack it over the mountains. And some of them still carried such items of debatable value as pajamas, bathrobe, bedroom slippers, and blow-dryer.

The following checklist is based on two decades of cycling experience in France. If you follow this guideline, the total weight—excluding camera and film—will be slightly less than 12 pounds.

Clothing is minimal; the list is predicated on frequent laundering. Items made of synthetic fibers or a blend of these and cotton will dry quickly if certain techniques are followed— which will be discussed. Even pure cotton will dry in a few hours unless the humidity is 100%. Wool shorts with chamois inserts take forever to dry and should be avoided.

Many cyclists have the idea that they must dress up for dinner. In Paris and certain big city restaurants—yes, perhaps. But generally, in the provinces, cycling garb is acceptable even in fairly formal dining rooms and the 'better' restaurants, provided one does not offend with semi-nudity. Tank tops and short-shorts would be offensive.

To make yourself acceptable in restaurants (and churches), you should wear leg coverings of some sort—stretch pants, heavy gauge 'pantyhose,' Danskins, something. These serve a multiplicity of purposes: They protect the legs from sunburn. Exposure to the sun, hour after hour, day after day, is an invitation to skin cancer. Secondly, if it should be cool, the leg covering prevents chill. Thirdly, wearing something on the legs prevents the appearance of over-exposure and makes one acceptable in churches (where long bare legs are in extremely poor taste) into which one may wish to look along the way, and in restaurants and hotel dining rooms.

Over these should be worn shorts with pockets. Pockets are extremely handy while on a cycling tour. In them you can put your change purse, a pocket-pack of Kleenex, your pocket-knife, and in the hip pocket, a folded plastic grocery bag or two. Grocery stores in France do not automatically supply bags. Shoppers, especially in villages, where you might be buying picnic supplies, are expected to supply their own bags.

You should wear an undershirt, preferably cotton or a mixture of cotton and acrylic. This helps keep you cool or warm, as the need may be, and prevents the nipples from becoming chafed (which can be quite painful). Over this, a shirt with button-down flap pockets, one on either side. In one, carry your wallet with your credit cards and paper money of your own country. Keep the flap buttoned. In the other, carry a small notebook, your pen, and a comb. If you have hotel reservations, it's a good idea to have the names and addresses and phone numbers of each hotel recorded in your notebook, along with the dates of your reservations. I have met cyclists who have arrived in a town where they were supposed to spend a night but who had completely forgotten the name of their hotel.

Over this, wear a nylon shell jacket with at least two large inner pockets and at least two outer pockets. All of these should close with snaps or Velcro, and the use of a safety pin for additional security is an excellent idea.

In one of the inner pockets, carry your passport (protected from rain and perspiration by being wrapped in a plastic sleeve or pouch) and your return airplane ticket, similarly protected. In the other inner pocket, carry your traveller's checks in a flat wallet also protected by a plastic sleeve. Some banks will not accept checks that are wet. I wrap my checks in two plastic sleeves and secure them with rubber bands. These pockets should close and should then be safety pinned for added protection. Getting lost or stolen checks replaced is not as simple as television commercials would have you believe. And pickpockets, who ply their trade at airports and train stations where you are apt to be distracted or tired, are extremely skillful.

The outer pockets are for French cash on one side and for odds and ends such as Rantex (discussed below) on the other side. In addition to these, my jacket has a small pocket which I find ideal for carrying Metro or commuter train tickets, both of which are needed for getting through turnstiles and which are therefore best kept handily accessible.

If France is having a heat-wave, I protect my neck from sunburn with a filmy scarf that is virtually weightless. I have learned to knot it and tuck it into my shirt like a foulard, which looks nice in restaurants.

It's better to wear the jacket or keep it in sight all the time. Don't ever drape it over the back of a chair in which you are sitting. That's an invitation to potential thieves. I wear the jacket all the time, except in bed or in the shower. American passports are a hot commodity abroad. They sell for up to $10,000 and in 1985, a year when Americans flocked to France because of the advantageous exchange rate, the US Embassy received 23,000 reports of lost or stolen passports. Replacement travel papers permit you to go home only; not to continue traveling. Getting a lost or stolen airline ticket reissued can also be tough and time consuming.

Finally, a head-covering. In the blazing sun, it's a good idea to wear something. In the pouring rain, a visor helps keep the rain out of your eyes. Many American cyclists consider helmets essential. They become glassy-eyed when evangelizing the gospel of the helmet. There's no point in arguing with rabid fanatics, but helmets aren't necessary in France. French cyclists don't wear them and few bicycle shops stock them. The Bell helmet is advertised to withstand an impact of 2,000 pounds per square inch. It may, for all I know. But the vertebrae in the neck won't. If a cyclist crashes head-first into something with enough force to shatter an unprotected skull, that impact will assuredly smash the vertebrae in the neck. The helmets made for race car drivers protect both the head and the neck, but cyclists don't wear that sort of helmet. The sort they do wear serves to fend off bird droppings, but are otherwise of dubious value.

Over the course of the many years I've been cycling in France, I've taken five spills, all of them the result of my own carelessness. In two of them, I ripped the elbows out of my jacket. In one, I skinned the base of my right thumb. In another, I broke my right thumb. In the fifth, only my dignity was injured. I have never run headfirst into a tree—I simply don't think it sounds like fun—nor have I tangled with an automobile. I abide by French traffic laws and cycle sensibly. Challenging an automobile for the right-of-way, which many demented Americans do, is worse than silly: it's idiotic.

If you insist on wearing a cycling helmet you'll have to take it along, because they are hard to find in France. (Moped and motorcycle riders are required by law to wear helmets, but these are akin to those worn by race car drivers.)

There is no rain gear on the checklist. The only rain gear that actually works is made of GoreTex, the material developed to make diaphragms for kidney dialysis machines. Garments made of GoreTex are very expensive. If one were planning to cycle in the rainy parts of France, or in Ireland, a GoreTex jacket, and possibly even GoreTex pants, might be worth the investment. But in addition to being expensive, such gear is also bulky, and occupies a lot of pannier space when not in use.

Other materials don't breathe. Consequently, perspiration does not evaporate and you wind up getting just as wet as if you wore no rain gear at all. I have never worn rain gear in France. I wear clothes that dry out quickly. If it rains and I am unavoidably caught out in it, I simply get wet. Then I get dry again.

It is advisable to take along at least one credit card. Many hotels and restaurants accept them, but chiefly they are handy to have in case of an emergency, such as if you need to rent a car. If you pay a bill with a credit card, the exchange rate you get will be that which prevailed at the time your purchase or charge cleared the international clearing house. In addition,

The author with all his luggage on a Pyrénées trip.

you will be charged a five percent fee for the conversion. So don't use your credit card recklessly, unless money is no object.

In France, the credit card most widely accepted is VISA, also known there as *Carte Bleue*. VISA is welcomed almost everywhere, and can also be used to obtain cash advances. MasterCard is next in recognition and acceptance. It now approaches VISA's position. American Express traveler's checks are still by far the most widely accepted checks (some banks there won't accept any other), but the AmEx card has dropped to third place in acceptability in France. Diners Club, like AmEx, is a charge card—not a credit card. It is accepted at many big-city restaurants and at some hotels. Carte Blanche is useful as a bookmark. I have not so far seen the relatively new Discovery Card used in France, but I suppose it will be accepted there as soon as an overseas marketing set-up can be created.

At the time this was written, France no longer required Americans to have a French visa (entry permit, not the credit card). Until the fall of 1986, a passport sufficed, and it does again. But when the Reagan administration became petulant because France refused to allow American planes to fly over France on their way to bomb Libya, France responded by requiring American visitors to have visas. Check with a travel agent to find out whether they are required at the time of your trip. If so, they are easily obtained through travel agencies for a fee (which is sometimes as much as $40) or directly from any French consulate for about one fourth of that.

Cleated cycling shoes are a nuisance. They do increase cycling efficiency, but are hardly necessary for touring at a relaxed pace. Moreover, they must be removed before entering a château or museum. The small amount of energy they save is dissipated by changing shoes each time you stop to see something.

The Latex gloves mentioned on the list are the type physicians use: thin and disposable. They can be obtained in many drugstores and in all home health care supply houses. They are for use in case you have a flat tire on the rear wheel and must therefore handle the chain—which is usually dirty. Wear the gloves while removing and replacing the chain, then throw them away. (Into a trash receptacle. The French countryside—and roadsides—are remarkably free from litter; you should help keep it that way.) Incidentally, a trash receptacle is called a *poubelle*. It is named for a Préfect [governor] of the

Département de la Seine—the area around and including Paris—who decreed, in 1884, that trash cans be placed where citizens could use them for the disposal of all sorts of garbage. By 1890, Monsieur Poubelle's name had become a noun in the language, meaning trash can or waste basket.

Rantex is a 'personal wipe' also obtained in some drugstores and all home health care supply houses. They are excellent in preventing rear-end discomfort such as hemorrhoids. They come individually packaged, 100 to a box, and cost about five cents a piece. A physician cycling in France with me in 1978 introduced me to them. I have never been without them since—whether at home or abroad.

Frisbees are rarely seen in France, but fascinate the French and are thus an excellent way to make friends. It's relaxing to toss a Frisbee in the park or town square after a day of cycling. If you do this, you will soon be surrounded by curious (and envious) onlookers. Let a couple of them try it—show them how to launch it—and you will soon have made a friend or two.

The spoon is for eating yoghurt. French yoghurt, called—*yaourt*, is excellent, and is available in even the smallest village *épiceries* (grocery stores). Yoplait and Danone are the most popular brands. Those brand names are found in American stores—with Danone spelled 'Dannon'—but in France, the taste and texture are much different and—I think—better.

Rearview mirrors that attach to the earpiece of eyeglasses or sunglasses are not sold in French bike shops. These are, in my estimation, far more essential to safety than helmets. They also arouse French curiosity and are thus a bridge to friendship. I take along a few extra to give away. The most popular of these to be found in American bike shops these days is the Third Eye brand made of black plastic in two models—one that attaches to helmets and one that attaches to glasses.

My objection to Third Eye mirrors is that their extension arm (on the model that attaches to glasses) is about ¼ to ⅜ inch too short. The maker of these is Dr. Jack Greenlaw, a dentist in Walnut Creek, California. Dr. and Mrs. Greenlaw were on a tour with me in 1980. I've mentioned to them the desirability of extending the arm slightly, but so far as I know, this has never been done.

I prefer the wire model that 'wraps' onto the left earpiece of one's glasses. These can be homemade from a bicycle spoke and a small mirror. Mirrors of suitable size are available at science hobby shops. Bend the spoke into the proper configuration with alligator-nose pliers, clip off the surplus portion with wire cutters, and attach the mirror with Krazy glue. *Voilà:* You have a rearview mirror for a few cents.

You will be asked in France, "Qu'est-ce que c'est ça, Monsieur?" (What's that, sir?)

In French, it is a *rtroviseur.* Let your interrogator have a look for himself. He will be amazed at the field of view and you will have made another friend.

If you want to coat a portion of the wire in plastic, find anything made of pliable plastic, cut it into bits with shears, and melt the bits in something such as a washed tuna fish can over low heat. Then dip the wire into the melted plastic, and remove it immediately, then let it dry. It's best to do this after the wire has been shaped and cut to size. Even simpler: dip the shaped wire into rubber cement, then let it dry. Dip it and dry it again. This will wear off, but recoating the wire is easy.

Many panniers are advertised as being waterproof. I have yet to find one that is totally impervious to water in a rainstorm. It is, therefore, advisable to enclose all items of clothing in plastic bags and seal them shut with strong rubber bands. Anything else that can be damaged by water, such as your address book, your pocket calculator, film for your camera, maps, anything electronic or made of cloth or paper, should be similarly protected. On a long trip, bags may wear out or get torn, so taking along a few extra is a good idea. Take extra rubber bands as well. (Heavy duty 'zip-lock' bags will serve this purpose for many items.)

Anyone taking his or her own bike should take along whatever additional tools are necessary as well as those on the checklist. The same tools used to take the bike apart will be needed to put it back together.

The two most convenient handlebar bags I know of are those made by Kirkland and by Rhode Gear. Both snap securely into place and do not require bungee cords. The map case on the Rhode Gear bag has the added advantage of being attached by Velcro, which permits it to be turned to whatever angle that makes the map easiest to read. (Kirkland has gone out of business, but some bike shops still have Kirkland bags in stock.)

Additional luggage for use in Paris or for traveling elsewhere in Europe can be stored at your first hotel if you are returning to it, or with the bike supplier if you are renting a bike, or in the train station baggage *consigne*. However, the items on the list below are adequate for a protracted stay abroad and suffice for almost any situation other than a formal dress reception.

If you are taking a camera, take more film than you think you'll need. Film is available everywhere in France, but it is more costly there than in the United States or England. In addition to the Value Added Tax—approximately 18%—there is also a luxury tax on film, which varies according to the political climate, and in addition, film cost there includes processing costs. Some shops in the USA honor this processing charge, but many (if not most) do not.

Some travelers take along Woolite for laundering clothes, shampoo for washing their hair, and their favorite brand of soap for bathing. Using Woolite for all three purposes saves weight and space. Woolite will not harm your scalp or skin.

All the other items on the checklist are self-explanatory, but a word is in order about quality of clothing. Items that rip, tear, or fall apart at the seams are a nuisance. The best biking and hiking clothing in the world is made by Alex Tilley of Canada and called 'Tilley Endurables.' For a catalog, dial (from the USA) 1-800-338-2797. In Canada: 1-800-387-0110.

When you pack your clothes, roll them as tightly as you can, put them into plastic bags, roll these also to eliminate air bubbles, and secure the bags with rubber bands. This reduces bulk and protects the clothing from rain.

To pack a shirt, first fold it neatly (to look as it did when you bought it), then lay it front-side down and roll it, starting from the bottom and ending with the collar. For socks, lay them flat, fold lengthwise, then put them in a plastic bag lengthwise across the bottom, and roll the bag as tightly as possible. Roll and pack T-shirts the same as shirts.

I have found bread bags excellent for this purpose. They are strong and are practical in size. If you use them, turn them inside out and shake them to get rid of crumbs, then turn them back again because the colors and inks on the outside rub off. Pack carefully and thoughtfully, utilizing every niche, every cubic centimeter of space. You'll be amazed at how much can be packed into a very small bag.

I now pack everything I need for a stay of three or four weeks into my Rhode Gear handlebar bag. That's the only piece of luggage I take to France. But I used to use 'day-glo' panniers because they showed up well in the mists that often envelope France, especially on autumn mornings. I marked on the pannier tops and pockets with an indelible laundry marker what each part of the bag contained, such as *clothes*, *toiletries*, etc. It might not look aesthetically pleasing, but it was handy when I wanted to get something from a pannier.

I almost always mount the bike from the left side. So when I stop, I lean the right side against a tree or wall. For this reason, I carried in the left-side pannier anything I might want en route, such as a pocket pack of Kleenex or a Band-Aid. A bike can be parked against a curb by putting the curbside pedal rearward and on top of the curb, with the front wheel angled into the curb at a very slight angle.

The most important items are in my pockets; those of next importance were (when I used panniers) in the handlebar bag: items such as spare pens, camera, film, address book, maps, and tools.

If you take anything to France in a bottle, put it in the top of a pannier or handlebar bag because security checkpoint monitors at the airport will want to see it. They are looking for volatile fluids that can be used as bombs.

When you start packing for the trip, it helps to lay out everything in related groups. Then place items in the panniers and handlebar bag in logical sequence. Items least likely to be needed for a few days go in first, on the bottom. Anything you may need en route, such as your toothbrush, razor, Rantex, etc., goes in last. Packing intelligently and logically results not only in convenience, but also in peace-of-mind, enhancing your enjoyment of the trip.

Checklist

Clothing:

Cap or helmet

2 T-shirts (or turtlenecks if you're going in early spring or late autumn)

2 shirts

3 undershorts

3 pairs of socks

All-purpose shoes

1 pair of cycling shorts with pockets (Tilley shorts have seven)

1 pair of leg coverings

Jacket with at least four pockets

Cycling gloves

Thin slacks and /or wraparound skirt for women

Toiletries:

Comb

Toothbrush

Toothpaste

Dental floss

Razor (men)

Extra blades

16-oz. bottle of Woolite

Rantex (2 per day of stay in France)

Visine

Chapstick

Sunblock gel

Pocket packs of Kleenex (one pack per two days)

Miscellaneous:

Passport (with visa if required)

Travelers checks (in both French francs and dollars)

French francs in cash (about 500 on hand is adequate)

Cash of your own country (for use when you return)

Hotel list: names, addresses, and phone numbers, with date of stay noted

Maps—if you have them

Address book

Permanent ink ball-point pens (several)

Small notebook

Camera and film

Band-Aids

Antiseptic

Sunglasses

Rearview mirror

Small sewing kit

Personal medicines

Spare plastic bags

Extra rubber bands

Smallest possible flashlight

Wristwatch (preferably with dual time and 24-hour time)

Pocket calculator (one that converts to metrics is handy)

Pocket knife

Spoon

Credit card(s)

Any necessary hardware for attaching panniers and handlebar bag

Pocket phrasebook if you don't speak French

Pocket French dictionary, if you do

Crescent wrench

Tire/tube repair kit if you are taking your own bike

Pump if you are taking your own bike

Photocopy of English-French bike terms and phrases (see Chapter 10)

CHAPTER 5

Getting There . . . and Staying Well

From the US or Canada, the best way to go to France is by a major airline that flies directly to Paris. These include American Airlines, Delta, TWA, Northwest, and Air France. American Airlines and Delta land at Orly Airport south of the city of Paris. TWA lands at Roissy-Charles de Gaulle Terminal 1; Air France at Terminal 2, north of the city. Both airports are served by commuter trains that leave every 15 minutes. The train from Orly arrives at the Gare Austerlitz in the 12th arrondissement. The train from Roissy-Charles de Gaulle arrives at the Gare du Nord in the 10th arrondissement. (Shuttle buses take you from the terminal building to the train station.) The old airport, Le Bourget, where Charles Augustus Lindbergh, the first man to fly across the Atlantic alone, landed in May of 1927, is now a military airport and a museum.

Many American visitors to France make the mistake of taking some cheap flight to Luxembourg, Frankfurt, or London. This may save $200, but involves train travel that eats into

This couple, Naomi and Eli Goldstein, took their custom-built bikes to France—uncrated.

that, and also involves time and energy that leaves the traveler exhausted and thus unable to enjoy the beginning of the trip. Icelandic Air from New York to Luxembourg is the worst mistake. The flight stops in Iceland for a few hours where passengers are encouraged to spend all their money in the airport shops. Then it moseys on to Luxembourg, from which you must take a bus into town, then a train to Paris. The trip is exhausting. Lufthansa to Frankfort is better, but it involves a long train ride from Frankfort to Paris.

The various carriers that go to London sometimes have special prices. They land at Heathrow, the major airport and as busy as Chicago's O'Hare, or at Gatwick, nearly 50 miles south of London. To get from either to London involves a hassle. Then you must change stations to get the boat train to France. It takes forever and costs a fortune. (When the English Channel Tunnel opens, it will be quicker, but not cheaper.)

Charter flights to Paris advertise blatently in major newspapers. A few of them are reliable. Most are disasters. They cancel flights without notice, and you are stuck with the choice of abandoning the trip or buying a very expensive ticket on a real airline. (An early purchace means a reduced rate. A last-minute purchase can cost twice as much.)

If you live in the 'Deep South,' Delta from Atlanta makes sense. If you live near North Carolina, New York or Chicago, American (from Raleigh in North Carolina, from Chicago, and also from New York) is the best choice. The planes are staffed by courteous flight attendants and the service is excellent.

Service on TWA flights has declined since that airline was acquired by Carl Icahn. The food is awful, and the personnel seem detached, as though they wished they were somewhere else. Most of the passengers seem to share that wish.

Air France has the food (American Airlines is tops in this department) —but who flies for the food? Its 7 p.m. departure from New York gets you to France in the early morning. The later flight gets you there about midday. American flights from Raleigh-Durham arrive at Orly around 10:30 a.m.

Roissy-Charles de Gaulle Airport was built in the 1970s and is exceptionally efficient. Orly grew by increments over many decades, and is a sprawling mess. However, if you fly American or Delta, you will hardly notice this.

At either airport, once you land, the first thing you do is go through passport control. There will be long lines at the head of which are officers sitting in glassed-in booths. Glance over the lines. Do not get into a line in which there is someone wearing flowing robes, a turban, or anything else that indicates the person may be from the Middle East or Africa. These travelers have bizarre travel papers, and the French officers examine them at great length. The line may remain motionless for half an hour.

After you clear passport control, you will go to the baggage claims area. If you have traveled wisely, you will not have checked any luggage, so you will not have anything there to wait for. You will go directly to the exit to take the shuttle bus to the train station. The bus is free. Just get on. If you missed it, another will be there within ten minutes.

At Roissy-Charles de Gaulle, the bus is marked *Roissy-Rail* and is found just outside the exit door marked *30*; at Orly, the bus is just outside the door marked *sortie aux autocars et navettes* and the bus is marked *Orly Rail* and stops at the concrete island marked *1*. If you have taken your bike with you, put it in the aisle in the back of the bus, and stand there holding it. At Roissy, you buy your ticket to Paris at the train station. At Orly, from a coin-operated machine near the exit at the airport.

From either airport, the shuttle bus (*navette*) takes about ten minutes to get to the rail-head, the train station. To purchase a ticket at Roissy, go to the ticket window and ask for a ticket to Paris. Say: *"Aller-simple, Paris-Nord, deuxième classe, s'il vous plaît."* (pronounced *Ah-lay sam-pluh, Pah-ree Norr, duh zyeem clhass, seel voo play*.) That means: "One way to Paris, second class, please."

Tickets cost—at this writing, mid-1991—about 25 francs from Roissy; about 20 francs from Orly. The trip from Roissy to the Gare du Nord usually takes 28 minutes. From Orly (Pont de Rungis), 18 minutes.

At Roissy, please remember, you buy the ticket at the train station. At Orly, you buy it at the airport. This is important because the tickets operate the turnstiles at the departure station and also at the station where you arrive in Paris.

When you get to France, you will be pumped up on adrenalin. If you have taken a typical evening flight from the US, it will be early in the morning: between 7 and 10 a.m. Your body will be far more tired than your mind. Or than you think. In France, 7 a.m. is 1 a.m. in New York; midnight in Chicago; 11 p.m. in Denver, and 10 p.m. in Los Angeles. Most likely, you will not have slept. Your body is accustomed to ingesting and processing nourishment at certain times. It is used to being rested—asleep—at certain times. Breaking this schedule is going to cause your body considerable grief. This is called jetlag. Your body has been jetted to Europe; its functions lag behind in wherever you live in the USA.

When Dr. Henry Kissinger was Secretary of State for President Richard Nixon, and was flitting all over the world, the Argonne National Laboratory experimented with methods of minimizing jet lag so that Kissinger might function effectively as soon as he touched the ground.

The system works for some, but not for all. However, it's worth trying. The idea is to boost your circadian rhythms into a new phase. Here is how it works:

Let's suppose that June 10 is your departure date—the day you are going to board the plane for France. June 6 is a day of fasting. Orange juice, toast, and tea. June 7 is a day of feasting with a lot of carbohydrates. June 8 is a fasting day; June 9 is a feasting day.

On June 10, the day of departure, a glass of orange juice only—plus as much water as you want. But no food. When dinner is served on the plane, skip it (this takes a lot of willpower on an American Airlines or Air France flight) but do drink two cups of black coffee. No sugar, no cream.

While others watch the in-flight movie, take a nap if you possibly can. When the movie is finished, and the others are napping, take a walk and do isometric exercises.

When breakfast is served, eat everything offered, and ask the flight attendant for seconds—another pastry, another glass of juice, another cup of coffee (with cream and sugar).

At lunchtime in France—midnight in New York—sit down and have a high-calorie, high carbohydrate lunch. The process of digestion and the time zone difference will make you very sleepy in the afternoon, but resist the urge to take a nap. Don't do anything strenuous, but try to stay awake. Take a leisurely walk.

That evening, have dinner at 7 p.m., something easily digestible (no fried foods, no cheese) then go to bed no later than 9 p.m. If this procedure works for you as it did for Dr. Kissinger and does for many other travelers, you will wake up the next morning alert, fully recovered, with your body adjusted to the new time zone. It is impossible to overemphasize the importance of adapting as smoothly as possible to the new time zone.

The strong temptation is to run around and see everything as soon as you arrive. Resist. Don't do it. To do so will burn up all your reserves of energy and in a couple of days you will succumb to what are called 'the bonks.' You will feel physically exhausted and emotionally depressed. I have seen people in this condition weeping, wanting to go home right then and there, truly pathetic. But they recovered.

If you disregard this advice and do become exhausted and depressed, take a day off and do nothing but rest. For some reason or other, eating honey seems to help. Honey in France is called *miel* and is found in most grocery stores.

The best thing, of course, is to avoid this. When you get to France, relax. Rest. Sit on a park bench. Let the day flow by.

Tap water in France is just as pure as your own—wherever you may be. But all tap water contains a trace of coliform bacteria, the bugs that cause diarrhea. We develop an immunity to the bacteria prevalent where we live, and some Americans are immune to the bacteria in France.

But if you're there for a short vacation—two or three weeks —it isn't worth the risk to find out whether you are or not. Because if you are not, bang, there goes your vacation. Drink Evian water. Evian water comes from a spring in southeastern France. It is so pure that pediatricians recommend it as the water to use for mixing baby formulas. It is tasteless (naturally) and should be consumed in quantity: at least a liter and a half a day.

When you first arrive in France, the best thing to do is ... nothing. Relax.

I owe the following advice to Mrs. Pamela Vandyke Price, an English woman who writes about France and is an expert on French wines. Her husband was a physician. Mrs. Price says her friends are amazed by the fact that she never gets sick when she goes abroad. She attributes her immunity to the ills that plague travelers to the fact that she drinks six to eight British pints of bottled water daily. Perhaps it drowns the bugs, I don't know. But it works for me and it has worked for all my clients who have adhered to this regimen while in France with me.

Evian water is sold in 1.5 litre bottles. The cost in France is negligible. I suggest drinking at least one bottle every day, and if you can manage it, drink two. Drink it in your hotel room in the morning and at night, and put it in your water bottle and drink it during the day.

Volvic is another bottled water that serves the same purpose. Contrexeville works—but it is a diuretic. Badoit is slightly prickly and contains mild natural salts, but it is also equally beneficent. In fact, I find Badoit particularly refreshing after a long ride. France is awash in bottled waters; most of them are bubbly and most are minerally. Vichy-St. Yorre and Vichy-Celestins are examples of the bubbly, minerally variety. Perrier is the most bubbly and the most expensive. (It is nice, though, for making mixed drink cocktails, such as Perrier and Picon.) Vittel is ubiquitous and although it has a slight taste, is not bubbly and is almost equal to Evian. Hepar is a laxative: helpful if you've eaten too much French bread and cheese. The food of France is one of the reasons for going there; French cuisine is the best in the world, with certain exceptions. (The French produce the best beef in the world—but don't know how to cook it! They serve it almost raw!) The temptations are irresistible. However, your American diet is not nearly so rich as what confronts you in France, and indulgence is one of the reasons Americans get sick there—in addition to drinking tap water or too much wine. Rich sauces will do you in quite quickly. Especially sauces made with eggs and/or cream. Beware.

Bread and cheese are virtually a cliché. The French make between 350 and 400 kinds of cheese, and of course French bread is acknowledged as the best in the world. Although it isn't as good as it used to be, unless you find a village bakery that adheres to traditional methods.

Americans tend to overindulge in this department. Too much bread and too much cheese. The effect is constipation, and this can lead to hemorrhoids—which, on a bicycle tour, are not pleasant.

Wine is an aid to digestion, especially red wine, which is high in tannin. (White wine contains almost no tannin.) In moderation, wine is healthy. But all alcoholic beverages, please remember, are dehydrating. Wine is no substitute for water.

For years, wine merchants in America have scoffed at the red-wine-with-red-meat adage and the correlative. They say you can drink any wine you like without regard to what you are eating. That advice comes from ignorance and greed. There is a very logical reason for having white wine with fish and red wine with beef and lamb. If you eat seafood often, you are accustomed to seeing it served with lemon wedges. You probably squeeze the wedges and dribble lemon juice over your platter of clams or crabcakes or shrimp or flounder or oysters…. Did you ever stop to wonder why lemon juice enhances the flavor of seafood? You don't squeeze lemon juice on your steak (I hope). Why on fish?

Because the acid combines with the molecular structure of the fat cells in the seafood in such a way that it enhances the taste. The fat in red meat (even the leanest) has a different molecular structure and is not improved in taste by lemon juice.

White wine, because of the way it is vinified—the way the grape juice is made into wine—contains a natural fruit acid in greater proportion than does red wine. This is why white wine tastes great with fish—but not with beef.

Red wine contains tannin. Tannin is bitter. It enhances the flavor of beef and lamb, just as certain spicy sauces do. But it is inimical to the more delicate flesh of fish and shellfish.

What about chicken and pork and *foie de veau* (calf's liver)? A light red wine, or a good rosé, goes best with chicken. Sancerre rosé, made from the Pinot grape, is the best rosé in the world. It is very dry. Unfortunately, it has been 'discovered' and is now expensive. Chinon rosé, made from the cabernet franc grape, is a very close second and can usually be found in restaurants in the Chinon area. With veal and pork, try a Beaujolais. With foie de veau, any light red wine goes down well. Incidentally, in France, foie de veau is usually served with a melting pat of butter which has been sprinkled with freshly chopped parsley, and with a slice of lemon. When asked how you want it cooked, say: "*À point. C'est à dire, rosé dans l'interieur."* This means pink in the center but browned outside.

When you order any sort of steak in France, from the lowliest (and ubiquitous) *steack pommes frites* (steak with French-fried potatoes) in some humble village restaurant, to the lordly Châteaubriand at Le Taillevent in Paris, you will be asked politely how you wish to have it cooked. There are four standard replies: *bleu, saignant, à point,* and (shudder) *bien cuit.*

Bleu means blue. The meat is gray and faintly warm on the outside. It is totally raw and cool on the inside. This is the preference of sophisticated French diners who fancy raw beef.

Saignant means bleeding. The meat is lightly browned on the outside and nearly hot. It is blood-red rare on the inside and barely warm. This is the degree of doneness preferred by a majority of French diners.

À point means, more or less, 'just enough.' This is supposed to be the equivalent of medium rare but is more often congruent with what Americans would deem rare. Nevertheless, this is the reply to use because it is as far as the chef is willing to go.

Bien cuit means well-cooked. If you send this message to the chef, one of three things will happen: (1) The steak will arrive at the table very rare; (2) the steak will not arrive at all and you will be ordered out of the restaurant; (3) the chef will decapitate you with a cleaver, then go home and meditate upon the dietary idiocy of Americans.

Steack haché is the French term for hamburger. For obvious reasons, good restaurants do not feature this on their menus. In those less-than-good, what passes for hamburger is more likely than not to be pretty awful: a little meat, a lot of fat, and virtually raw.

Steak tartare, on the other hand, is served in many fine restaurants. This is good beef, ground up, with an assortment of toppings such as a raw egg, capers, green peppercorns, cracked black or white peppercorns, Tabasco sauce, chopped onions, etc.

Brie and Chablis—the phrase used to designate a certain elitist element of pretentious society—are not particularly good together. Brie tastes much better with a light red wine. Chablis—a really good Chablis, such as Chablis Fourchaume—goes best with raw oysters.

Raw oysters in the United States are an invitation to hepatitis. Fortunately, the oyster beds (called *parcs*) in France are not polluted. You can safely eat raw oysters in France. There are five major kinds if oysters: *Fines de clair*, *Belons*, *Marennes*, *Arcachons*, and *Portuguaises*. They are graded in size by numbers. The largest are designated 00; then 0, 1, 2, 3, 4, and possibly 5. The best sizes for eating raw are the 2s and 3s. What is the finest oyster is a hotly debated question, but since I am not French and am 4,000 miles away as I write this—thus out of reach —I can tell you without hesitation: the best are the *Fines de clair*. The flanges of this oblong oyster are pale green, somewhat like a kiwi fruit. The body is light gray. It is delicious. A few drops of lemon juice, or of the sauce sometimes served, made of red wine vinegar, finely chopped shallots, and black pepper, enhances the flavor. Thinly sliced dark bread, akin to pumpernickel, and butter, are invariably served with oysters, and a bite of this between oysters also enhances the taste and enjoyment.

With beef, the best wine to have is the best Bordeaux you can afford. It is highest in tannin, and the Cabernet-Sauvignon grape from which comes most of the juice imparts a flavor that is wonderful with red meat. The red wines from the Côtes du Rhône in southeastern France are also great with red meat, especially the Châteauneuf du Pape and Hermitage wines, made from the Petit Syrah grape, brought back to France by Crusaders in medieval times.

Great Burgundian wines cost about as much as a Mercedes convertible. The best are Romanée Conti, La Romanée, Grands Echezeaux, and Chambertin. Echezeaux, Nuits St. Georges, Clos de Vougeot, and Mercurey are also excellent.

The greatest wines from the Bordeaux area have been bought up by foreign investors and the processes of vinification have been altered to ensure a return on the investment. The great names from the Médoc, Graves, Pomerol and St. Emilion, are no longer made in the tradition that prevailed in the earlier decades of this century and that produced the great vintages of 1929, 1934, 1937, 1945, 1947, 1949, 1952, 1953, 1961, and 1964. British beer companies, distillers, and Greek grocery-store chains have acquired such great properties as Latour and Margaux, and quality has not always been maintained. Meanwhile, the Japanese have come to France with their multi-millions and purchased a château's entire production before the grapes were harvested! This drives up prices of even medium quality Bordeaux wines, of course.

Château Haut-Brion, owned by the daughter of the former (and now deceased) American ambassador to France, Douglas Dillon, who bought the property, is one of the best and most reliable wines from Bordeaux. It is a Graves from Pessac; the property is contiguous to the city. It makes both red and white wines. The estate was already famous in the 18th century and it was one of Thomas Jefferson's favorite wines. He mentions it by name in the journal he kept while visiting France.

What has all this to do with cycling? A great deal. If you are going to France to do nothing but ride around on a bicycle, stay home. Ride around the block. France is meant to be savored, and nothing is more savorsome than French wines.

In the Loire Valley, try the red wines of Chinon and Bourgueil and the white wines of Vouvray and Saumur. They are superb. The sparkling white wines of Vouvray and Saumur come very close to the quality of the best Champagnes. If, however, you are rich, and want to have a real Champagne with your dinner, find a place that has in its cellars Laurent & Perrier Cuvée Rosé Brut. It is, I think, the finest Champagne in the world.

CHAPTER 6

Selecting a Route

You have already decided the area of France you want to see. Now you want to select a route. That involves distances between overnight stops, and picking the best possible roads. This means being able to read a map—and reading a map means more than being able to get from one place to another with the help of a map; it means understanding and correlating the information the map conveys to you.

But first, to get to the area you want to see, you must go to the right train station. Paris has six major train stations and probably the best train service of any country in the world. The trains are frequent, fast, punctual, comfortable, and clean. The TGV (*Train à Grande Vitesse*, which means high-speed train) now serves most of the major long-distance lines in France. These sleek, orange bullets travel at about 166 miles per hour. Except in first class, they are as cramped as the cheap section of an airplane, and you must make reservations to ride them. The TEE (*Trans-Europe Express*) is the luxury long-distance train. To ride it requires paying a small supplement over the regular first-class fare, and it travels at about 110 miles per hour. The *Corail*, a nice train that serves intermediate stops as

Train stations in France are often elegant, like this one in Tours.

well as long-distance destinations, has both first and second class coaches and compartments. You can reserve a seat if you want to, but it isn't necessary. Simply buy a ticket and get on board. These trains travel at about 86 miles per hour. The TGV's and TEE's have luxurious dining cars; most Corails have cafeteria-style grill cars. Those that do not offer instead sandwich and beverage service from carts pushed through the aisles. Meals and beverages aboard the trains are expensive; smart travelers concerned about economizing buy what they want for the journey and take it on board with them.

The word for station in French is *gare*. If you are going to the north of France, for example to Amiens to see the great cathedral there, or to Belgium, Holland or London, you leave from the *Gare du Nord*. If you are going east, to Reims and the Champagne country, or to Strasbourg and Alsace, you leave from the *Gare de l'Est*. If you are going west to Rouen or elsewhere in Normandy, you leave from the *Gare St. Lazare* (the one depicted in several paintings by Claude Monet). If you are going west to Brittany, you leave from the *Gare Montparnasse*. (Commuter trains go from here to Chartres, also, if you care to visit the greatest of all the Gothic cathedrals.)

To go to the southwest, a huge region that includes such destinations as Châteaudun, Vendôme, Blois, Orléans, Tours, Chinon, Saumur, Angers, Poitiers, Limoges, La Rochelle, Niort, Perigueux, Angoulême, and Bordeaux, among others, from the Loire Valley to the Pyrénées, you leave from the *Gare d'Austerlitz*. The TGVs leave from Gare Montparnasse.

To go to the southeast, also with divers (and diverse) destinations, including Clermont-Ferrand and the Auvergne, Lyon, Dijon and the Burgundy area, plus Nîmes, Avignon, Ar les, Marseille, Nice, Cannes, and the Riviera, Montpellier, Toulon, and Perpignan, you leave from the *Gare de Lyon*.

Maps for Touring

There are several series of suitable maps for bicycle touring in France. The Institut Geographique National (IGN) publishes 72 maps that cover all of continental France at a scale of 1 : 100,000. That means one centimeter on the map represents one kilometer on the ground. These are topographic maps and are excruciatingly detailed. I find them excellent for reference but cumbersome to use while cycling. '

The Michelin Tire Company publishes two series. The most popular one includes 36 maps that cover continental France at a scale of 1 : 200,000. The second series, to the same scale, covers the country with 16 (very large) regional maps. At scale 1 : 200,000, one centimeter on the map represents two kilometers on the ground. These maps do not show some of the tiniest roads that are included in the IGN maps, but they are nevertheless highly detailed, accurate, and provide a wealth of information. I find them ideal for practical use.

Michelin maps are sold in bookstores, newsstands, and train stations. In Paris, you will find a large selection at Smith's Book Store on the rue Rivoli, and at Brentanos on the avenue de l'Opéra. The maps are numbered and the outside cover shows the area included.

Segmented distances are shown in small red numerals between small red pins with solid heads. These pins mark an intersection or village. Overall distances between two major towns, marked with larger pins with doughnut heads, are shown in larger red numerals. In either case, the numerals represent kilometers.

The maps have symbols and markings to show altitude, the height and steepness of hills, the location of châteaux, ruins, abbeys, chapels, churches, cemeteries, swimming pools, monuments, rural restaurants and hotels, emergency telephones, hospitals, water towers, even panoramic views. The maps also show—quite accurately—the location of rivers, creeks, even small streams. All these features, and more, are explained in the legend on the inside cover of each map.

The roads are shown in three colors: red means high density traffic; yellow means moderate traffic; white means low density traffic. The roads are also shown in various widths which correspond accurately to what you will find to be the actual case. Roads that appear tiny on the map will be narrow on the ground. Scenic routes are designated with a green border beside them—but remember, these maps are intended primarily for motorists. Many small white roads are more scenic—and far more pleasant for cyclists—than a yellow or red road with a green stripe beside it.

When you see the symbol for a panoramic view, like the ribs of a collapsible fan, on the map, you can be sure that the view exists because of altitude. This means that to get there, you will have to pedal up a hill. The arrowhead markings tell you how steep the hill is. One arrowhead means a strenuous climb. Two arrowheads mean an arduous climb even with low-ratio gearing. Three arrowheads mean you might as well dismount and push the bike up the hill.

When you see that the road you are thinking about crosses the wiggly blue line that indicates a small stream, you know that you are going to descend to cross the stream and ascend on the other side. If the road you are thinking about parallels a solid black line, or crosses back and forth over it frequently, you may be sure the road is virtually flat. The solid black line is a railway line, and trains do not go up- and downhill much.

Hamlets and villages, in addition to being named, are indicated with small black rectangles which represent stores and houses. If you are looking at a road with a hamlet or village every four or five kilometers or so, you may be sure the road was built for the use of farmers and has very low density traffic. This is especially true if the road is curvy or wavy. Such roads are used only by an occasional farmer and the postman.

Low density traffic is usually coincident with a smooth surface. And it invariably means no billboards, no litter, and most often, no power poles or fences. Just a small lane meandering through open countryside —vineyards, meadows, forests, farms, pastures—and past an occasional château. The villages along these roads are often ancient, and in some of them you will find a church that dates back five or six centuries.

Michelin maps indicate distances between small pins to within 0.5 km (500 meters). Along the roads themselves, particularly at intersections, you will occasionally see signs that say the distance to the next village is perhaps 4.2 or 3.8 km—a very specific distance. You may wonder: what is the distance measured to, so precisely?

All distances in France (except to Paris) are measured from city hall to city hall, or town hall to town hall. If the village is too small to have even the most modest town hall, then it is measured to the village church. If the hamlet is so insignificant that it doesn't even have a church, then distances are measured to the cross-roads at which the hamlet is formed.

All distances to Paris, the one exception to the above, are measured to the front of the Cathedral of Notre Dame.

City Hall in French is *Hôtel de Ville*. It does not rent out rooms. Town Hall is *Mairie*. What more logical place for the office of *Monsieur le Maire*? (The Mayor.) Of course, it may be the office of *Madame la Maire*. France has many women mayors.

How far is a good day's ride? The answer to that depends on several considerations, not the least important of which is your attitude, your reason for going to France in the first place. If you are an easy-going person, someone who rides at an easy pace, the sort of person who wants to explore each village, to sit in the village tavern a few minutes and listen to the habitués, this will affect how far you ride per day.

If you are a photographer and like to stop and compose your photographs carefully, this, too, is a distance determinant.

If you want to stop and visit every château along the route, that takes time. Whatever your interests are—architecture, history, language, village life, agriculture, scenery—if you indulge them (and you certainly should: why else go there?) then the average daily distance is going to be less than what you are capable of riding.

Other factors to take into account are weather, terrain, whether you plan on having a picnic or prefer a sit-down-and-be-served lunch, what there is of special interest to see at your destination, and even such minor details as whether you must do laundry or not.

The Château at Chambord is part of the Loire Valley's Renaissance splendor.

The type of terrain you can expect to encounter can be estimated by the discussion of the various regions of France in Chapter 2, and by reading your map carefully. An abundance of hills will impede your pace. You might think that what you lose on the climb you would regain by zooming down the other side, but it doesn't work that way, for this reason: in France, you must descend hills cautiously. French cowherds, goat-herds, and shepherds often drive their herds along these country lanes. If you come flying down a hill at top speed, round a curve, and find yourself confronted by thirty cows occupying the entire road, including the shoulders, you're in big trouble. It is, therefore, imperative to descend hills cautiously, so you cannot make up the time you lose pedaling slowly up them.

Weather is an imponderable until you get there and start cycling. You may encounter an enervating heat wave that lasts for days and makes it necessary to set out early in the morning and stop for the day no later than noon. Or you may run into several days of unseasonably cold rain. Worst of all—whether the sun is shining brightly or the rain is coming down in torrents—you may encounter headwinds of discouraging force. All these elements are capricious and completely unpredictable. And they all affect the distance you can comfortably cycle in a day, during which you take the time to see what you want to see, and arrive at your day's destination at a reasonable hour.

Originally, I averaged close to 50 miles a day. Now, I've cut that back to thirty. When I was actively leading tours in France, I designed routes that averaged just slightly more than 30 miles for each day's ride, with no stage longer than 45 miles.

I find it pleasant to leave the hotel at a reasonable hour, which is around 8 a.m. for me; to cycle at 18 to 20 kilometers per hour (with a tail wind, I've averaged 30 km/h; against a strong headwind, 15 is the best I can do), and to stop in almost every village— I enjoy observing the degree to which rural France has retained its traditional customs. I like to look into the ancient churches and to think of all the generations that have worshipped in them. After 40-some tours, I've become indifferent to all but a few of the great Renaissance châteaux, but old abbeys, and the ruins of ancient castles and monasteries never lose their appeal for me.

I am not a picnic person; I am not fond of ants, flies, wasps, sunshine, and dust. The aspect of French civilization that attracts me most is the attitude the French have toward lunch. It is something to be enjoyed leisurely and in comfort. I share that regard for the culinary artistry of the country and for its gastronomical amenities. I have had many, many picnics in France, a few of which were enjoyable. But given a choice, 12:30 p.m. will find me comfortably ensconced in some attractive country inn or village restaurant.

After lunch, I like to rest, relax, do laundry, take a shower, change clothes, look around town, and sit at a sidewalk café and study the people who pass by. Whether for a private vacation or as the leader of a tour group, I have never gone to France to hurry from one place to another.

Late afternoon rides have their own special cachet of charm, particularly if there has been an afternoon rain. When it lets up, and the fields smell sweet and fresh, and steam is rising from the wet road surface, and towering cumulus clouds are billowing on the horizon, it is mysteriously beautiful to come riding into the town where you will stop for the evening and find it glowing in the slanting rays of the descending sun. This has occurred when I have waited out a rainstorm in some village restaurant, then have ridden on after the clouds have dispersed. Sometimes, there's a rainbow.

The final determinant in deciding how far you want to ride on any given day is the distance between where you start from and where you are going to stop. If your itinerary requires that you ride from one city to another, than that's it. The distance between them is the minimum you will ride that day. For this reason—and all of the reasons above—if you are making hotel reservations and adhering to an itinerary, it is wise to keep the daily stages to a reasonable length. If you err, it is better to err on the short side than to plan a ride that's too long. Better 20 miles than 60. I've made 60 and even 80-mile rides in France. Despite the softening effect time has on our memories, I look back on these rides, even now, with a shudder. A 65-mile ride from Rochechouart to Perigueux, most of it in a drenching downpour of cold rain, wasn't fun. An 83-mile ride against a headwind all the way from near Cognac to Mirebeau one September Sunday was an endurance test, not a pleasure trip.

If you are traveling without hotel reservations and are thus unencumbered by the obligation to arrive at a particular destination by a certain time (unsecured hotel reservations are held until 6 p.m.; then the room is rented to whoever asks for it), you have the freedom to deviate from your planned route and take any road that looks appealing. Even if you plan to end up in a certain town or city, don't allow the pleasure of impulsive exploring to slip by. If you come upon an especially beautiful road, take it. See where it goes. Don't worry about getting lost. If you have a map, you can't possibly get seriously lost in France. The roads are too well marked for that.

Besides, getting lost can be a pleasant adventure itself. One rainy autumn day in 1984, a man who seemed to have been right behind me (and one of ten persons in the group) was suddenly nowhere to be seen. I rode back to look for him but couldn't find him.

Don't worry about Ben, his wife said. He is the best navigator in the group. He was the chief pilot for one of America's major corporations. He had been a military pilot during one of the wars. He was so cool that he would make an iceberg look like a tropical island.

The whole group stopped for a pre-arranged lunch. Ben didn't show up. I promised his wife that if he was still missing when we reached our destination that afternoon, I'd borrow a car and look for him.

When we reached the hotel, there stood Ben, wearing gray flannel slacks, a cashmere sweater, a silk scarf loosely tucked into his collar, and a broad smile.

"What happened?" we asked him, practically in unison.

"I wasn't paying attention and took a wrong turn somewhere," he said. "The next thing I knew—I looked up and nobody was there. Pretty soon, I came to a village. I remembered what you said about finding a bar near the church so I headed for the church— I could see the steeple—and sure enough, there beside it was a bar.

"I went in and asked if anyone could speak English. One man said he could speak a *'leetul beet.'* I told him I was lost and was looking for the road to Loudun.

"He said, instead of trying to explain, he would take me there in his truck. But first he took me to his house—a farmhouse —and showed me his *cave.* He's a wine-maker. We tasted wine straight from the barrel for half an hour, then he put a case of wine in the back of the truck with my bike and drove me to the hotel. The wine is for everybody. I've been here three hours. I hope you weren't worried."

The late Dr. Clifford Graves, who pioneered bicycle touring in France for Americans long before it became so popular, used to tell about a young married couple on one of his tours who got separated from the group. When they got to the next town, they sat down at one of those tables shaded by an umbrella to have a bite of lunch and study their map.

They were poring over the map when a woman came out and asked if there were anything she could get for them. The young man said he'd like a bottle of beer and a ham sandwich. His wife asked for a glass of white wine and some cheese and bread.

It came in due time. They ate, figured out their route, and called to the woman who had served them.

"*L'addition, s'il vous plaît!*"

"There's no charge," the woman said with a smile. "You're in my garden."

According to Dr. Graves, the woman waved aside their embarrassment; they exchanged names and addresses, and remained pen-pals for many years.

In short, if you do get lost, get lost creatively, and make the most of the opportunity.

CHAPTER 7

Where to Stay

During the hours of darkness, *la nuit* in French (night), the sensible cyclist sleeps. The question is: Where? Basically, there are five choices:

☐ In a château;

☐ In a youth hostel;

☐ In a small hotel or inn;

☐ In a chambre d'hôte;

☐ In a field or forest (camping).

Numerous châteaux in France have been converted to hotels. Some of them are extremely gracious places, with such amenities as tennis courts and swimming pools in addition to the suave, silken service. Compared with the cost of a room in a New York hotel, the price is not exorbitant. The cost of a double room in a typical château-hotel—at the time this book was written (in the summer of 1991)—ranged from around $150 to $200.

To stay in one, reservations are necessary and should be made well in advance. Once you have decided on the area in which you wish to cycle, talk with a travel agent. All good agencies have reference books that list the names of all the châteaux that are now hotels, their addresses (and even small maps showing their exact locations), and their prices. The agent will make the reservation for you (eight percent of the cost will be paid by the château to the agent). If you cannot find an agent who has the information about such places, you can obtain it yourself by contacting:

Relais et Châteaux
Centre d'Information
17 Place Vendôme
75001 Paris
F R A N C E
Tel. (from the USA): 011 33 1 42 61 56 50

Except in the Loire Valley, these places are too spaced out (in many ways) to make them your destination every night. But if you have worked out your general itinerary, you could arrange one such reservation, and then plan your specific itinerary around that date and destination.

The principal drawback to staying in a château-hotel (apart from the cost) is that almost all of them are a considerable distance from the nearest town. There is not a great deal to do at these places except eat, drink, and contemplate the evaporation of your money.

Youth hostels are also usually found out in the country. They are extremely inexpensive—and rightly so: They are little more than barracks. Staying in youth hostels restricts your freedom: you must check in at opening time which is 4 p.m. They fill up fast, and if you arrive late, you will be out of luck. And out, period.

Hosteling ('Youth' is no longer appropriate, because vagabonds —free spirits—of all ages are hostelers) requires a resilient personality and an abundant tolerance for noise and inconvenience. Most of them have communal showers and too few toilets. Their managers are often misanthropic, a condition acquired, no doubt, by protracted association with certain types who elect to stay in hostels.

They are regularly sprayed with disinfectants and the odor is unpleasant, to put it mildly. This astringent odor combines

The Château de Marçay is now a hotel.

with that of unwashed bodies (the communal shower does not appeal to many) and misused toilet facilities, and the general effect makes one prefer to be at the North Pole without a blanket, if that were the only other choice. The decibel level of 'conversation' and rock music from radios is just fractionally less than that of a major earthquake.

The appeal of hostels is beyond my comprehension. The argument has been put forth that they are great places 'to meet people.' No doubt they are. But I do not care to meet the sort of people who voluntarily stay in such places. Not all of them are necessarily as bad as I have described them. (I have not visited all of them, of course.) But the conditions described are those that seem generally to prevail, I regret to say.

In fairness to the concept, I should add that all this does not stem from a flaw intrinsic to the idea (other than it was, like other utopian ideas, premised on the intrinsic goodness of mankind). Nor are all hostelers the bane of civilized society. But in a hostel that accommodates, let's say, forty persons, it only takes five or six to make a mess of the place, to create the unsanitary conditions, to generate the noise, and there seems to be no shortage of such types, alas....

The small hotel or inn (*auberge* is the French word for 'inn') is, in my opinion, the best choice for an overnight resting place. Such places are found in every town and in most villages throughout France. They may have as few as six rooms, and rarely have more than twenty or thirty. They are family-owned as a rule, and often have been operated by the same family for generations. Each place has its own particular charm and character. Some of them do not have baths and toilets in every room—but the facilities, 'down the hall,' are kept spotlessly clean. And the prices of rooms without these amenities are incredibly low. Even the rooms with the 'comforts' are inexpensive. In the city of Blois, for example, in 1991, one could have a very comfortable room for two persons with bath and toilet for slightly more than $29 a night. Not $29 each; $29 for both. (The cost of the room was 180 francs; the value of the franc was $0.163.)

Naturally, these hotels are popular with European travelers, the result of which is that they are filled almost every night—especially during the cycling season. If you want to stay in a small hotel or auberge, during the late spring, summer, or early fall, it would be highly advisable to make reservations well in advance. Figure out your itinerary from a general map of France (the highly-detailed Michelin maps are available in some American book stores, such as Brentanos) then write to the Syndicat d'Initiative in the towns where you want to spend the night and request the names and addresses of hotels. Enclose a self-addressed envelope and international postage coupons (available at your post office). You should do this at least six months in advance of your trip.

Once you obtain the names and addresses of hotels, write for reservations. You will probably be asked to make a deposit. You can do this with a travelers check in French francs. Many banks sell American Express checks in French francs; they are also obtainable at AAA (American Automobile Association) offices if you are a member of the local club that is associated with AAA. At banks, you will be charged a fee of one percent for the checks. At AAA offices, there is no charge for members. The checks are available in 200-franc and 500-franc denominations.

For one room in a small hotel, the deposit usually requested is 200 francs. This is applied to the cost of the room, of course, which may be anywhere from 140 to 350 francs, depending on the location of the hotel and its quality. Any excess will be applied to breakfast or refunded.

The star rating system is not necessarily an accurate guide to the quality of a hotel. Of course, a hotel with no stars or one star is apt to be a very plain place, and a hotel with four stars is apt to be elegant, and will invariably be expensive. But many two-star hotels are rat-traps, while many others with two stars are idyllic places with great charm. For example, the *Hôtel du Grand Monarque* in Azay-le-Rideau has been host to two American presidents—Truman and Eisenhower—and to the Duke of Kent. It has only two stars (as of this writing). It could add a third star if it wanted to, but that would put it into a higher tax bracket.

The *Hôtel Diderot* in Chinon is another example of the capriciousness of the French star system. It is one of the most charming small hotels in the Loire Valley. Its owner is a Greek Cypriot and a civil engineer by profession; his wife was formerly a nurse specializing in tropical diseases. The building was an 18th century residence—a town mansion —which was converted into a hotel. The present owner bought it after this conversion and added modern plumbing. It had a one-star rating.

Because the star system is generally misunderstood by foreigners (such as us Americans) the hotel did not have the clientele it deserved. So the owner applied for, and was given, an additional star. Now the Hôtel Diderot is rated ** NN and is filled up every night. The owner is permitted to charge more for the rooms than he formerly charged, and is required to pay more taxes. He could have three stars if he wished, but he doesn't. Three-star hotels are seldom better than good two-star hotels, but are higher priced.

The French spelling, incidentally, is the same as the English, except for the circumflex over the 'o'—hôtel. This indicates that the letter that used to follow the 'o' has been dropped. Hôtel was formerly 'hostel.' The word château was once 'chastel.'

To write for a room reservation, follow the model letter shown below.

What you have said is: "Sir, I plan to make a bike trip in France and I would like to stay in your hotel. Therefore, I would like to reserve a room with shower or bath, and toilet,

---

Your Name   *Your street address*
                               Your town, state, and Zip
                               U.S.A.

La Direction Hôtel (name of hotel)
Street address
01234 French Town
FRANCE

Monsieur,

Je compte de faire une randonnée au vélo en France, et je voudrais bien rester dans votre hôtel. Aussi, je voudrais reserver une chambre avec douche ou bain, et W.C., pour la nuit de mercredi, du 6 au 7 Septembre, 1992, s'il vous plaît.

Voudriez vous bien me faire savoir si cela vous convient, et le prix de la chambre. Si vous désirez des arrhes, je les envoyerai immediament.

Dans l'attente du plaisir de la visite, je vous prie d'agréer, Monsieur, l'expression de mes salutations distinguées.

Your name   *Your signature*

---

for the night of Wednesday, from the 6th to the 7th, of September. Please let me know if this is acceptable. If you want a deposit, I'll send it right away. Sincerely yours…."

The days of the week, in French, are:		The cycling months, in French, are:	
dimanche	Sunday	*avril*	April
lundi	Monday	*mai*	May
mardi	Tuesday	*juin*	June
mercredi	Wednesday	*juillet*	July
jeudi	Thursday	*août*	August
vendredi	Friday	*septembre*	September
samedi	Saturday	*octobre*	October

Note that in specifying the date of your stay, you write *du*, a contraction of *de le* meaning 'from the,' and *au*, a contraction of *à le* meaning 'to the'. The French are very logical: You go to bed on one date; you rise on the following date.

Many of the small hotels and most of the auberges have dining rooms. If they do, you can almost always rely on the quality of the cuisine. Minimally, it will be very good; often, it will be outstanding; occasionally, superb. An example of 'very good' is the *Hôtel de la Gare et Terminus* in Blois. It is so good that many of the residents of the city have lunch there every day and dine there on Sunday nights. An example of outstanding is the restaurant *Diane de Méridor*, an adjunct of the *Hôtel Le Bussy* (Diane and Le Bussy were historic personnages and are characters in a novel by Alexandre Dumas, père) in Montsoreau, a river port village on the Loire. The *Hôtel La Loire*, also in Montsoreau, has an outstanding dining room. An example of 'superb' is the cuisine at the *Hôtel Central* in St. Jean-Pied-de-Port near the Spanish border.

If the hotel has a dining room, overnight guests are expected to dine there—but it is rarely mandatory. Where it is, the price of the room is designated as being demi-pension which means that one major meal is included. (Your choice of beverage is not included, for obvious reasons.) The *Grand Monarque* in Azay-le-Rideau, for example, where the cuisine is somewhere between outstanding and superb, quotes prices 'demi-pension.' The same is true of the *Hôtel Lion d'Or* in Amboise.

Many small hotels do not have a *salle à manger*, (dining room) which leaves you free to search out an attractive restaurant. The hotel owner will be glad to recommend places to you, and you can rely on the recommendations, because the hotel owner wants you to be happy —and will not recommend a place that serves bad or overpriced food.

All hotels serve breakfast. This is usually the so-called 'continental breakfast,' which consists of a choice of beverages (coffee, tea, or hot chocolate) plus bread, butter, and jam. Some times the 'bread' is a croissant. Such a breakfast may seem inadequate by American or British standards, but it is high in carbohydrates and suffices to fuel any normal human being for a morning of cycling. (Actually, it is what you had for dinner the night before that provides the fuel for morning ride.)

Curiously, the French word for lunch, the midday meal (which is often the largest meal of the day) is literally 'breakfast': *déjeuner*. (*Jeuner* means 'to fast.' The prefix *dé* means 'un' to 'unfast'—to break the fast.) The French term that corresponds to our breakfast is *le petit déjeuner*, ('the little breakfast'). Which brings us to the fourth choice, the *chambre d'hôte*, the French expression for what the British have popularized as 'bed and breakfast.'

In France, all places classified as chambres d'hôte ('bedrooms of the host') must meet certain standards set by the French government, and are regularly inspected on an unannounced basis to insure conformance to these standards. To find out in advance the location of such places, use the model letter asking for the names and addresses of hotels. Simply substitute *chambre d'hôte* for *hôtel*.

Such places usually have only two or three guest rooms, but a few have as many as twelve. The parallel with the British bed and breakfast is misleading, since many serve family-style dinners as well. That is to say, all the guests staying overnight sit around one large table and are served whatever the host— or, more usually, the hostess —has prepared. At those places that do serve dinner, the meals are often wonderful. But not always.

In the village of Monts-sur-Guesnes, 10 miles from the town of Loudun, there is a chambre d'hôte operated by a former Parisian where the dinners (in my experience) have been dreadful.

On the other hand, the chambre d'hôte called *La Guertière* near the town of Richelieu, 13 miles south of Chinon, serves meals that are veritable regal feasts, with apéritifs and wines included. Room, dinner, and breakfast, all of it, costs approximately $30.

If you are cycling in France without reservations and want to spend the night in a chambre d'hôte, stop in the village bar and ask where one might be found. The bartender can almost invariably supply you with the name and address of the place, and even sketch a map for you, showing how to find it. He (or she) will, in most cases, telephone to make a reservation for you if you appear 'serious.' In that case, you should go immediately to confirm your intention of spending the night there.

If you are in a town or city that has an *Office du Tourisme*, you can obtain a booklet that lists all the chambres d'hôte in the area from the office. Also, if you stay in one, you can ask the host at that one for the name and address of another one near your next destination. The host will be glad to telephone to make a reservation for you if you wish.

The cost of a room at a chambre d'hôte is usually a pittance compared with hotel prices. I have stayed in such places where (in 1985) $12 paid for the room, dinner, and breakfast. And the room had a modern private bathroom with a glassed-in shower.

Most of these chambres d'hôte are, in fact, farmhouses that accept guests. Typical is *La Tallanderie* near the château and village of Villandry. This farm is owned by a retired French army colonel named William Hausser, who raises horses (and supplies manure for the gardens of the Château de Villandry). The farm is located on the flat expanse of land between and high above the Cher and Indre rivers. In 1991, a room for two there cost $18, including breakfast. They do not serve dinner. When I stayed there, I bought picnic supplies at the village grocery store and had a private picnic on an umbrella-shaded table on the beautifully tended and flower-bordered lawn.

If you want to obtain the names and addresses of all the chambres d'hôtes in any given area, get a good overall map of France, such as the Michelin 1 : 1,000,000 scale road map, and write a letter to the Office du Tourisme in the chief city of the area asking for the brochure that lists them. The chief city in any given *Département* has the name shown in boldface type, in capital letters, and the circle that represents the city has a 'P' in it, which stands for *Préfecture*. Request that it be sent by airmail (*poste aérienne*) and enclose $5 worth of international postage coupons. Otherwise, it will be sent by surface mail which takes up to two months. You can write in English.

Finally, camping. This is the least expensive choice, the one that permits the most freedom, and it is the most uncomfortable. (There has to be some sort of trade-off...)

When my wife and I made our first cycling tour in France, the 720-mile trip from Mirebeau to Spain and back, we camped out most of the way. Only once did we stay in a designated camping area, and that was in Vieux Boucau on the Atlantic Coast. The rest of the time we simply stopped at some appealing meadow or woodland, and spread out our ground-cloth (an oil-cloth, actually) and unrolled our sleeping bags.

The back roads of France are so lightly traveled that this can be done safely and practically. But, as we quickly learned, there are certain techniques which, if followed, make camping out much more pleasant than doing it haphazardly.

First of all, take a look at the map—your highly detailed Michelin 1 : 200,000 map—and estimate where you are going to be at mid-afternoon. What you want to do is stop in a village grocery store before you get to where you think you will camp and buy what you want for supper. Make it simple: a vegetable that can be eaten raw, such as a carrot or turnip or tomato (yes, I know a tomato is actually a berry and thus a fruit); a piece of fruit such as an apple, pear, or banana; some meat that does not require cooking, such as slices of *saucisson sec* or boiled ham, known in France as *jambon de Paris* or *jambon blanc*; plus a bottle of inexpensive wine; perhaps some cheese; and a *baguette* (or, better yet, a *pain complet*—whole-grain bread: unsliced and delicious, as well as good for you).

Then continue on, looking for a likely campsite, such as the far corner of a meadow, or a patch of woods with a stream running through it, but in any case, between five to ten kilometers from the next village. Stop for the night a few miles short of the next village or town. This way, when you get up the next morning, pack up, clean up the site (you should not leave the slightest trace of your having been there), and ride on, you will quickly come to the next village or town, and there you can have breakfast in the village café, and, more importantly, in this café you can use the toilet.

With proper diet, your body will adapt itself to this schedule, the importance of which, on a cycling trip on roads that do not have service stations with toilets, can hardly be over-emphasized.

But even if you plan a trip that involves camping, you will want to stay in a hotel occasionally—to wash yourself and your clothes. My wife and I found that five nights of camping out was enough to make a hotel highly desirable on the sixth.

On our trip from Mirebeau to Spain, by the sixth night out, we were grimy, weary, and very much in need of the comforts afforded by a hotel. We pushed our bikes up a terribly steep hill into a town called St. Sever. Near the top of the hill, we came to a hotel called, *Hôtel de France et des Ambassadeurs*.

"Wait here and watch the bikes," I said to Janie, who was wearing jeans, a windbreaker, and a cheap 'cowboy hat' to shield her face from the sun. "I'll go in and get us a room."

The woman at the desk took one look at me (or caught a whiff of me) and informed me that the hotel was 'complet' (filled). I was so disappointed that I almost broke out in tears. It was now seven o'clock in the evening and we were too tired to ride on and look for a place to camp.

"Please! don't you have anything at all?" I pleaded.

"Non, Monsieur; nous sommes complet." (No, sir. The hotel is filled.)

Another woman emerged from the back office. She was stately and moved with grace and elegance. Very calmly she said: "We have Room Three."

The first woman, the clerk, looked stunned.

"Chambre trois?" she exclaimed, increduously.

"Yes, chambre trois," said the other woman, obviously the owner of the hotel. Then she whispered to the clerk, all of this in French, of course, "Go outside and see who he has with him."

While the clerk was gone, I registered for the room. When she returned, she whispered to the smiling, gracious owner: "He has his little boy with him."

When we came down to dinner, well-scrubbed and wearing clean clothes, the hotel staff was surprised by the magical transformation of this 'little boy' into an attractive young woman.

What was so special about Room Three? A marble fireplace; original oil paintings on the walls; a polished oval mahogany table with six high-back chairs upholstered in red velvet in the center of the room; a huge canopied bed in an alcove; an ultra-modern bath room with a glass-door shower, and a balcony. The cost of the room, that August in 1972, was 35 francs. Translated into dollars, $7.35. Ten years later, inflation had pushed prices in France to double or triple what they had formerly been. Hotel rooms that had once been incredible bargains were now priced at three times their former cost.

In 1981 I made another trip—with a tour-group—through south-western France and across the Pyrénées into Spain. This time I wrote to the Hôtel de France et des Ambassadeurs for reservations and asked if I might again have Room Three.

The hotel owner, who had been charmed by the transformation of my 'son' into my wife, charged me the current rate for the rooms occupied by my companions on the trip, but for Room Three, charged me only 35 francs, the same price I'd paid in 1972. Except that the exchange rate in 1981, made this only $6.48. The French are a very sentimental and generous people.

A word about laundering clothes at hotels. First of all, many hotels will do this for you if you have checked in early enough, or are staying two nights. To launder socks, underwear, and a shirt or two, the usual charge is 20 to 30 francs. Simply ask at the registration desk.

If you do it yourself, there are techniques that reduce the drying time, and there are also certain rules that should be followed. Let the items soak a few minutes in water to which you have added Woolite. (A little is quite enough.) Then wring out the items, and soak them in a change of water. (I use both the hand basin and the bidet.) Wring them out again, and soak them again in a change of water.

Now, ring them out as hard as you can, then flap the items as though you were cracking a whip until there is no more spray to be felt when you do this.

Hang the items on clothes hangers and, wherever possible, prevent one surface from touching another. For example, if you put a pair of undershorts on the hanger by placing the ends of the hanger in the waist-band, you can then separate the surfaces by carefully placing a pocket pack of Kleenex crossways in the center of the waistband. This allows the air to circulate on all sides of all surfaces, which accelerates evaporation of the moisture and reduces drying time to a couple of hours.

There are several prohibitions which should be strictly observed:

☐ Do not allow clothes to drip onto the floor or rug. Put a towel under them.

☐ Do not place wet clothes on furniture, because the wetness will cause stains.

☐ Do not hang clothes in the window. It looks tacky and the hotel owners don't like it. Many small hotels have clotheslines 'out back,' where you can hang clothes; some of them have laundry drying rooms which you may be permitted to use.

Towns and cities have laundromats with dryers. If you are staying at a hotel in a city, the concierge at the desk can give you the location of the *laverie automatique*.

Incidentally, every major city in France has been accurately mapped by a company called *Plans-Guides Blay*. These maps include every street—and if the street is one-way, arrows show which direction— plus commentary about the city, including its history, places of interest (museums, historic churches, etc.), and the names and addresses of all hotels. They also give the address of the *Office du Tourisme*. These maps are inexpensive, and can be purchased at railway station newsstands, and at bookstores.

CHAPTER 8

Manners and Customs

One of the pleasures of traveling to a foreign country is that when you get there, you become the foreigner. If you are observant, you can learn what—apart from the language—differentiates the culture and customs of the country you are visiting from your own. Unfortunately, there are those who go abroad insisting that everything conform to American standards or usage, and who ridicule anything that doesn't. Because they make so much noise, it takes only a few such ill-bred boors to persuade the native population that Americans in general are a bunch of bad-mannered morons. Once that perception has been formed, it requires a great amount of tact and diplomacy to efface it.

Customs and culture differ somewhat from one region of France to another. Bretons, Normands, Alsatians, Provençals, Basques, and Gascons all have their distinct patterns of life, their own habits, and characteristics. But there are certain

French etiquette requires that both hands be on the table. Everything is 'above board.'

ingrained traits that are pervasive throughout France. One of these has to do with table manners.

Americans are taught to sit up straight at the dining room table, chew with their mouths closed, hold their fork in the right hand, to rest the knife on the rim of the plate when it is not in use, and to keep the left hand in their lap out of sight.

In France, some of these 'rules' are drastically different, as indeed they are in most other European countries. Putting one's left hand in one's lap is so rude that it makes a French person very uncomfortable when you do that. In France, both hands should be in sight at all times.

This bit of etiquette goes back to medieval times, when rival knights and barons sat together with the lord of the castle to partake of a meal and iron out their differences.

Until a few decades ago, in any American city you could see a sign tacked to a house saying: 'Room and board.' These places, called 'boarding houses,' rented rooms by the week or month to single men and sometimes women, and provided meals. The 'board' referred to the meals; more precisely, to the dining room table.

We still have the expression: 'Everything was above board,' meaning out-in-the-open, honest, with nothing hidden or suspicious. Again, the 'board' refers to the dining table. Everyone's hands were on the table in plain view when such and such transpired. There was no hanky-panky under the table.

The medieval lord's table usually was made, in fact, of a few long, wide, thick boards supported by trestles. The lord of the manor sat in a highbacked chair; his distinguished guests of honor sat in (or on) smaller chairs; everyone else sat on benches along the length of the table.

Motion pictures present a distorted view of the medieval feast. More often, the main dish, indeed, quite often the only dish, was a stew of 'gamy' meat (there was no refrigeration in the crude castles of the minor nobility; great lords such as dukes and kings might have a small room packed with snow and ice that would last well into summer) and vegetables. Wooden bowls or sometimes pieces of hard bread served as 'plates'; the stew was eaten by skewering solid pieces of meat or vegetables with one's dagger; the liquid was sopped up with bread. Forks were introduced to France by the entourage of Catherine de Medici when she came across the Alps from Italy to marry Henri II, king of France, in 1533.

Every man carried a dagger in a scabbard hanging from his belt or 'girdle.' Occasionally, when tempers flared, fights erupted and one participant would stab the other. When arch-rivals were seated close together at these gatherings, it was not unknown for one of them to hold his dagger under the table and, at an opportune moment, stab his foe in the stomach with a hard back-hand thrust.

Whereupon the foe usually fell forward into the mashed potatoes and gravy, making a terrible mess and spoiling everyone's appetite —for a few minutes at least.

To curb this sort of thing, the custom was promulgated and adopted requiring every person at the table to keep both hands in sight at all times. This would prevent surreptitious stabbing-in-the-stomach under the table. In time, this became the keystone of French table manners and although very few guests today would actually murder anyone during dinner, the requirement of keeping both hands in full view is now so thoroughly ingrained that to do otherwise is deemed unspeakably rude. Therefore, when you are in France, never put your 'free' left hand in your lap. Keep it 'above board.'

The fork is held upside-down in the left hand; the knife—used both to cut and as a 'pusher'—is held, rather like a pencil, in the right hand. Even when the knife is not being used, both hands should remain in view.

American cyclists enjoy a dinner party with a French friend. At the head of the table is the celebrated artist Jackie Tanvier.

Bread is placed on the table, not on the plate. It is broken off into smaller pieces and used—as it was in medieval times—to sop up gravy or sauces, even the vinaigrette sauce that accompanies raw vegetables and salads.

The French clean their plates thoroughly. Nothing remains but the bones—if there were any to begin with. To leave food on the plate indicates that what the chef or your host (or hostess) served you was inedible or poorly prepared. For this reason, the American visitor should choose wisely, and take small portions.

The French do not rush through a meal, and they think Americans are barbaric if they do so. Almost everyone in France gets two hours off for lunch; many take two-and-a-half or even three. Lunch is a leisurely meal, the highlight of the day, something to be savored and appreciated, not wolfed down. No French person has lunch alone if she or he can help it. The very word 'companion' means someone to break bread with, i.e., share a meal with, and the French like companionship at the table.

Conversation is as important to the meal as the main dish or the wine. The French love to discuss things—anything: politics, weather, economics, love, travel, philosophy, art, music, wine, the end of the world, and what's wrong these days with Paris (this has been a topic of conversation for centuries; something is always wrong with Paris).

However, not everyone is fortunate enough to have a companion for lunch or dinner, so some must dine alone. Usually, he or she brings along a book or magazine or the daily paper to supply the intellectual stimulation that is the role of conversation.

Seats at tables are not wasted. In small French restaurants, a person entering alone will often be seated at the table of someone in similar circumstances. In such instances, it is polite to acknowledge the other person's presence by wishing him or her *"Bon appétit,"* after which it is polite (for us foreigners) to remain silent, except to ask the other person to pass the salt or the mustard. If you are seated at a Frenchman's table, or he at yours, and he strikes up a conversation (*"Vous êtes Américain?"*), then of course it is polite to respond. But it is not polite for us to interrupt the train of thought of the French person by making idle observations such as *"Il fait beau temps, non?"* (Nice weather, isn't it?)

In Spain, to summon a waiter it is perfectly all right to snap your fingers or to clap your hands to get his attention. In France, this is not done. You may call to the waiter, or raise an index finger beckoningly, but no clapping, snapping, or whistling.

French waiters, knowing the spiritual and aesthetic importance of the meal, never hurry anyone. On the contrary, you may begin to suspect that the place will close for remodeling before someone gives you the check. When you want to settle up and go, it is acceptable to call to the waiter or waitress and say, *"L'addition, s'il vous plaît!"* (The check, please.)

In America, men hold the door open and allow their female companions to enter first. In France, the man leads the way. This also harks back to the Middle Ages when the man entered a room first to make sure no evil-doer was lurking in the shadows, then, when safety was assured, allowed his female companion to join him.

Upon entering a restaurant—any restaurant other than American fast-food franchise clones—one will be greeted by a waiter or waitress, head-waiter, host, hostess, chef, somebody. You announce your desires by requesting the appropriate number of place settings.

Instead of saying, *"Une table pour deux personnes, s'il vous plaît,"* (A table for two, please), the correct phrase is: *"Deux couverts, s'il vous plaît."* (Two place settings, please). The table may be big enough for four, six, eight, or even ten persons. So it isn't a 'table for two' you want; it's two places at a table.

Small grocery stores are called *épiceries,* (spice shops) an echo over the centuries from the days when most of the meat was in the process of rotting and, after the Crusades opened up trade with the East, the source of most spices, these were used to mask the taste and smell of the meat. Ginger was particularly popular. Once it arrived in Western Europe, there was hardly a dish that didn't incorporate it.

Nowadays, most village épiceries are *libre service* (self service), but not all. Unless you see the sign in the window that says LIBRE SERVICE, you should take a look and see what other customers are doing before you start helping yourself. There are still quite a few grocery stores where the proprietor or clerk gets for you the items you specify.

Upon entering a small store, or bakery, or delicatessen, if there are other customers there ahead of you, it is polite to greet them by saying, *"Messieurs, dames..."* When departing, it is polite to take leave of those still there by saying, *"Au revoir, messieurs, dames."* Listen carefully and you'll quickly pick up the pronunciation and tone of voice in which these greetings and farewells are expressed.

Charcuteries (delicatessens) and *pâtisseries* (bakeries that produce cakes, tarts, pies, etc., and often bread as well) are never self-service. Customers wait in line for their turn to be served. This is also true in *boulangeries*, the bakeries that sell only bread. (Some bakeries also sell boxes of snack crackers.)

Laiteries sell milk and butter; *boucheries* sell meat to be cooked; *fruiteries* sell fresh fruits; *fromageries* sell scores of kinds of cheeses. These specialized shops are giving way now to minimarkets and supermarkets, but may still be encountered here and there. The épiceries have greatly expanded the range of items they stock, and in a village's sole épicerie may be found needles and threads, school supplies, jigsaw puzzles, kitchen utensils, milk, wine, bottled water, canned foods, fresh vegetables and fruits, cooked or cured meats, digital watches, playing cards, cigarette lighters, candy, and much more, all of this crammed into a store probably not as large as your living room.

Sadly, these traditional stores and specialty shops are fading from the scene. They still exist in villages and small towns, but supermarkets are now ubiquitous, and the hypermarkets that sell everything from radishes to real estate are increasingly commonplace.

It is quite all right in France to buy one apple, one pear, one banana, one carrot, one tomato, or one of anything else you want for your picnic.

Shops such as those described here are open on Sunday morning; they usually close around 12:30 or 1:00 p.m. and remain closed until Tuesday. Monday is the traditional 'closing day' for all sorts of shops, including pharmacies and bike shops. (Many pharmacies are closed on Sunday as well as on Monday.)

Tuesday through Saturday, these shops are generally open from early morning until 12:30, then they close for lunch and reopen at 3:00 or 3:30 or whenever they feel like it, and remain open until 7:00 or so. Except in a few very large cities, banks and department stores close promptly at noon and reopen at 2 p.m. The lights go out; customers are hustled out the door (sometimes the back door), and everyone dashes off to a leisurely lunch.

For national monuments, such as châteaux, museums, historic abbeys, and the like, Tuesday is usually the closing day. Some of the great châteaux remain open every day of the week, but most of them are closed on Tuesday, and a few are closed part of Monday or Wednesday as well. Châteaux that provide guided tours close for lunch. Those that permit self-guided tours usually remain open during the two-hour lunch period. Almost all museums are closed on Tuesdays. This custom should be borne in mind when you are planning your itinerary. Post offices in villages and small towns also close for the two-hour lunch. Most of them remain open until 6 p.m., sometimes until 6:30.

Banks in France usually open at 8:30 a.m.; a few as early as 8:00. This is convenient if you need to cash a traveler's check before you set out on the morning ride.

Main post offices in cities will cash travelers checks. The fee is approximately the same as in commercial banks such as the Crédit Agricole, Banque Nationale de Paris, Société Générale, Crédit Lyonnais, Banque Populaire, and so forth. Not all branches of these commercial banks handle travelers checks. Those that do usually have a small sign somewhere on the front of the building or in a window that says CHANGE.

The Banque de France, which corresponds to the United States Federal Reserve System or the Bank of England, and which prints and distributes the money (it does not deal in

Every town in France has an open-air market like this one in Poitiers, at least one day a week.

such matters as checking accounts, savings accounts, loans, the sort of business handled by commercial banks), will exchange French currency for traveler's checks, but for American Express checks only. For anyone exchanging a sizable sum (suppose you have been designated 'treasurer' for a group composed of several couples on a cycling excursion in France) it makes sense to exchange your checks at the Banque de France because it gives the exact rate and does not append a service charge. You will get more francs for your dollars.

The Banque de France in Paris is located on the rue Croix de Petits Champs, diagonally behind (north of) the Palais Royal, off the rue de Rivoli, which runs along the north side of the Louvre.

Most major cities have branches. The one in Blois, for example, is on the avenue Jean Laigret about 150 meters from the train station. (These banks are shown on city maps, such as Michelin, Plans-Guides Blay, Leconte, etc. Other banks do not enjoy this distinction.)

But remember, banks in France close for the lunch 'deux-heures,' and they close for all national and religious holidays as well, which, in France, are far more numerous than in the United States. For example: May Day; Ascension Day; Joan of Arc Festival Day; the Monday after Pentecost; Assumption Day; and, of course, the 'Fête Nationale,' Bastille Day, which is like the American Fourth. of July but ten days later. This is just a partial list of official holidays when all banks and many stores are closed.

If you have travelers checks in French francs, you can use them to pay your hotel bill and keep the change. For example, if you hotel bill is 240 F, you can pay with a 500 F check and thus acquire 260 F in cash without having to go to the bank and fill out forms.

Hotels are less eager to accept checks in dollars because, after all, they are not banks, and do not have the information on exchange rates that banks have. Large hotels will, however, accept checks in dollars (not personal checks; travelers checks only) as a courtesy to their clients. The exchange rate, however, will be less favorable than you would get at a bank.

While on the subject of banks and post offices (post offices also exchange francs for checks) it might prove handy to know that when post offices are closed for the evening, the weekend, or for a holiday, you can still buy postage stamps if you need them. Just look for the two red cones attached at their large ends that designate a bar licensed to sell tobacco products and is therefore a *tabac* as well as a bar or café or tavern. All tabacs sell postage stamps. They do not sell the beautiful commemorative ones you can find in the post offices, but they have the standard '*Mariannes*' (comparable to the American 'flag' stamps) in several commonly used denominations. So if you've written a dozen postcards and want to mail them before setting off tomorrow but are out of stamps, simply look for a *tabac*. Since the owner sells stamps at face value and makes no profit on them, it is polite to have a drink at the bar—a glass of beer or wine, or a cup of coffee or a soft drink—then to buy the stamps when paying the tab.

Stamps are called *timbres poste*. To buy a few, simply ask for "*des timbres-poste, s'il vous plaît.*" (Some stamps, please).

The cashier will ask you what denomination you want and how many. Two ordinary stamps used for letters in France will suffice to send one postcard to the States via airmail, so simply reply that you want (the number of postcards times two) "*timbres tarif ordinaires.*" Be sure to mark your postcards PAR AVION. Otherwise, they may go by surface mail (boat) which can take anywhere from four weeks to four months.

Café-bars and taverns abound in France; there is scarely any village so humble as not to have a café-bar. Many of these serve simple meals, such as sandwiches, crêpes, or pizzas heated in a microwave oven, and sometimes omelettes, but more importantly, they take the place of service stations with respect to toilet facilities.

Many villages and most towns have public toilets, but unless they have attendants, these are often revoltingly unsanitary. The bar's toilet is usually better maintained. If you are cycling and develop an increasingly urgent need to visit a restroom, the choice is between taking to the woods or waiting until you arrive at the next village. In the areas that are most suitable for cycling—because of the multiplicity of untrafficked roads—villages are seldom more than three to five miles apart.

To find the toilet quickly, look for the church steeple and head for it. Near the church will be a bar. Sometimes across the street or village square, sometimes next door. But never very far away. The reason for this is that on Sundays wives go to church, while their husbands gather in the bars to pass the time talking. Women worship; men drink. So the bar is never far from the church.

Go in; order anything you like—but something; then you are entitled to use the restroom. It will be labeled on the door *Toilettes* (the word is always plural in French) or *W.C.* which stands for water closet, the British expression. If you don't see a door thus labeled, ask the bartender. *"Où se trouve le W.C., s'il vous plaît?"* (Where is the toilet, please?) That is pronounced: *Oo suh troove luh vay-say, seel voo play?*

In an emergency, don't hesitate to use the field or forest (always keep a pocket pack of Kleenex with you). It is not considered immodest in France. In fact, public urinals are often open to plain view. No one thinks anything about it. I have seen a truck driver, stopped for a red light, descend from his truck, urinate in the street, then get back in and drive away when the light turned green. The French have a much more rational attitude toward natural functions than we have.

You may find a commode with the seat missing. Think nothing of it. Seats get broken and are thrown away. Why replace them? The next one would just get broken, too. The porcelain feels cold to the thighs, but it's better than no commode at all, and that's something you will also encounter: the '*trou Africain*,' the 'African hole.' This is a hole with slightly raised platforms for the feet on either side. Using these is uncomfortable and annoying, especially for the uninitiated.

Many public toilets (with attendants who keep them clean in exchange for tips) have these holes for men and stalls with commodes for women. When I encounter this arrangement, I suddenly become a wounded war veteran with one leg that won't bend at the knee. War veterans are greatly respected in France, especially those who have been wounded. I mention my infirmity to the attendant and, invariably, she graciously waves me to one of the stalls for women.

It is customary to tip the toilet attendant—usually a middleaged woman who will be reading and knitting—50 centimes or one franc for using the urinal; two or three francs for using a stall with a commode. She earns her money: she keeps the place clean and disinfected, and keeps the hand-washing area supplied with soap and towels.

Town and village public toilets are usually found near the town hall, the *mairie*. Small villages do not have them; in these, you must take recourse to the café-bar.

Finally, the French custom of kissing family members and close friends of both sexes, and handshaking. The kissing looks like the courtship dance of certain birds. Actually, the participants don't really kiss; they bob back and forth touching cheeks. Were it done correctly, Person No. 1 would kiss Person No. 2 first on the left cheek then on the right, whereupon Person No. 2 would reciprocate. Nowadays, Person No. 1 brushes perfunctorilly the cheeks of Person No. 2, who then 'replies' with a bob close to the right cheek of Person No. 1, and that suffices. The whole procedure takes about three seconds.

As a foreigner in France, you will not be involved in this sort of greeting unless you are returning to see a close friend for the tenth time, but you will see others engaged in this ritual.

Handshaking is universal. School children shake hands with classmates upon arrival at school and again when departing for home. The habitué of the village tavern shakes hands with all the other regulars upon entering and again upon leaving. Workers in offices, factories, anywhere and everywhere, shake hands upon arrival and departure. This is not a 'How do you do? So pleased to meet you,' handshake. More often it is merely a touching of three or four fingers, although the one-shake handshake does persist among traditionalists in the provinces.

The origin of the handshake is similar to keeping both hands in sight at the dining table, but goes back into the dim

Courtesy is engrained in French custom. Whenever friends meet, they ritually shake hands.

reaches of history, and quite likely to prehistory. The significance is: "You see? I come in friendship; my hand holds no weapon. I am not going to harm you. Not yet, anyway." This probably originated as far back as Neanderthal Man when a stone could be concealed in the hand and used to crack a skull. The hand was offered in greeting to show that it didn't contain a rock.

At any rate, it is a gesture of politeness, and is universal in France among those not 'close' enough to engage in the bobbing back and forth routine. If you are introduced to anyone, naturally you shake hands. In the United States, that suffices. But in France, you shake hands again when taking leave of that person.

Small courtesies serve to reduce friction and make society work more smoothly. As remarked before, France is only four-fifths the size of the state of Texas, but has a population four times that of Texas. The city of Paris, with a population of 2.8 million persons crammed into 26,044 acres, is one of the most densely populated national capitals in the world. (That's 108 persons per acre. By comparison, Washington DC has a surface area of 44,800 acres and a population of approximately 700,000, or about 16 persons per acre.) Good manners, small courtesies, and politeness, even when ritualized and perfunctory, help compressed populations to function. When civilities are abandoned, the fabric of society rips apart. America's cities are examples of this.

CHAPTER 9

Eating Out

Every true-blue Frenchman, if asked to name the most important part of the human body, will snap to attention, salute smartly, and reply: *"L'estomac, bien entendu!"* (The stomach, of course).

Except for farmers and those confined by illness, almost every French man and woman eats out once a day. They do not 'run grab a bite' or gulp down a sandwich at their desks; they sit down in a restaurant and savor a lunch that contains a minimum of three courses, and more likely four or even five. They start with an apéritif, then have an hors-d'oeuvre. My own favorite hors-d'oeuvre is a plate of raw vegetables, such as sliced tomatoes, sliced cucumbers, radishes, shredded carrots, and sometimes shredded cabbage in a vinaigrette sauce. Other possibilities are soup (usually a creamy vegetable soup), an assortment of sliced 'dry sausages' (a bit like salami but much better) or cured ham, or (in season) raw oysters, or smoked salmon….

Then comes the main dish—meat or fish, accompanied by appropriate vegetables served separately. A few hearty eaters will have both fish and meat, but usually one or the other suffices. The fish dish may be something such as *Coquille St. Jacques gratinée*, which consists of scallops cooked in a cream sauce usually flavored with sherry or Vermouth and topped with a crust of breadcrumbs and grated cheese.

Meat dishes run the gamut from roast wild boar to steak and French fried potatoes. (If all the fried potatoes the French eat in one day were piled up, it would make Mount Everest look like a molehill.) Roast pork, veal cutlets, *foie de veau* (calf's liver), *rognons* (kidneys), *jambonneau* (boiled ham hocks)—the choices are multitudinous, as you will see when you glance over the glossary at the end of this chapter.

Then comes the cheese course. To the French, cheese is an essential part of the meal. Every meal. Many farmers and country folk even have cheese with breakfast. The various regions of France produce more than 350 kinds of cheese, made from cows' milk, goats' milk, and sheeps' milk. The French lean toward blue-veined cheeses, such as Roquefort or Bleu de Bresse or Bleu d'Auvergne, or toward soft-ripening cheeses typified by Camembert and Brie, but not limited to those two well-known names by any means.

After the cheese comes dessert. A piece of fruit selected from a large *compôte* containing apples, pears, oranges, bananas, and grapes is a popular choice. So is a piece of fruit tart, or a *crème caramel*, or chocolate mousse, or a dish of *sorbet* (sherbet).

Coffee—strong black coffee—is the finishing touch to every French lunch or dinner. This may be accompanied by a liqueur, euphemistically called a *digestif*.

All of this is washed down with wine, ranging from a small brown pitcher of ordinary red wine to an expensive bottle of red or white wine. A bottle of mineral water, such as Badoit or Vittel, is also usually on the table. (Waiters and waitresses do not automatically serve water to customers, but will bring a carafe of tap water to the table if asked to do so. Mineral water, though, is preferable.)

Time out for refreshments on a sunny autumn day in Panzoult.

Each course is enjoyed leisurely. Not only is this good for the digestion; it is good for morale as well.

As mentioned earlier, all hotels serve breakfast, whether they serve any other meals or not. Restaurants do not serve breakfast, but café-bars do—the simple but adequate continental breakfast consisting of croissants with coffee and milk. Sometimes, when France is in the grip of a heat-wave, my friends and I have left hotels long before the breakfast service begins, in order to avoid riding in the heat of the day. We stop for breakfast in some village café. The cafés usually open by 6 a.m.—some of them even earlier.

In the United States, there is no clear distinction between a café and a restaurant. In France, there are several clear distinctions:

☐ The *café* serves mainly coffee and alcoholic beverages such as beer, wine, pastis, rum, calvados, cognac, etc.

☐ The *café-bar* serves coffee and a full range of alcoholic beverages (although the French do not care much for mixed drinks).

Neither of these two, as a rule, serve food of any sort, not even peanuts or potato chips. There are occasional exceptions that serve simple sandwiches, such as boiled ham on bread or something like Camembert cheese on bread. They also serve pâté on bread and often sliced 'dry sausage.' But in general, cafés and café-bars do not serve food except for croissants with coffee in the mornings. They stay open from 6 a.m. until perhaps 11 p.m. and do not close for lunch.

☐ *Brasseries* are like café-bars, except that they serve sandwiches and snacks at all hours. Among the most popular of items is the *Croque Monsieur*. This is a grilled ham-and-cheese sandwich made with two large slices of bread that resembles American white bread (of the kind used in restaurants to make sandwiches), boiled ham, a bit of mayonnaise and mustard, topped with a partially melted slice of Gouda-like cheese. The *Croque Madame* is identical but contains one addition: a fried egg on top.

Brasseries also often serve sauerkraut (*choucroute*) with frankfurters (*saucisses*), and sometimes what they call 'hot-dogs,' which consist of a hard roll with a hole punched lengthwise with a spike made especially for that purpose, and what passes in France for a wiener stuffed into that hole.

They often have a selection of salads and several hors-d'oeuvres. They open early and close late, and you can eat there any hour of the day or night. The standard beverage is beer, but wine in a carafe is also available. Certain brasseries have retained their old-time charm and have become, in fact, restaurants. They serve regular meals, and only at the usual lunch and dinner hours.

☐ *Restaurants* usually open at noon (never earlier, and often not until 12:30) and will not serve guests who arrive later than 1:30 or 2:00, although those already there may linger as long as they like. They reopen for dinner no earlier than 7:00, more often at 7:30, and discontinue service at 9:00, except in large cities where a restaurant may remain open until midnight.

Restaurants range from the most humble sort of place, where there is no menu—you sit down and take whatever the cook has prepared—to the most elegant temples of gourmandize imaginable. But the typical French restaurant is closer to the lower end of the scale than the higher. The multitude of restaurants to which office workers and business people repair every day are, by and large, simple places with a few special-ties and a hand-written menu that is apt to change every day.

Prices of relatively simple lunches are high by American standards, but the quality of the food itself and the preparation is far superior to that of most American restaurants. Between French inflation and the Federal Government's manipulation of the value of the dollar, the most inexpensive lunch one can find at an out-of-the-way country restaurant costs slightly more than nine dollars. In towns, the normal price of a lunch is the equivalent of $12 to $15, and these are good but not elaborate lunches. In a moderately up-scale establishment, $25 for lunch is a reasonable price, and that doesn't include the wine.

Fortunately, you can inform yourself of restaurant prices without going inside. Every restaurant has a menu posted in the window or in a special glassed-in box. These menus usual-ly show three *prix fixe* (fixed price) menus, ranging from the simple to the fairly elaborate, which allow a choice of hors-d'oeuvre, main course, and dessert, and sometimes they show the *à la carte* menu as well.

Hardly anyone in France orders à la carte, unless he or she wants even less than the simplest prix fixe menu, such as an omelette and nothing else, or wants some very special dish that is not included on any of these menus. Almost everyone selects his or her meal from one of the several fixed-price menus.

At a modest restaurant, the simplest of these usually starts at the equivalent of $9 to $10, but once in a while you may chance upon one with a 'menu' at $8 that even includes *vin ordinaire,* such as at the Hotel-Restaurant *La Gaieté* in Savigny-en-Véron, six miles west of Chinon. In either event, this will be a three-course meal: a limited choice of hors-d'oeuvre, followed by a main dish garnished with vegetables, then a limited choice of desserts. (At the Gaieté, there are no choices; you take whatever the cook has prepared.)

The next step up, at about $12 or $13, offers a greater selection among the hors-d'oeuvres, a better choice of main dishes, and both cheese and a dessert.

The best prix fixe menu offers a considerable range among the hors-d'oeuvres; a fish course followed by a meat course; then cheese and a choice of desserts. The cost will be $15 to $18. (These estimates of costs are based on the mid-1991 exchange rate and prices in France. They may escalate but they are unlikely to diminish.)

Suppose you want a main dish from the intermediate menu but the hors-d'oeuvre from the simplest menu. You must pay the cost of the intermediate menu, but the waiter or waitress will be glad to bring you the hors-d'oeuvre from the less expensive menu. The main dish governs your choice of menu and consequently what you pay.

A quarter-carafe (or pitcher) of red wine is sometimes included, sometimes not. The menu will tell you: 'Boisson non-compris' means it is not included. If it is included, the menu will state that it is. For example: 'Quart de vin rouge compris.' That 'quart' does not mean a quarter of a gallon, as we know the word: it means a 'quarter portion.'

If the beverage is not included and you want just a bit of wine, red or white, you ask for *"un quart du rouge"* or *'blanc.'* It is not necessary to insert the word *vin.* If you want more than that, which is about the equivalent of two glasses, you ask for *"un demi du rouge"* (or *'blanc'*). This is a half-carafe or pitcher and contains the equivalent of about four glasses.

If you are under the impression that the waiter is called *garçon,* disabuse yourself of any such notion unless you are eighty years old and the waiter is a lad of fifteen. The word *garçon* means 'boy.' Waiters are no longer thus degraded. You may still hear it, occasionally, but it is impolite. He is *Monsieur*. If it is a waitress, she is *Madame* regardless of age or marital status unless she tells you she is *Mademoiselle*.

I know very few restaurants in France that do not automatically tack on a service charge ranging from 12 to 20 percent, with 15 percent the standard. The menu prices may be printed with or without the surcharge. At the top or bottom of the menu will be a note: '*Service (15%) compris*,' meaning the price of the menu includes the service charge, or '*Service (15%) non-compris*' which means the price you see does not include the service charge. In either case, it will be included on your bill.

If the service has been very good, helpful, and pleasant, it is customary, but not obligatory, to leave a few coins in addition to the automatic service charge. On the other hand, if it has been perfunctory, minimal, barely adequate, or disdainful, you should not leave anything extra.

If you visit a very fine restaurant and consult with the wine steward about the choice of wines, and he serves it properly, he should be given his own special gratuity.

Monsieur Roy (standing, left), headwaiter at the Diane de Méridor in Montsoreau, and Monsieur Wurffel, chef, counsel patrons about lunch.

The best guide as to whether you should 'leave a little something extra' is how you feel after the lunch or dinner. If it has been a very pleasant meal and you feel happy, then yes, leave a tip. If you feel something was unsatisfactory, then don't.

But remember, what you may think of as lack of attention on the part of the waiter may be what the French would consider courtesy. He has not neglected you; he has been careful to avoid 'rushing' you. The next dish should be brought with reasonable promptness when you have finished a course, but the check, *l'addition*, is rarely presented until you ask for it.

One thing is certain: if you apply the information contained in this chapter, and use discretion, you will enjoy some of the best meals of your life.

The following explanation of terms will help you understand the menus.

Menu Terminology

Agneau	Lamb
Ananas	Pineapple
Andouillette	Pig intestines stuffed with chopped intestines.
Aubergine	Eggplant
Banane	Banana
Bar	Sea bass
Beurre	Butter
Brochet	Pike (usually *quenelles de brochet*; breaded ground pike dumplings served with tomato sauce).
Brochette	Shish kebab
Canard	Duck (*magret de canard* is broiled breast of duck; *confit de canard* is preserved duck.
Cassoullet	White beans in a casserole cooked with bacon, sausages, and preserved goose
Champignons	White mushrooms; others frequently on menus are cepes and morels.
Chou	Cabbage
Choucroute	Sauerkraut, usually served with sausages.

Choufleur	Cauliflower
Choux de Bruxelles	Brussels sprouts
Citron	Lemon
Citron vert	Lime
Civet	Thick stew usually made with rabbit.
Concombres	Cucumbers
Coquillages	Shell-fish, especially clams and oysters.
Coquille St. Jacques	Scallops, served either 'gratinée' in a cream sauce, or 'provençale' cooked with garlic, tomatoes, and herbs.
Courgette	Zucchini
Crudités	Assorted raw vegetables in a vinaigrette sauce, served as an hors-d'oeuvre.
Daurade	Sea bream
Dinde	Turkey; native to America, this bird was first thought to come from India, thus was called *'d'Inde'*.
Écrevisse	Crayfish, usually cooked, chilled, and served with mayonnaise.
Entrecôte	Rib steak
Farci(e)	Stuffed
Foie	Liver, usually *foie de veau*, grilled calf's liver.
Fraise	Strawberry
Framboise	Raspberry
Frites	French-fried potatoes
Fromage	Cheese (in the plural, it is an assortment of cheeses).
Garni(e)	Garnished; accompanied by something.
Gigot	Leg of lamb
Glace	Ice cream
Glaçon	Ice cube
Haricots verts	Green beans
Huîtres	Oysters, almost always served raw with dark bread, butter, and lemon

	or with a sauce made of vinegar, chopped shallots, and black pepper.
Jambon	Ham; *jambon cru* is raw cured ham; *jambon blanc* is thinly sliced boiled ham; *jambon de Bayonne* and *d'Auvergne* are highly prized cured hams.
Jambonneau	Ham hocks, boiled
Lapin	Rabbit, usually roasted and served with a delicate mustard sauce.
Lard	Bacon
Lardons	Diced bacon, usually served in a salad made with curly endive.
Lièvre	Hare, as in *'civet de lièvre'*
Limande	Lemon sole
Lotte	Turbot
Merlan	Whitefish
Meunière	Sauce made with pan scrapings, butter, parsley, and lemon juice.
Moules	Mussels (cooked in white wine with chopped shallots and herbs).
Moutarde	Mustard; ubiquitous on tables in small restaurants.
Navet	Turnip
Oeuf	Egg; *oeufs en plat*: fried eggs; oeuf-dur: hard-boiled egg served with mustard-flavored mayonnaise.
Pain	Bread; 'French bread' is called *baguette*; *pain complet* is whole wheat bread.
Pavé	A thick steak, e.g. a rumpsteak
Petits pois	Green peas
Poivre	Black pepper
Poivron	Green pepper, usually stuffed with ground meat, bread crumbs, chopped onions, herbs, and baked.
Pomme	Apple
Pomme de terre	Potato
Pommes frites	French fried potatoes
Potage	Thin vegetable soup made with

99

	meat stock and flavored with herbs.
Prune	Plum
Pruneaux	Prunes
Radis	Radishes, served with butter
Raisin	Grape
Raisins-secs	Raisins
Ratatouille	Vegetable casserole from Provence made with eggplant, zucchini, onions, tomatoes, parsley, garlic, and olive oil.
Rillettes	Shredded pork pâté, often flavored brandy.
Rillons	A chunkier version of *rillettes*.
Ris	Sweetbreads, e.g., *ris de veau*
Riz	Rice
Rognons	Kidneys; *rognons flambés* are

Robbie and Leslie Jones at l'Ancre in Ile-Bouchard.

	broiled kidneys with brandy poured over them and ignited. Colorful, but they still taste the way urine smells.
Salade	Green leafy lettuce salad with a vinaigrette dressing.
Sanglier	Wild boar (*marcassin* is wild piglet roasted whole).
Saucisson	Sometimes a frankfurter, but more often like salami, particularly if called *saucisson sec*.
Saumon	Salmon, usually served with a cream sauce flavored with sorrel.
Seau	Ice bucket, e.g. *seau à glace* or *seau à Champagne*.
Sel	Salt
Sorbet	Sherbet, usually made on the premises; delicious, and very expensive ($4 or so for two small scoops).
Thé	Tea; herbal teas are called *infusion*.
Thon	Tuna
Tomate	Tomato; *salade de tomates* consists of sliced tomatoes sprinkled with finely chopped shallots and parsley in a vinaigrette sauce.
Tournedos	Medaillon of filet mignon served with Bearnaise sauce flavored with tarragon.
Veau	Veal; *côte de veau*: veal cutlet.
Vinaigrette	Salad dressing made with light oil, wine vinegar, chopped parsley, sometimes chopped shallots, and seasoned with salt and pepper.

Ordering Drinks

- To order inexpensive wine, ask for a *carafe* or a *pichet*.
- *Quart* means a quarter portion: 18.75 centiliters (about ⅓ pint).
- *Demi* means a half portion; for wine, 37.5 cl (about ⅔ pint); for beer, 25 cl (about ½ pint.

- To order a glass of wine at a bar, ask for *un petit rouge* (or *blanc*).
- For a draft beer, ask for *"un demi, s'il vous plaît." Une pression* is also a draft beer, but the former term is more commonly used.
- *Panaché* is a mixture of carbonated lemonade and draft beer, very refreshing.
- France makes good beers, most of them from the Alsace. Kronenbourg is to France what Budweiser is to the United States. Kanterbrau is next in popularity. Pelforth is like a stout (e.g. Guinness). Imported beers, especially from Denmark, such as Carlsburg, are found almost everywhere.

Common Phrases

C'est combien?	How much is this?
Combien je vous dois?	How much do I owe you?
Merci beaucoup.	Thank you. (*'Merci'* alone often means 'no, thank you.')
De rien.	You're welcome.
Il n'y à pas de quoi.	You're welcome.
Plaisir!	My pleasure, You're welcome.
On s'arrose?	Shall we have a drink?
Volontiers!	Gladly.
Enchanté!	Pleased to meet you.
Au revoir!	Good-bye.
À bientôt.	See you soon.
À toute à l'heure.	See you later.
Ou se trouvent les toilettes?	Where are the toilets?
Le W.C., s'il vous plaît?	Where is the toilet?
Je suis perdu.	I'm lost.
Je suis crevé.	I'm done in.
J'ai soif.	I'm thirsty.
J'ai faim.	I'm hungry.
J'ai froid.	I'm cold.
On cherche la gare.	I'm looking for the train station
Où se trouve la route de…?	Where is the way to…
Vite!	Quickly.
Va t'en!	Scram. Beat it.
Fiche le camp!	Let's get out of here.
Zut!	Damn!
Merde alors!	Damn it!

CHAPTER 10

In the Bike Shop

Sooner or later during your trip, the odds are that you will visit a bike shop. Perhaps you will be buying a bike shortly after your arrival. Perhaps you will be renting one. Perhaps the bike you are riding will develop some problem that needs to be eliminated, such a broken spoke (which, if it occurs at all, only occurs on the (inaccessible) freewheel side of the rear wheel—such is the perversity of inanimate objects), or perhaps you want something adjusted, such as the derailleur cable.

Bike shops are abundant in France. As mentioned earlier, even a town of 10,000 is apt to have two or three bike shops, because so many of the French themselves depend on bicycles for their daily routine transportation. Bike shops also sell and service *mopeds*, so called because they have both a motor and pedals, and mopeds rival bicycles for ubiquity in France.

I confess to a strong dislike for repairing flat tires, especially when they occur on the rear wheel—which is usually the case. I don't like removing and replacing the chain; I don't like getting the tire off the rim and on again; I don't like reseating the valve. A good bike mechanic can do in three minutes what takes me twenty to accomplish. So unless I'm miles from the

Heavily loaded bikes are prone to tire problems.

next town or village when a flat occurs, I much prefer to take the bike to a shop and have a professional mechanic replace the tube for me. During the course of this, he will also determine and remove the cause of the puncture —if it was something still in the tire. The charge is negligible; the time saved is appreciable, and my hands are not stained with grease.

Whatever the reason for your visit, it will be helpful to know the terminology. Sign language would suffice, but words are better. First of all, you must find the shop. The best way to do this, of course, is to ask. Go into the bar or the épicerie, and inquire, thus:

"Pardon, Monsieur [Madame], mais où se trouve une maison de vélo, s'il vous plaît?" (Pardon me, sir [madam], where is a bike shop?) There are several ways to ask, but this is probably the simplest.

The person will tell you, and if he or she perceives that you don't understand, will almost certainly show you where it is.

When you go in the shop, you will most likely find only one person there—the owner, who is also the manager, the clerk, the mechanic, the janitor, the bookkeeper, and everything else. Let's suppose you want your rear derailleur adjusted.

"Bonjour, Monsieur!" you say. *"J'en ai un petit problème. Voudriez-vous regarder mon derailleur en arrière, s'il vous plaît? Ce truc ne marche pas trop bien."* (Hello. I have a small problem. Would you take a look at my rear derailleur, please? The thing isn't working too well.)

He will have a look, spot the problem, ask you a few questions you may or may not understand, then fix it, and when it's done, he will say, *"Et voilà!"* (There!)

"Ah, bon!" you say (Good!) *"Merci beaucoup!"* (Thank you very much!) *"Combien je vous dois?"* (How much do I owe you?)

He will reply saying a certain number of francs—usually much less than you expected to pay, because French workmen, artisans, craftsmen, mechanics, anything, are extremely honest. (I once had an automobile distributor repaired. The mechanic refused to charge me anything at all because the problem, he said, was of no consequence. It most assuredly was to me: Until he fixed it, the car wouldn't start.)

In these cases, when the mechanic tells you a number of francs, it is a courtesy to give him several francs more than he said, and insist that he keep the change:

"Gardez-vous la monnaie, Monsieur."

Then you say goodby: *"Au revoir, Monsieur. Merci!"*

Here are some sentences that cover just about any situation, and their English equivalents. Following these sentences is a glossary of bicycle terminology in English and French, arranged alphabetically in English.

Helpful Sentences

The handlebars are loose.	*Le guidon est dévissé.*
There's a noise in the crankset.	*Le pedalier fait un tric-trac.*
The brake cable is loose.	*Le cable de frein est dévissé.*
The derailleur cable is loose.	*Le cable de command est dévissé.*
The cable is too tight.	*Le cable est trop serré.*
The cable is stuck (pinched).	*Le cable est bloqué (coincé).*
I have a broken spoke.	*Il y a un rayon caissé.*
On the freewheel side, of course.	*A côté de la roue-libre, bien entendu.*
Would you please straighten this?	*Voudriez-vous redresser ceci, s'il vous plaît?*
Would you please tighten this?	*Voudriez-vous serrer ceci, s'il vous plaît?*
Would you please loosen this?	*Voudriez-vous deserrer ceci, s'il vous plaît?*
Would you please raise this a little?	*Voudriez-vous soulever ceci un peu, s'il vous plaît?*
Would you please lower this a little?	*Voudriez-vous baisser ceci un peu, s'il vous plaît?*
I would like to have smaller sprockets, please.	*Je voudrais des pignons moins grands, s'il vous plaît.*
I would like to have larger sprockets, please.	*Je voudrais des pignons plus grands, s'il vous plaît.*
I would like to have one chainring with 40 teeth, the other with 48 teeth, please.	*Je voudrais un plateau de quarante dents, s'il vous plait; l'autre avec quarante-huit dents. Voilà!*

Could you raise the saddle just a bit?	*Pourriez-vous monter la selle un petit peu?*
Please put in a new inner-tube.	*Voudriez-vous bien remplacer la chambre à air, s'il vous plaît.*
This tire is worn-out.	*Cette enveloppe est toute usée.*
The toe strap is broken.	*La courroie est rompue.*
The chain is broken.	*La chaine est caissée.*
I need new brake pads.	*J'en ai besoin des patins nouveaux.*
Do you have a restroom here?	*Y-a-t-il un vay-say ici? ['vay-say' is actually WC, water closet, but 'vay-say' is the way to say it.]*
How much do I owe you?	*Combien je vous dois, Monsieur?*
Here you are, and keep the change.	*Voilà! Et gardez-vous la monnaie.*
Thank you.	*Merci bien!*
I appreciate it very much.	*Je suis bien reconnaissant.*
That is very kind of you.	*Vous êtes bien gentil.*
Can you tell me which is the road to ...?	*Pourriez-vous me dire, ou se trouve la route de ...?*
Goodbye, and thanks.	*Au revoir! Merci!*

Parts of the Bike

The following bike nomenclature was compiled with the help of Monsieur Pierre-Alain Deride, an insurance company executive in Niort, and Claude Leblond, a bike shop owner and builder of fine bicycles in Blois.

Aluminum alloy	*alliage d'aluminum*
Ball bearings	*les billes*
Bicycle	*la bicyclette*
Bike	*le vélo*
Blow out	*l'éclatement*
Bottom bracket	*la boîte de pedalier*

Brake cable	*le cable de frein*
Brake lever	*la poignée (la cocotte)*
Brake lever hood	*le repose-main*
Brake pads	*les patins*
Brakes	*les freins*
Bungee cord	*le sandow*
Butterfly (Wing) nuts	*les papillons*
Centerpull brake	*frein à tirage central*
Chain	*la chaine*
Chain ring	*le plateau*
Chain stays	*les bases*
Clincher (wired-on tire)	*le pneu*
Crank arm	*la manivelle*
Crankset	*le pédalier*
Derailleur cable	*cable de command*
Derailleur (front)	*derailleur à plateau*
Derailleur (rear)	*derailleur en arrière*
Down tube	*le tube diagonal*
Drop-outs	*les pattes*
Fender	*le garde-boue*
Flat (noun)	*la crevaison*
Flat (adjective)	*degonflé[e]; crevé[e]*
Frame	*le cadre*

Freewheel cluster	*la roue libre*
Front fork	*la fourche avant*
Gear	*la vitesse* *
Gooseneck	*la potence*
Handlebar bag	*le sac avant*
Handlebars	*le guidon*
Handlebars	*les cintres*
Handlebar tape	*la guidoline*
Handlebar tape [alt.]	*la bande collante en toile*
Head tube	*la douille*
Hub	*le moyeu*
Inner tube	*la chambre à air*
Light (noun)	*la phare*
Light (red, rear)	*le feu rouge*
Light (weight)	*leger*
Locking cable	*l'antivol*
Luggage rack	*le porte-bagages*
Lugs	*les raccords*
Nut	*l'ecrou*
Odometer	*le compteur kilométrique*
Pannier	*la sacoche*
Pedal	*la pédale*
Pinched (e.g. cable)	*coincé[e]*
Pump	*la pompe*
Puncture	*la crevaison*
Quick-release	*le blocage rapide*
Racing bike frame	*cadre course*
Rearview mirror	*le retroviseur*
Recreational (touring) frame	*cadre demi-course*
Reflector	*le catadioptre*
Rim	*la jante*
Saddle	*la selle*
Saddle (narrow)	*la selle à course*
Saddle (wide)	*la grande selle*
Saddle mount (frame)	*le chariot*
Screw	*la vis*
Screwdriver	*le tournevis*
Seat post	*la tige de selle*

Seat stays	*les haubans*
Seat tube	*le tube de selle*
Set screws	*les vis de reglage*
Sew-up(s)	*le boyau (les boyaux)*
Shifter lever	*levier de derailleur*
Side pull	*à tirage lateral*
Size (frame size)	*la taille; hauteur de cadre*
Spoke	*le rayon*
Spoke wrench	*le clé à rayon*
Sprocket	*le pignon*
Steel	*acier*
Steel rim	*la jante en acier*
Sticky fluid (to fix flats)	*la dissolution*
Teeth	*dents*
Tire (outer casing)	*l'enveloppe*
Tire repair kit	*le necessaire de réparation*
Tire tools	*les demonte-pneus*
Toe cage	*le cale-pied*
Toe cage strap	*la courroie*
Top tube	*le tube horizontal*
Tube patches	*les Rustines (trade-marked)*
Tube scraper	*la rape en toile emeri*
Valve	*la valve*
Water bottle	*le bidon*
Water bottle cage	*le porte-bidon*
Wheel	*la roue*
Wrench	*la clé*
Wrench (crescent)	*la clé anglaise*

Notes:

The tire and inner tube are collectively called *le pneumatique,* or *le pneu.*

The handlebars—the whole works—are called *le guidon.* Drops (dropped handlebars) are *guidon course.* Flat handlebars are *guidon plat.*

A short-frame racing bike is a *vélo course.* The more conventional touring bike or recreational bike is a *vélo demi-course.* A woman's bike frame (as opposed to the conventional diamond frame) is a *cadre mixte.*

To ride a bike is *rouler* or *faire le vélo.* The bike ride itself is called *la randonnée.* To go for a leisurely ride is *faire une randonnée.* To ride as fast as possible is *rouler à toute allure.*

Gearing and Speed

An alternate term for 'gear' is *le developpement.* This refers to the distance the bike travels for one complete turn of the cranks. With the standard French 700 mm wheel, it is 2.2 meters times the ratio. Ratio is determined by dividing the number of teeth on the chainring by the number of teeth on the sprocket. To determine your speed with a pocket calculator, multiply the development by the number of crank revolutions per minute, then multiply that by sixty.

For example: Suppose you have the chain on a 48-tooth chainring and a 17-tooth sprocket. Thus your ratio is 2.82. Multiply that by 2.2 [meters] and you get 6.21. That's the number of meters you move the bike with each complete turn of the cranks, or the 'development.'

Now suppose your pedaling speed, or cadence, is 70 revolutions per minute. Multiply the development by 70 and you get 434.8 meters per minute of cycling. Times 60 [minutes] gives you 26.1 kilometers per hour, which translates into 16.2 miles per hour.

A much simpler way of determining speed, however, is to look at your watch when you pass a kilometer marker, then again when you pass the next one. Let's say the elapsed time was three minutes. Divide the number of minutes in an hour (60) by 3 and you get 20. That's the number of kilometers you are covering in an hour—at this speed. That's just slightly less than 12.5 miles per hour, a very comfortable pace on flat or gently rolling ground with no wind to impede your progress.

CHAPTER 11

Before You Go …
Bone Up!

Wherever you choose to cycle in France, you will find a beauty that borders on enchantment, a beauty that will envelope you and permeate your senses, and perhaps even your soul. You will feel this regardless of what you know—or do not know—about France. But the more you know, the more aware you will be, and the more deeply you will perceive the mesmerizing mystique of this lovely land.

Thousands upon thousands of books about every aspect of France have beguiled generations of readers. One lifetime is too short to read them all. During the past two decades, I have read a few more than three hundred books about French art, wine, food, and history—especially history. All of them were informative, but some were interesting; others were dull.

What follows is a selection of those I particularly liked, in various categories, with a brief summary explaining why. I have divided them into categories, since not everybody likes the same things. The appearance of a book title here does not mean it is 'the best' (although it may well be) in its category. I have not read all the books about France that exist. It means that the book is well-written, informative, accurate (if it pertains to history, unless otherwise noted), or that the illustrations are exceptionally good.

Architecture

Form, Function & Design, by Paul Jacques Grillo. This is a slender volume, amply illustrated in black and white, by a French architect who is also a very good (and persuasive) writer. He explains why certain buildings look 'right,' while others strike us as monstrosities. Non-technical, this is entertaining to read, and also highly instructive.

Master Builders of the Middle Ages, by David Jacobs. Ostensibly a book for young people, this is one of the most emotionally moving books about the great cathedrals ever written. It explains why the cathedrals were built, how they were built, and who built them. It is well-illustrated in both color and black and white.

Châteaux of the Loire, Michelin Green Guide. This book, well-illustrated with line drawings, is an excellent introduction to the distinctions between architectural details as they evolved from the Middle Ages through the Neo-Classical period, in both châteaux and churches. (There is much more in this book as well.) It is flawed, however, by several errors of historical 'fact.' (See below under 'Châteaux'.)

Impressionism, by Jean Leymarie. Of the scores, if not hundreds, of books on Impressionism, this may well be the best on account of its insights, accuracy, good sense, and brevity. Impressionism, the all-pervasive school of painting that flourished in the last quarter of the 19th century, soon informed the other arts as well, notably music and poetry, and influenced artists throughout the Western World. This book has excellent illustrations, all of them in color.

The Impressionists at First Hand, edited by Bernard Denvir. This is a collection of letters, reviews, articles, and diary excerpts by the artists themselves (about themselves and each other), by their friends (and sometimes their detractors) and by the mem-

The château at Azay-le-Rideau is considered the finest example of French Renaissance architecture.

bers of their families. Profusely illustrated with photographs, cartoons, plus black-and-white and color reproductions.

The Hidden World of Misericords, by Dorothy and Henry Kraus. Misericords are, in the strict ecclesiastical sense, pardons, mercies, graces, but they are also wood carvings found under the fold-down choir seats in many French churches and cathedrals. In effect, they are cartoon-like commentaries sculpted in wood. Some are illustrative of the tasks of daily life—such as butchering a hog. Some are satirical—such as a cleric who has over-indulged in wine. And some are even salacious—such as ... well, never mind. This book explains the misericords, tells where to find the best ones, and describes the life of their creators, a guild of itinerant artisans who flourished in the late Middle Ages.

Châteaux

Châteaux of the Loire, Michelin Green Guide. This slender book manages to be both compact and comprehensive. Some of the historical detail is factually inaccurate, e.g., the statement that all three sons of Henri II died violent deaths (Francois II and Charles IX both died of illness; only Henri III died a violent death —he was assassinated) and that Richard the Lion-Heart died at Chinon (remarkable, in view of the fact that his intestines and brains were buried at Chalus before the remainder of his body was carted first to Chinon then to Fontevrault Abbey—except his heart, which was sent to Rouen), but this guide is nevertheless an almost indispensible source of information about the châteaux, fortresses, churches, and cathedrals of the Loire Valley.

The Châteaux of France, by Daniel Wheeler. Of the great profusion of books on this subject, this one rises above the others on the basis of its clarity of text, relevancy of detail, and abundance of illustrations.

Court Life

The World of Watteau, by Pierre Schneider. Although this is about a particular artist, Jean-Antoine Watteau, it is extremely valuable for the insights it provides into the world in which he lived, the over-ripe world of the royal court during the Regency after Louis XV, still a child, succeeded his great-grandfather to the throne of France. This book, illustrated in color, halftones, and black and white, describes the aristocrats who, far from being mere twits and fops, perceived all too well the impending cataclysm, and warded off their dread with elaborate diversions so poignantly depicted by Watteau, Fragonard, and Boucher.

Cuisine

The Foods of France, by Waverly Root. Root was an American war correspondant who took up residence in Paris and remained there until his death in the 1970s. He wrote with enthusiasm, but also with great good sense about food. In this book, he explains the differences in the regional cooking of France better than anyone else has done. **Note:** This is not a cookbook.

History

The Birth of France: Warriors, Bishops and Long-Haired Kings, by Katharine [cq] Scherman. This is an anecdotal, 'popular', but accurate and immensely readable history of early France from Roman times to the end of the Merovingian Dynasty.

Fleur de Lys: The Kings of France, by Joy Law. Superbly illustrated in color, this book by a British historian combines extracts from contemporary documents with Mrs. Law's own incisive commentary. It presents the views of court officials, ambassadors, and others who were intimately involved in the destiny of France over a period of nine centuries. (It begins with the election of Hugues Capet in AD 987.) Although these biographies are necessarily compressed, the amount of detail is both fascinating and amazing. For example, rather than say, 'died in 1367,' Mrs. Law provides the precise cause of death, such as malaria or dysentery, and the exact date.

The History of the Franks, by Gregory of Tours. During his 21-year reign as Bishop of Tours, AD 573-594, this remarkable ecclesiastic resolved disputes among the various members of the savage Merovingian clan, served as ambassador and negotiator for numerous kings, instructed the clergy and nipped heresies in the bud, and chronicled it all in highly readable fashion. In this excellent translation (by Lewis Thorpe) from the original Latin, we can read for ourselves the machinations and shennanigans of the unscrupulous clan of warrior-kings who ruled embryonic France during what are now called—with good reason—The Dark Ages.

Prince of the Renaissance, by Desmond Seward. Scholarly books are usually stuffy and often more deadly dull than cold oatmeal. Desmond Seward is a British scholar who writes to entertain rather than to impress; to keep the reader excited rather than sleepy. This is a short, enjoyable biography of François I, the king during whose reign the Renaissance flowered in France. François was a warrior-king, but also a patron of the arts. He was a close friend of Leonardo da Vinci and provided him a home. He and his ministers built almost all the great châteaux in the Loire Valley and the Ile de France. François was also a patron of scholarship and literature, and put together the nucleus of what is now the Bibliothèque Nationale, the French equivalent of the US Library of Congress. This book contains a wealth of illustrations, mostly in color.

The Splendid Century, by W. H. Lewis. This book does a remarkable job of describing everyday life in France, and particularly life in the royal court, during the 72-year reign of Louis XIV (he acceded to the throne at the age of five). It discusses the king's appetites for war, food, and women, and his patronage of the arts. Professor Lewis includes some absorbing details, such as how the king's day progressed, minute by minute (even getting out of bed was a public ceremony) and what the king liked for breakfast (a far cry from ham and eggs).

The Sun King: Louis XIV, by Nancy Mitford. Alice Roosevelt Longworth, the daughter of President Theodore Roosevelt, once said, "If you can't say anything nice about somebody, come sit by me." If she ever met Miss Mitford, I'm sure they were side-by-side all evening. Nancy Mitford has nothing nice to say about Louis XIV, but her stinging portrayal of the king who was the apotheosis of monarchial France includes such a plenitude of detail that it fascinates us—just as gossip did Mrs. Longworth.

Versailles, by the editors of *Newsweek*. Gorgeously illustrated in color, this is an overview of the kings and their courts, and the unparalleled splendor that made Versailles a paradise for the favored few, but purgatory for those fallen from grace.

Paris

Paris, by John Russell. Although it may exist, I cannot imagine any book about Paris that even comes close to this one for insights, historical accuracy, and its plethora of details. Russell, art critic for *The New York Times,* lived in Paris for decades. He knows the city intimately, and although he obviously loves it, he does not gloss over its flaws. An over-size book, it is copiously illustrated in both color and black and white.

Paris, Michelin Green Guide. This is an excellent (and emotionally neutral) guide to the history, architecture, and neighborhoods of Paris, as well as an abundant source of helpful (practical) information.

Plan de Paris par Arrondissement et Communes de Banlieue edited by the firm of A. Leconte. Here, in handy size, is a guide that gives the specific location of every museum, church, post office, police station, embassy, etc. etc. in Paris, as well as the location of every street. The maps are the most easily 'read' of all the many guides to Paris. The maps are based on aerial photographs and are completely detailed and precisely accurate. It also contains the Métro (subway) and RER (suburban line) system, and every bus route. There are many imitations, but none of them approach the Leconte 'Plan' for uncompromising quality.

Wine

Wines of France, by Alexis Lichine. This book has been in print (periodically revised) for more than four decades! It is unquestionably superior to any other book on the subject. Lichine is a Russian-born American citizen who has lived most of his life in France as a château owner, wine grower, and wine exporter. No other writer can equal his knowledge of every facet of this fascinating subject. Unfortunately, he did not write the whole book; much of it was researched by knowledgeable young men and women, and written by various writers under Lichine's general supervision. Portions were written by Lichine, of course. Recent editions tend to become 'cute' when cleverness was the objective. The classic editions are those of 1953 and 1955, when most of the writing was by Alexis Lichine himself and was based on his incredibly extensive knowledge as well as on his assistants' research. The evaluation of vintages in the early editions is now a matter of historical rather than practical interest; the great old vintages are now as absurdly priced as Van Gogh paintings. Nevertheless, the older editions are extremely well-written, and you can get a current vintage chart simply by asking for it from almost any wine merchant.

Miscellaneous

Eating and Drinking in France, Today by Pamela Vandyke-Price. Mrs. Price is the widow of a British physician and for many years has been one of Britain's leading authorities on the subject of French wine. Yet, this is not just a wine book, or wine and food book, despite the title. It is, rather, an eminently sensible book on how to enjoy France and how to get along there. It even tells you how to stay healthy and how to shop for presents, and—the ultimate in 'how to's'—how to use those French toilets that are simply holes between two footrests. It covers all this and more, including a brief description of all the bottled waters you may encounter in France, valuable information indeed since some of them have a laxative effect.

A Little Tour in France, by Henry James. The quality of the writing and the insights remain unsurpassed even though this book was first published in 1884—more than a century ago! It is superbly illustrated with color reproductions by numerous great artists. James had an unerring eye for significant detail, and the ability to write so beautifully that it makes many modern travel books seem trivial by comparison. It is a wonderful book to own, and can be read with just as much appreciation after a trip to France as beforehand.

Richard the Lion Heart, by John Gillingham This Richard was a king of England, not France, but he spent most of his life in France (his childhood with his mother, Eleanor of Aquitaine), spoke French (he never learned English), and this excellent biography is a highly valuable adjunct to the study of French history.

CHAPTER 12

Cycling Safely in France

The beautiful byways of France that so beguile the visiting cyclist don't, alas, extend to infinity. In the larger towns and in all cities, you will encounter frenetic, nerve-wracking traffic. French drivers observe the laws of France, not the opinions of American cyclists. I want to stress that point, because I've seen all too many American cyclists who, in asserting their 'rights' on city streets, such as riding in the middle of a lane, or two or three abreast, make insufferable nuisances of themselves, and annoy motorists to the point of madness. This is not tolerated in France, and anyone who tries it there will simply be *bouleversé, écrasé, et répandu sur les pavés.* (Knocked over, wiped out, and spread upon the pavement.)

French drivers—even those driving tractor-trailers—respect the rights of cyclists to the extent required by law. These same laws—which are national, not local—define the manner in which the cyclist must ride in traffic. Being a foreigner does not excuse you from compliance. French motorists justifiably expect all cyclists to conform to the national regulations, the *Code de la Route.* Every person who obtains a driver's license in France must attend driver's school, must virtually memorize

Cows in the streets are an occasional hazard in rural France.

this *Code*, part of which applies to cyclists, and must pass a stiff examination. No matter where you go in France, the rules remain the same. For your own safety, and for the safety of your companions, it is of paramount importance to learn these rules and to obey them without the slightest deviation.

Here is a translation and interpretation of the articles in the *Code de la Route* that pertain to cycling. This will be followed by observations based on two decades of cycling in France. (In addition to these observations, cyclists from Britain and other countries with LH traffic will have to get used to riding on the RH side of the street—train yourself to look first left, then right then left again, instead of what you were taught at home.)

☐ In all populated areas [cities, towns, and villages], cyclists must ride on the far right-hand side of the road or street, unless it is a mandatory right turn lane and the cyclist intends to go straight ahead or turn left, in which case the cyclist will ride on the far right-hand edge of the appropriate lane.

☐ The cyclist preparing to turn right must extend the right arm to signal this intention to motorists. The cyclist preparing to turn left must extend the left arm. The cyclist preparing to slow down or stop must extend the left arm out and downward away from the body at an angle of approximately fifty degrees. If several cyclists are riding in a line and are all going to make the same turn, or slow down, they must all give the same signal. When turning, the appropriate arm must remain extended until the turn is begun.

☐ At an intersection, cyclists must yield the right of way to all vehicles approaching from the right, unless the cyclist is on a priority road, or unless there is a *STOP* sign controlling traffic approaching from the right.

☐ The cyclist making a left turn must yield the right of way to vehicles approaching from the opposite direction.

☐ Two or more cyclists riding together in populated areas must ride in single file on the far right-hand side of the road or street.

☐ Cyclists must obey all traffic-control signs and signals, including one-way street signs.

☐ Cyclists must yield the right-of-way to pedestrians in cross-walks.

☐ Cyclists are prohibited from riding in bus-lanes, or on sidewalks. Cyclists are prohibited from riding on *départementale* or *nationale* routes if a parallel lane designated for cyclists is provided. Cyclists are prohibited from riding on *autoroutes* under any circumstances whatsoever.

☐ On *nationale* routes [roads designated *RN* or simply *N*], cyclists must ride on the far right-hand side of the road. Two or more cyclists riding together must ride in single file on these roads.

☐ On *départementale* or *communale* routes [roads designated *D* or *C*], cylists may ride two abreast, but must get in single file when approached from behind by one or more motor vehicles. Cyclists riding two abreast must ride on the far right-hand side of the road. To ride more than two abreast is not permitted.

Commentary

Ride in a straight line. Do not swerve or deviate from a straight line. This is especially important in traffic. Cars, trucks, and tourist buses will miss you, but not by much. They do not get into the adjacent lane to pass you. They may miss you by 39 inches or so. That's legal and that's what they do. Many, but by no means all, truck and bus drivers will swing out a bit wider because they are aware of the 'suction' caused by their vehicles—but don't count on it. Truck drivers are nicer than tour bus drivers. Regular bus drivers are more courteous than tour bus drivers. Belgian and German tour bus drivers, for reasons upon which I will not speculate, appear to be the worst, that is, they seem to delight in passing a cyclist with perhaps 12 inches of clearance. Cycling in urban traffic or on a main highway, you will encounter such situations. The most practical solution to the problem is to get onto a small road as soon as you can.

Never zigzag to climb a hill. To do so subjects you to the possibility —in fact, the likelihood—of being wiped out by a fast moving car cresting the hill while you are on the wrong side. Stay on the far right and ride in a straight line. If you can't make it up the hill on the bike, walk.

When you are riding on an urban street along which cars are parked, watch carefully for drivers pulling away from the curb without signaling. The law requires drivers to signal their intention to pull out into traffic, and to yield to traffic approaching alongside, even to bicycles, but not all drivers do this, so be alert and ready to stop. If a car pulls out from the curb in front of you, slow down or stop. Do not swing out into the path of following cars.

Watch also for drivers opening doors on the street side just as you come along. Again, if it happens, stop. Don't swing wide into the path of following cars.

In two-way traffic on a two-lane street, watch for drivers who pass you, then immediately turn right, crossing your line of travel. This is illegal, but occasionally you may encounter an impatient or arrogant driver. (On the whole, however, you will find that French drivers are far more courteous to cyclists than are American or Canadian drivers.)

Do not run a *STOP* sign. (These are the same in France as in the USA: the letters STOP in white on a red background.) Come to a complete stop at the far right-hand side of the road. When a traffic light is changing, do not run the intersection on yellow.

Yielding to pedestrians is especially important—not just because it is required, but because it takes getting used to. In the United States, pedestrians don't step off the curb in front of traffic, but in France they do. Pedestrians know they have the right of way, and they take it. If you are in a line of vehicular traffic, you may not see the pedestrian who has stepped out in front of a car, causing the car to 'panic stop' directly in front of you. In traffic, you must be ready to stop instantly. Pedestrians will step off the curb directly in front of cyclists as well, of course. This annoying habit has inspired me to learn some very rough language, but it doesn't do any good.

Just remember: the pedestrian has the right of way, knows it, and takes it. If the car directly ahead of you makes a panic stop and you don't, or can't, you will ruin your front wheel, not to mention your disposition.

The following has been mentioned before but it bears repeating: When you are descending a long hill, keep the bike under control. If you have pedaled laboriously up the hill, the temptation is strong, after you crest it, to hunch over, hang on, and fly à toute allure down the other side.

Don't do it. Cow herds, shepherds, and goat-herds often walk their herds along the roads going from one pasture to another. If you round a curve at top speed and suddenly find yourself facing a bunch of farm animals completely blocking the road, the next few seconds can be very, very messy.

When you are riding in the rain, remember that wet wheel rims do not provide the braking friction that dry ones do. Consequently, stopping in the rain takes much longer than stopping in dry weather. Awareness of this is particularly important in traffic or when descending a hill.

Do not try to read a map while cycling. To glance briefly at the map is one thing; but to study it carefully is something else altogether. If you need to take a good look at the map, fine: stop, then look at it. (When you stop, make sure you are not impeding traffic.)

Morning mists, especially in the spring and fall when the atmospheric conditions are right, are so common in France that they are depicted on postcards. The French phrase is *brume matinale*. (*Brouillard* is fog.) The *brume* produces a lovely, softening effect, dissolving the edges of buildings, blending meadows with sky. But they also reduce visibility.

Under even the best of circumstances, it is a good idea to wear at least one highly visible article of clothing. On a misty morning, or in fog or rain, it is of utmost importance to make yourself as visible as you possibly can. A bright yellow or orange shell jacket helps. I wear a yellow reflecting triangle attached to the back of my jacket with Velcro patches. (Thus I can take it off when I am strolling around town and don't wish to be quite so conspicuous.) Reflective wear is available wherever surveyor's supplies and instruments are sold. Check the Yellow Pages in your telephone directory. (I got my reflecting triangle from Jog-a-Lite, Box 125, Silver Lake, NH 03875.)

From time to time, the French resurface their back roads by putting down a layer of oily tar, then spreading tiny gravel on top. This crushed gravel consists of pieces, often triangular with sharp points, scarcely larger than a match-head. Avoid riding on such surfaces. The gravel punctures high-pressure tires almost instantly. Moreover, it gets picked up and lodged in your chain and freewheel cluster, causing serious mechanical problems.

This sort of road patching or resurfacing usually is spotty or for a short stretch, in which case the gravel can be avoided by riding carefully around the patches or on the shoulder. But if that is not possible, get off the bike and carry it over the gravel. If that seems impractical, find another road.

If you encounter cobblestones, either ride on the shoulder or walk the bike to the far side of the cobbled portion. Bouncing along on the cobbles breaks spokes and damages kidneys.

High-pressure tires inflated to maximum capacity, thus very hard, reduce road friction, making cycling easier and faster. But they also are far more susceptible to punctures. If you run over a minute bit of glass or gravel, or even a thorn or spine from a chestnut burr, with a rock-hard tire, the bit you ran over has no place to go except into the tire, and bang: you have a puncture. A little less tire pressure and a little less speed is better than spending time replacing and reparing punctured tubes.

To establish the proper pressure for touring, put your index finger inside the rim and press the tire with your thumb. If you feel a slight 'give' when you are pressing as hard as you can, that's the right pressure. If the tire 'gives' easily, it's too soft. If it doesn't 'give' at all, it's too hard. It's a good idea to check the pressure on both wheels every morning before setting out for the day's ride. If the tire is soft, inflate it further. If it's too hard, release a small squirt of air by pressing the nipple of the valve for an instant. Don't forget to screw the valve nipple back in tightly. At the same time, check to make sure the ring nut at the base of the valve is tight. This protects the tube from shearing at the base of the valve.

In summation: Ride cautiously and cultivate an attitude of symbiotic cooperation with motorists. This inculcates better and safer cycling habits than an attitude of animosity or defiance. The more courteous we are to drivers, the more they will reciprocate the courtesy, and the safer and happier we'll all be.

Bonne route!

PART II
THE CYCLING TOURS

In the sections that follow, detailed route descriptions are given, each accompanied by an overall locator map and more detailed route maps for each stage. Although the essential information is given, you will also need the Michelin maps listed (or the corresponding regional maps) Refer to Chapter 6 for an introduction to the use of the Michelin maps. The following remarks apply specifically to the methodology used in drawing the route, or stage, maps printed on these pages.

☐ The route maps in this book are based on the Michelin France regional map series at 1:200,000 scale.

☐ Refer to the legend below for the symbols used on the route maps in this book.

☐ Cities or towns where routes start or end are shown in boldface type.

☐ Not all route numbers are shown on the maps because of space or placement limitations.

☐ Some of the route numbers are placed at the junction of the route, while others are placed at any point along the route.

☐ Consult the relevant Michelin map for the location of junctions along the route you choose.

☐ Some route numbers change at departemental boundaries. When you are cycling along a route, you may not find a physical boundary marker at the location indicated on the Michelin maps.

☐ Not all boundary markers and railroad crossings are shown on the maps used in this book. The ones that are shown are there for reference only.

Map Legend

(START)   Start of Route

(END)   End of Route

➤   to/from connecting route

++++++   Railroad

·—·—·—·   Departemental Boundary

:=:=:=:   International Boundary

▲   Point of Interest

△   Mountain Peak

Tour 1: The Sologne

Four-stage loop from Blois
Terrain: Essentially flat
Total Distance: 131 km (81 miles)
Michelin map No. 64

The Sologne is an eerlely quiet, flat, marsh-pond area teeming with wildlife. There are also numerous châteaux and charming villages. Four stages, starting and finishing in Blois. Three major châteaux and numerous lovely villages, plus hauntingly beautiful woodlands and ponds. Some of these ponds are more than a mile long. Romorantin has a cathedral.

Cycling two abreast is legal on rural roads, traffic permitting.

Blois to Neung-sur-Beuvron
42.5 km (26 miles)

Exit Blois on avenue des Déportes and Charles de Gaulle Bridge,
2 km. Turn right on cloverleaf after crossing Loire river, direction
Orléans.

Go under bridge; turn right into cloverleaf but bear left onto D72
and go to Les Noëls, 2 km. After slight uphill into Les Noëls, D72
turns left. Continue on D72 to Morest. Here D72 turns right; do not
turn.

Continue straight on D46 to Maslives, 4.5 km. Turn right onto D84;
go to Chambord, 3 km. Exit Chambord on D112; go to Bracieux,
7 km.

Turn left onto D923; go to Neung-sur-Beuvron, 21 km.

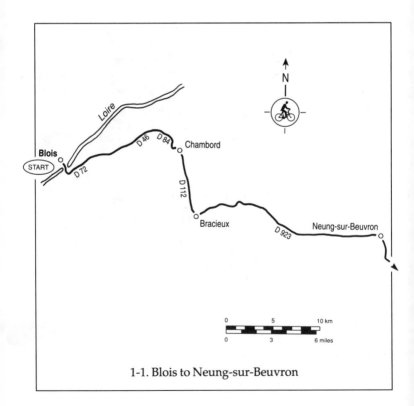

1-1. Blois to Neung-sur-Beuvron

Neung-sur-Beuvron to Romorantin-Lanthenay
29 km (18 miles)

Exit Neung southward on D925; go 1.5 km to INT with D922.

Go 1 km on D922; go to Marcilly-en-Gault on D121, 8.5 km. After passing church on your right, take second right turn onto D49; go to Loreux, 8.5 km.

Continue on D49 to Romorantin, 9.5 km.

Romorantin-Lanthenay to Contres
31.5 km (20 miles)

Exit Romorantin on D765 toward Blois. Go 1 km.

Turn left onto D59; go to Gy-en-Sologne, 13 km.

After passing the church on your left, turn right onto communal route (a cemetery will be on your right). Go to Soings-en-Sologne, 9.5 km.

In Soings, turn left onto D122; go to Contres, 8 km.

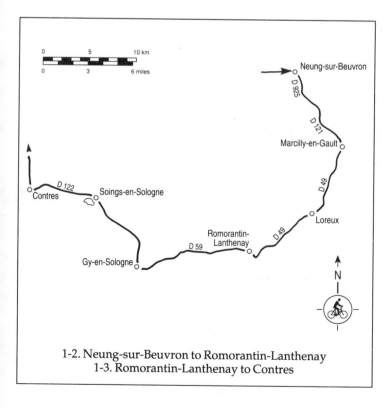

1-2. Neung-sur-Beuvron to Romorantin-Lanthenay
1-3. Romorantin-Lanthenay to Contres

Contres to Blois
26.5 km (16 miles)

Exit Contres on D956; go 0.5 km, then bear right onto D102.

Go to Château Cheverny, 9 km.

Leave Cheverny on communal road to Cellettes. Go 5 km to INT with D956.

Bear right onto D956; go to Celettes, 2 km. Follow signs to Château Beauregard, 1 km.

Return to D956, 1 km. Go to Blois, 8 km.

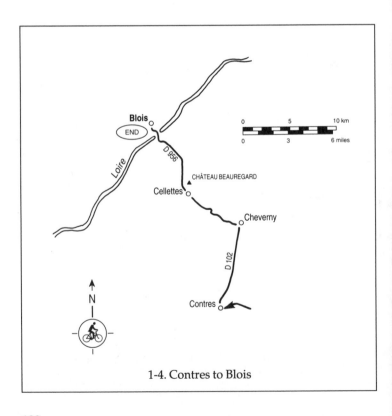

1-4. Contres to Blois

Tour 2: The Marais Poitevin

Poitiers to La Rochelle and back in five
stages
Terrain: Mostly flat
Total Distance: 346 km (215 miles)
Michelin maps 67, 68, and 71

The Marais Poitevin is an area reclaimed from
the sea by Dutch engineers during the reign of
Henri IV (late 16th and early 17th centuries). Five stages starting and
finishing in Poitiers. The first and last stages involve hills but not
severe ones, The Marais, also known as 'The Green Venice' because
of its canals, is flat.

Poitiers was the capital of the ancient duchy of Aquitaine and has a
cathedral the construction of which was financed by Eleanor of
Aquitaine. It also has the finest Romanesque church in France which
Richard the Lion-Heart attended as a teenager. Niort has a splendid
castle, now a museum, once one of Eleanor's residences.

Coulon is on the Sevre river and the canal system. La Rochelle is a
seaport; the inner city is a National Monument in which cars are not
allowed—only bicycles. It abounds with excellent seafood restaurants, the best of which is on the wharf where the fishing boats dock.
Fontenay, on the Vendée river, has a cathedral and a château. Parthenay has a fine old fortress and a medieval inner city.

*The old bridge and the church of St. André in Niort. Photo courtesy Office
de Tourisme de Niort.*

Poitiers to Niort
88.6 km (55 miles)

To exit Poitiers: Go one block south of the train station on blvd. du Pont Archard and turn right onto rue Georges Guynemer.

Go up the long hill and bear left onto rue Santos-Dumont which, with several name changes, will get you out of town and onto D6.

Follow D6 to Benassay, 25 km. Turn left onto D62 (you'll see a cemetery on your left) and go to Sanxay, 8.5 km.

After passing the church in Sanxay, turn right onto D3. You'll see a public swimming pool on your left.

After 1.5 km, note Roman ruins on your right. Slightly more than

1 km farther, you will cross the departemental boundary and D3 will become D21. Continue to Ménigoute, 2 km beyond boundary line.

After passing the church on your left, turn left onto D5. Go up the hill and continue to Fomperron. Exit Fomperron on D 121 to St. Maixent-l'École, 16.5 km. There is a very fine old church in St. Maixent.

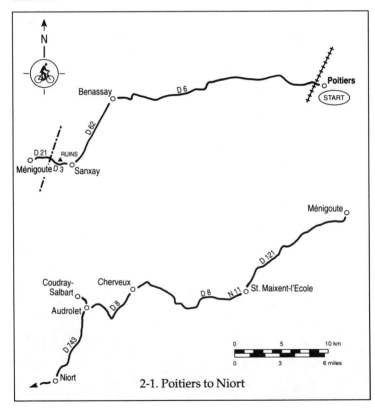

2-1. Poitiers to Niort

Exit St. Maixent on N11; go 1.5 km to INT with D8.

Turn right onto D8 and go to Cherveux, 12.5 km. There is a château in Cherveux.

Continue south on D8 exactly 4 km to INT with small communal road and turn right.

Follow this road to INT with D743 at Audrolet, 3 km.

Turn right onto D743 and go approximately 100 meters, then turn left to Coudray-Salbart, 2 km. The 12th Century castle ruins here are especially interesting.

Return to D743 and go to Niort, 11 km.

Niort to La Rochelle
74 km (46 miles)

Exit Niort on D9 (direction Magne and Coulon) and go to Coulon, 11 km.

Turn left onto D123 and go to INT with D102, 7 km.

Turn right onto D102 and go to Arçais, 4 km.

Exit Arçais on D102, which becomes D104 at the boundary line, and go to INT with D15, 8.5 km.

Turn left onto D15, which immediately becomes D116, and go to INT with D262 (E), 3 km. This is the road beside the Canal de la Banche.

Turn right onto D262 and go to Marans, 16 km. At Marans you will intersect D114 which takes you into town and connects with D105.

Take D105 to la Rochelle, 24.5 km.

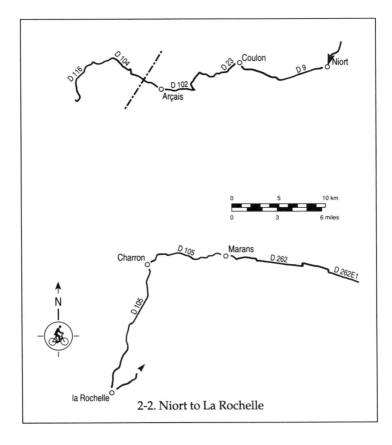

2-2. Niort to La Rochelle

La Rochelle to Fontenay-le-Comte
60.5 km (38 miles)

Exit la Rochelle on D9, which becomes D10A at Pont-de-Brault, and go north to Puyravault, 29.5 km.

Turn right onto D25 and go to Chaillé-lès-Marais. 8 km. In Chaillé, when you come to the church, D25 turns 90 degrees to the right. Turn, and stay on D25 to INT with D65, 7 km.

Turn left onto D65 and go to Fontenay, 16 km.

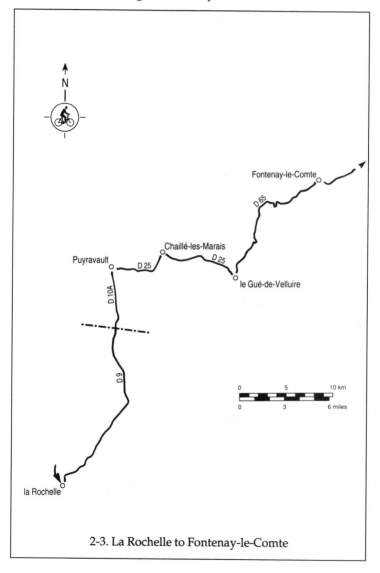

2-3. La Rochelle to Fontenay-le-Comte

Fontenay-le-Comte to Parthenay
60 km (37 miles)

Exit Fontenay on D49 and go to St. Hilaire-de-Voust, 19 km. Take the second right, D49E, after passing the church on your right, and go to L'Absie, 8 km. (D49 becomes D136 after crossing the departemental boundary.)

Continue on D136 from l'Absie to Largeasse, 10 km.

When you see the church on your left, turn right onto D140.

Take D140 to Parthenay, 23 km.

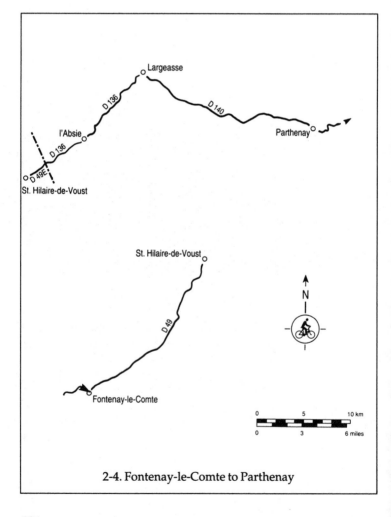

2-4. Fontenay-le-Comte to Parthenay

Parthenay to Poitiers
62.5 km (39 miles)

Exit Parthenay on D165 and go to Thénezay, 19.5 km. (By curious coincidence, midway between these towns, the elevation of D165 is 165 meters above sea-level.)

Getting out of Thénezay is a bit tricky. When you get into town, turn right and go past the church. One block past the church, turn right again and go one block, then turn left onto D141 (which, 4 km later, becomes D27).

Take D141/D27 through Ayron and Latillé (you'll go up a steep hill leaving Latillé) to the intersection with D6, 24.5 km.

Turn left onto D6 and go to Poitiers. 18.5 kms.

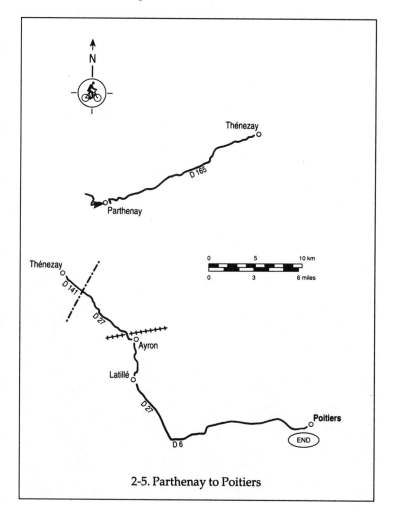

2-5. Parthenay to Poitiers

Tour 3: The Landes

Bordeaux to Mont-de-Marsan in five stages
Terrain virtually flat except leaving Bordeaux and approaching Mont-de-Marsan.
Total Distance: 400 km (248 miles)
Michelin maps No. 71, 78, 79

Flatness of roads and absence of traffic
make the long stages easy to ride.

The Landes is an immense pine forest, much of which is a national park. The roads are flat and straight and almost hypnotic. The only 'hills' are the sand dunes near the sea. Bordeaux is, of course, the most famous wine city in the world. Bazas is a cathedral city; on Saturdays there is a colorful open-air market on the square in front of the cathedral. On two sides of the square are arcaded streets.

Roquefort is not where the cheese comes from; that Roquefort is included in Tour 19. It is, however, a handsome old town at the edge of the forest where it meets the foothills of the Pyrénées. Sabres is in the middle of the forest, and has a large public swimming pool in which it's nice to cool off. Vieux Boucau has a beach with many hotels plus public camping areas It is not one of the famous beaches, so does not attract droves of foreigners—it is where the French go and thus is not as expensive as the more famous resorts such as St. Tropez.

Mont-de-Marsan on the Midourze river is the capital (*prefecture*) of the Landes Départment. One can return from there by train to Bordeaux, then to Paris.

Cycling through the forest of the Landes.

Bordeaux to Bazas
76 km (47 miles)

Exit Bordeaux on Font St. Jean. Turn right onto Quai de la Souys which becomes D113. Follow D113 to INT with D10, 9 km.

Take D10 to Cadillac, 23 km.

Shortly after passing the château on your left, turn right onto D117. Cross the Garonne river, then N113 at Cérons-Podensac, and go to where road forks, just after you cross the train tracks, 2 km.

Bear left onto D117E2; go to INT with D11, 3 km.

Bear left onto D11; cross A62 and go through Landiras to Balisac, 18 km.

Turn left onto D110; go to Villandraut, 7 kms. (**Note**: You will pass an ancient château, the former home of Pope Clement, on your left.)

Exit Villandraut on D3 (D11 on old map); turn right onto D110 after 1 km; go to Basas, 13 km (from turn).

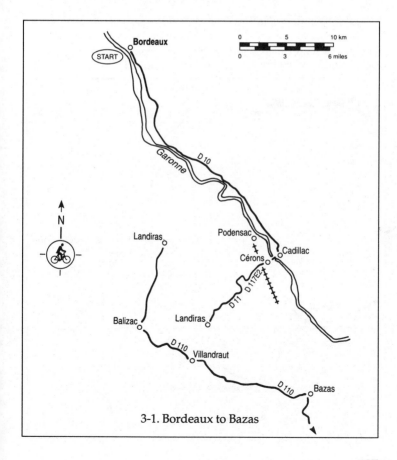

3-1. Bordeaux to Bazas

Bazas to Roquefort
91.5 km (57 miles)

Exit Bazas on D9 and D932 southward; go to INT with D12, 2 km.

Turn left onto D12; go to St. Michel-de-Castelnau, 17 km.

After passing the church on your right, swing right onto D10E5 (D12E on old map); go to Lartigue, 3.5 km.

Continue on D12E which becomes D433 at departmental boundary; go to Allons, 7 km.

Continue south to Losse, 12 km.

Exit Losse on D24 southward, direction Gabarret, to INT with D 35, 17.5 km.

Turn right onto D35; go to INT with D11, 13.5 km.

Turn left onto D111; go to Labastide-d'Armagnac, 4 km. (**Note:** this is a famous walled fortress-town and center of Armagnac production. The Bastide is well worth looking around.)

Exit Labastide-d'Armagnac on D626 westward; go to St. Justin, 4 km.

Exit St. Justin northwestward on D933; go approximately 800 meters and turn left onto D626; go to Roquefort, 11 km.

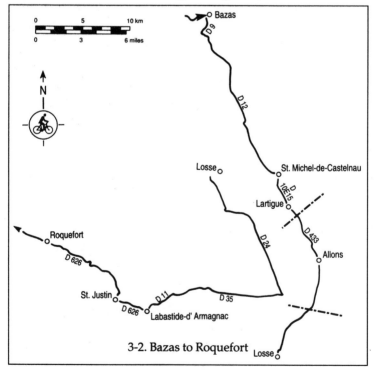

3-2. Bazas to Roquefort

Roquefort to Sabres
42 km (26 miles)

Exit Roquefort on D626 westward; go to Labrit, 20 km.

Exit Labrit on D57; go to Vert, 3 km.

Exit Vert on D57; go 300 meters to INT with D14. Bear right onto D14; go to les Basses, 11 km.

Turn right onto D327; go to Sabres, 6 km.

Note: Continuing on D626 from Labrit to Sabres is more direct, but the route described is more appealing. As you approach Sabres on D327, you'll see a public swimming pool on your right.

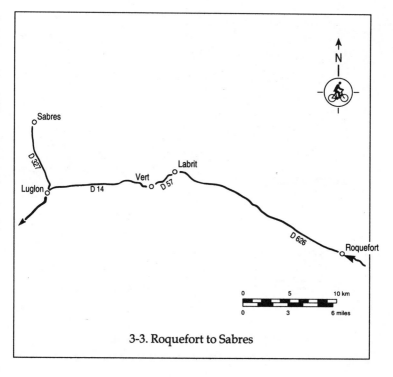

3-3. Roquefort to Sabres

Sabres to Vieux-Boucau-les-Bains
94.5 km (59 miles)

Exit Sabres the same way you came in, on D327; go to les Basses-Luglon, 8.5 km.

Turn right onto D14; go to Arengosse, 11 km.

Turn right onto D38; go 100 meters and turn left onto D14; go to Rion-des-Landes, 15 km.

Exit Rion on D41; go 300 meters and turn left onto D27; go to Laluque, 13 km.

Just after crossing the train tracks, turn sharp right onto D42; go to Taller, 7 km.

Turn left onto D140; go to INT with D947, 8 km.

When you cross D947, D140 becomcs D150. Take D150 through Herm to Magescq, 11 km.

Cross N10 and continue on D150 to Azur, 8 km. In Azur, when you see the church, turn left, so that the church is on your right. Weave through the forest past the Étang de Soustons to INT with D652, 8 km. Turn right onto D652; go to Vieux-Boucau, 5 km.

Note: In addition to the resort hotels and boarding houses, there is a public campground here with toilets, showers, and laundering facilities.

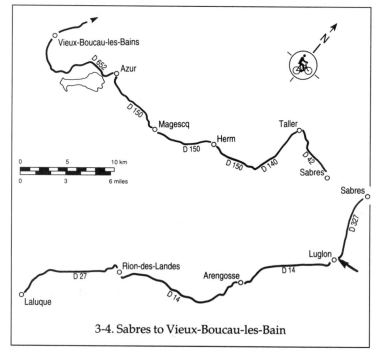

3-4. Sabres to Vieux-Boucau-les-Bain

Vieux-Boucau-les-Bains to Mont-de-Marsan
96 km (60 miles)

Exit Vieux-Boucau on D652 northward; go to Léon, 14 km.

Bear right onto D142; go to INT with D42, 11 km.

Turn right onto D42; go through Castets and Laluque to Pontonx-sur-l'Adour, 25.5 km.Cross N24 and take D10 to Mugron, 16 km.

Turn left onto D3; go to Souprosse, 7 km.

When you intersect D924 at Souprosse, turn right, go 1 km, then turn left onto D3.

Continue on D3 through Le Leuy and St. Perdon to INT with N124, 14.5 km. Turn right onto N124 and go to Mont-de-Marsan, 7 km.

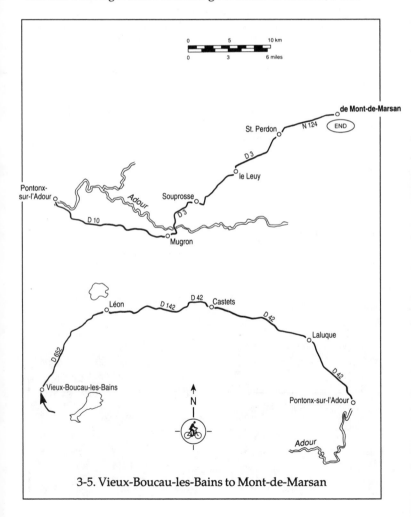

3-5. Vieux-Boucau-les-Bains to Mont-de-Marsan

Tour 4: Bordeaux Wine Route

A circuit through Bordeaux' major wine and
gastronomic areas in five stages
Terrain: Flat to rolling hills
Total Distance: 340 km (211 miles) via Cap
Ferret; 314 km (195 miles) stopping in Arès.
(Add 17 to either for extension to Margaux
and Cantenac.)
Michelin maps 71 and 75

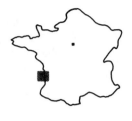

This route starts and finishes in Bordeaux. It can be tied in with the
preceding route. Cap Ferret has the Atlantic on one side and the Bay
of Arcachon on the other. Lesparre is the upper end of the Médoc
wine-growing area which produces the most famous red wines in the
world. The road to Blaye (which is reached by ferry), on the left bank
of the Gironde estuary, takes one by all the great vineyards and their
châteaux, e.g. Lafite-Rothschild; Mouton-Rothschild; La Tour; Margaux; etc.

The road to Castillon takes you through the Pomerol region (Château
Petrus is the best-known wine there) and St. Emilion (Château
Cheval-Blanc; Château Ausone whose vineyard has been in production for at least 2,000 years). Castillon, on the Dordogne river, is the
site of the last battle of the Hundred Year's War, and with its wrought-
iron grills, is reminiscent of New Orleans.

The Pont St. Jean at Bordeaux

Bordeaux to Cap Ferret
77 km (48 miles), or 51 km (32 miles) to Arès

The greatest wine property in Graves, Château Haut-Brion, and the next greatest, Château La Mission Haut-Brion, are both on ave. Jean-Jaures just north of the University of Bordeaux in the suburb of Pessac.

After visiting these châteaux, go southwest on ave. Jean-Jaures which becomes ave. Pasteur, then ave. Général Leclerc, then N250.

At a distance of 6 km from Pont St. Jean in downtown Bordeaux, turn right off N250 and onto D107; go to D106, 3 km.

Turn left onto D106; go to Arès, 42 km.

If you want great views of the Atlantic Ocean and the Arcachon Basin, plus great seafood, especially oysters, continue on D106 to Cap Ferret, 26 km. Otherwise, hold up in Arès.

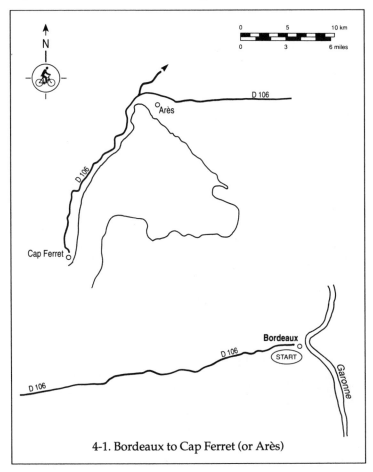

4-1. Bordeaux to Cap Ferret (or Arès)

Cap Ferret to Lesparre-Médoc
88 km (55 miles), or 66 km (41 km) from Arès

Return from Cap Ferret toward Arès on D106 to Lège, 24 km.

Turn left at Lège onto D3; go to Lesparre, 64 km. If you are leaving Arès, take D106 to Lège, 2 km. Turn right onto D3; go to Lesparre, 64 km.

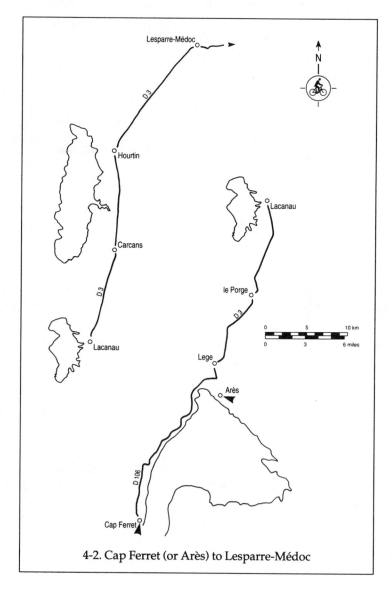

4-2. Cap Ferret (or Arès) to Lesparre-Médoc

Lesparre-Médoc to Blaye
44.5 km (28 miles), or 61.5 km (38 miles) with extension

Exit Lesparre on D2E (D204/D203); go to INT with D4E, 1.5 km.

Turn left onto D4E; go to Potensac, 5 km.

After you pass the cemetery on your left, turn left onto D4; go to St. Yzans-de-Médoc, 4 km. Turn left onto D2.

This is the 'Wine Road.' You'll see signs to *Cos d'Estournel*; *Châteaux Lafite-Rothchild, Mouton-Rothschild, Pontet-Canet, Haut Bages, Pichon-Longueville, Latour, Talbot*, and *Beychevelle*, inter alia. **Warning:** Tasting wine from the barrel makes you extremely thirsty because of the high tannin content (as well as the alcohol).

Whatever deviations you make to visit wine châteaux, follow D2 to Lamarque, 32 km from St. Yzans.

Note: Châteaux Margaux, Lascombes, Prieuré-Lichine, Brane-Cantenac, etc., are south of Lamarque on D2. To visit them, go 8.5 km farther south, then back to Lamarque, a 17-km extension.

At Lamarque, take D5 to Port de Lamarque on the Gironde estuary, 2 km. Take the ferry from here to Blaye.

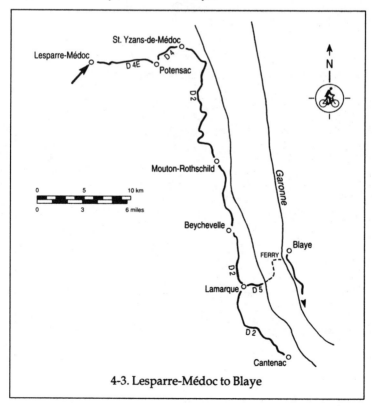

4-3. Lesparre-Médoc to Blaye

Blaye to Castillon-la-Bataille
84.5 km (53 miles)

Exit Blaye on D669; go to Roque-de-Thau, 6 km.

Turn right onto D9E; go to Bourg, 10 km.

Take D669 to St. Gervais, 9 km.

Turn left onto D115E; cross N137; go to INT with N10, 3.5 km.

Cross N10. D115E becomes D10. Take D10 to INT with D10E, 7 km.

Turn sharp right onto D1OE; go to INT with D121E, 10 km. (D 121E is a tiny road that turns left exactly 2 km north of Fronsac just before you start downhill, so watch for it; it's easy to miss.)

Turn left onto D121E. Cross the Isle river, the D674, then N89, and go to Pomerol, 6.5 km.

Here you will see signs to *Château Petrus,* the most famous name in Pomerol, and to *Château Cheval-Blanc,* one of the two most famous wine properties in St. Émilion. Although they are in different districts, they are only 1 km apart.

Continue to St. Émilion, 5.5 km. Château Ausone, the other of the two most famous wines from the St. Émilion district, is 120 meters south of St. Émilion on D122.

After visiting the wine chai, go 100 meters farther south and turn left onto D130E (D245); go to St. Étienne-de-Lisse, 6 km.

Turn right onto D130 and go to Castillon, 5 km.

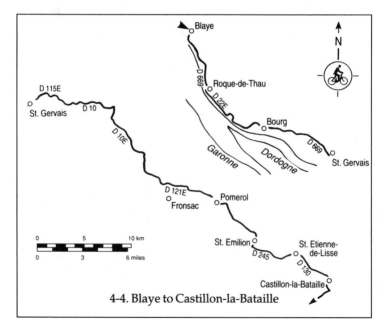

4-4. Blaye to Castillon-la-Bataille

Castillon-la-Bataille to Bordeaux
46 km (29 miles)

Exit Castillon on D119, on the south bank of the Dordogne river; go to St. Jean-de-Blaignac, 9 km.

Turn right and exit St. Jean on D18; go to Branne, 5 km.

Turn left onto D936; go to Bordeaux, 32 km.

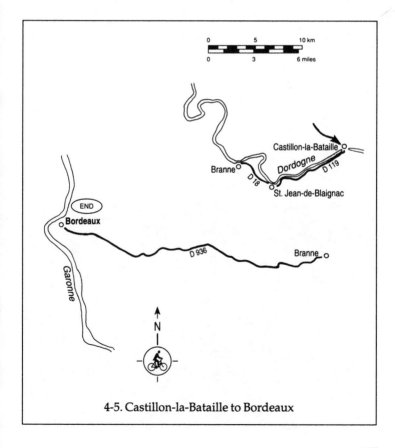

4-5. Castillon-la-Bataille to Bordeaux

Tour 5: The Dordogne

Bordeaux to Rocamadour and back in seven
stages
Terrain: Slightly to extremely hilly
Total Distance: 501 km (311 miles)
Michelin maps No 75 and 79

Note: The last two stages can be evened up
a bit by stopping at Sauveterre-de-Guyenne,
then riding from there to Bordeaux. This subtracts 22 km from the
long stage and adds it to the final stage.

This tour can be conbined with either or both of the two preceding
tours. The rides along the Dordogne and the Lot rivers are beautiful,
but the terrain, overall, is quite hilly. Ste. Foy straddles the Dordogne
river and is an old *bastide* (an arcaded, fortified town built around a
square). Les Éyzies is the site of the famous Cro-Magnon painted
caves. Sarlat is a story-book town and is enormously popular. Rocamadour is perched on cliffs and affords spectacular views. Cahors is
nestled in a horseshoe bend of the Lot river surrounded by craggy
hills. It is famous for its deep red, heady wine. Wednesdays and
Saturdays are market days here, when the open-air booths fill the
square and adjoining streets. Villeneuve occupies both sides of the
Lot river and has a lovely arcaded square. It is renowned for its plum
brandy. Marmande is on the Garonne river as is Cadillac. The Lot
flows into the Garonne; the Garonne and Dordogne meet near Bordeaux to form the Gironde estuary which flows into the Atlantic
Ocean.

The old gate once guarded medieval Bordeaux.

Bordeaux to Ste. Foy-la-Grande
71 km (44 miles)

Exit Bordeaux via Pont St. Jean and Blvd. Joliot Curie; bear right onto Cours Gambetta, which becomes Côte de Monrepos. This now does a question-mark turn. Swing right onto D936; go to Branne, 32 km (from downtown Bordeaux).

After passing the church on your right, turn right onto D18; go to INT with D130, 34 km.

Take D130 eastward to Ste. Foy, 5 km.

Note: When you go through Pujols, have a look into the church. The organ was made in Philadelphia.

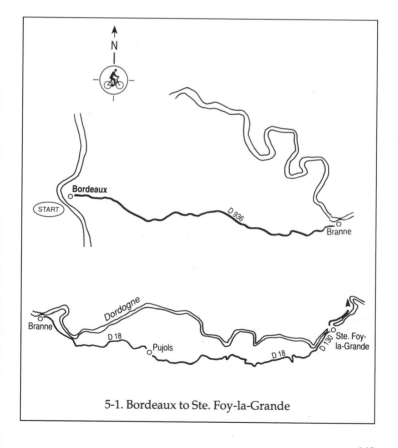

5-1. Bordeaux to Ste. Foy-la-Grande

Ste. Foy-la-Grande to les Eyzies-de-Tayac
79 km (39 miles)

Exit Ste. Foy on D20; go to le Fleix, 5.5 km.

Go right onto D32; go to Bergerac, 19.5 km. Continue on D32 to Ste. Alvère, 29 km.

Turn right onto D2; go to INT with D703, 3.5 km.

Turn left onto D703; go to Campagne, 14.5 km.

Turn left onto D706; go to les Eyzies, 7 km.

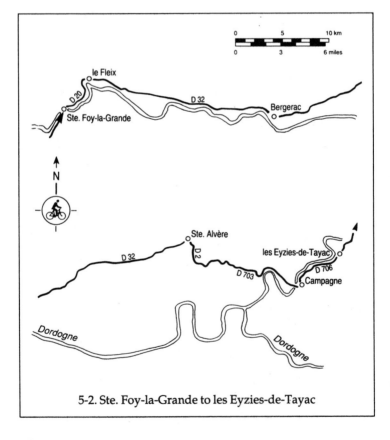

5-2. Ste. Foy-la-Grande to les Eyzies-de-Tayac

Les Eyzies-de-Tayac to Rocamadour
71 km (44 miles)

Exit les Eyzies on D47; go to Sarlat, 22 km.

Exit Sarlat on D704 southward; go to St. Cirq-Madelon, 12.5 km.

Turn left onto D101; go to Milhac, 3 km.

Turn right onto D128, go to Auniac, 5 km.

Cross the train tracks and turn sharp left onto D129; go to Payrac, 7.5 km.

Cross N20; go out of Payrac on D673; go to Rocamadour, 21 km.

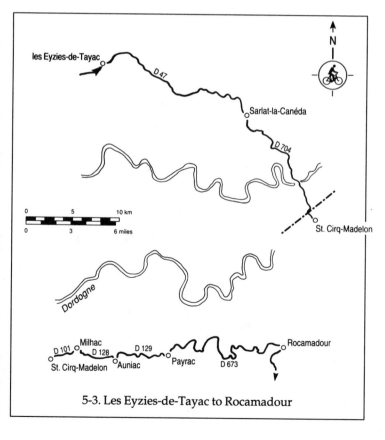

5-3. Les Eyzies-de-Tayac to Rocamadour

Rocamadour to Cahors
60.5 km (38 miles)

Exit Rocamadour on D32 southward; go to INT with D677, 16.5 km.

Turn right onto D677; go to Labastide-Murat, 8 km.

Bear left onto D32; go to INT with D653, 13.5 km.

Proceed into D653; go to Cahors, 22.5 km.

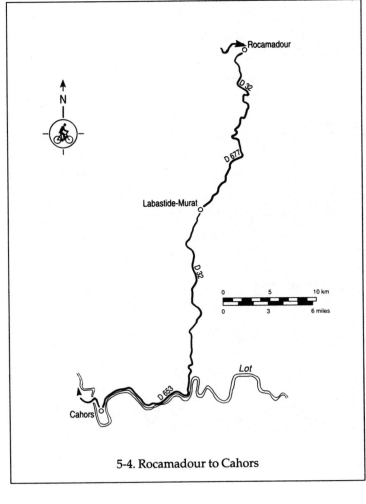

5-4. Rocamadour to Cahors

Cahors to Villeneuve-sur-Lot
77 km (48 miles)

Exit Cahors on D8 on the south bank of the Lot river; go to Fumel, 53 km.

After crossing the bridge into Fumel, turn left onto D911; go to Villeneuve, 24 km.

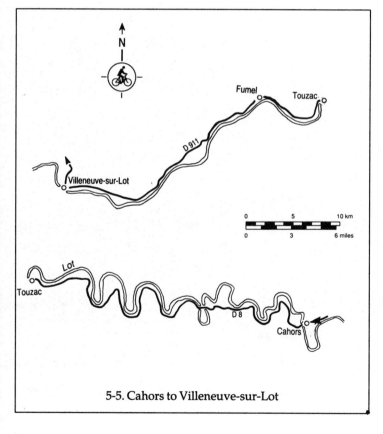

5-5. Cahors to Villeneuve-sur-Lot

153

Villeneuve-sur-Lot to Cadillac
107.5 km (67 miles)

Exit Villeneuve on N21 northward; go to Cancon, 19 km.

Turn left onto D124; go to Monbahus, 7.5 km.

At INT with D145, bear right onto it; go to INT with D227, 3.5 km.

Bear left onto D227; go to Miramont-de-Guyenne, 13 km.

Turn left, go one block, then turn right onto D668; go to Monsegur, 25.5 km.

Turn right, then left onto D21E; go to Castelmoron, 10 km.

D21E becomes D14; go to Sauveterre-de-Guyenne, 7 km.

Take D671 out of Sauveterre; go to St. Brice, 5.5 km.

Bear left onto D11E (D228/D230); go to Cadillac, 16.5 km.

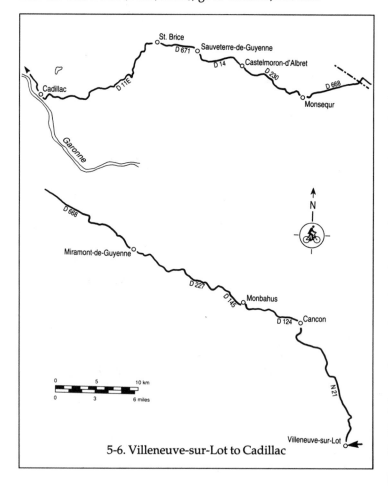

5-6. Villeneuve-sur-Lot to Cadillac

Cadillac to Bordeaux
35 km (22 miles)

Take D10 northwestward to Bordeaux, 35 km

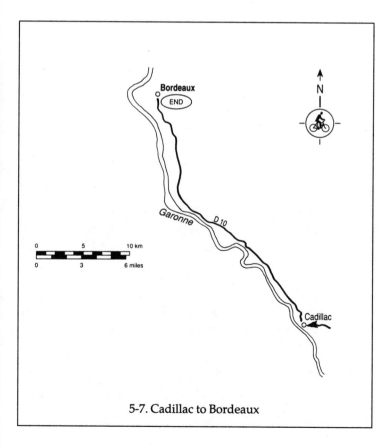

5-7. Cadillac to Bordeaux

Tour 6: The Loire Valley I

Six-stage circuit starting and ending in Blois
Terrain: Flat to moderately hilly
Total Distance: 380.5 km (236 miles)
Michelin maps No. 64, 65, and 69

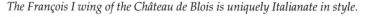

This first one of the three proposed Loire Valley route follows several rivers and includes
the great medieval Gothic cathedral in Bour-
ges, the famous vineyards around Sancerre, and picturesque châteaux
at Gien, Sully, and Beaugency as well as Blois. There are also excellent
museums of fine art in Bourges and Orléans.

Note: Any of the three Loire Valley tours can be combined with any
of the other.

The François I wing of the Château de Blois is uniquely Italianate in style.

Blois to Romorantin-Lanthenay
47.5 km (29.5 miles)

Exit Blois on rue Denis-Papin and Pont Jacques-Ange Gabriel, which becomes D765; go to INT with D923, 4 km.

Turn left onto D923; go to Bracieux, 14 km.

In Bracieux, just after passing the cemetery on your right, turn right onto D112. You'll see a swimming pool on your right and a church on your left.

At the south end of town (1 km), turn right onto D102, then left onto D120; go to Romorantin-Lanthenay via Fontaines-en-Sologne, Courmemin, and Veilleins, 28.5 km.

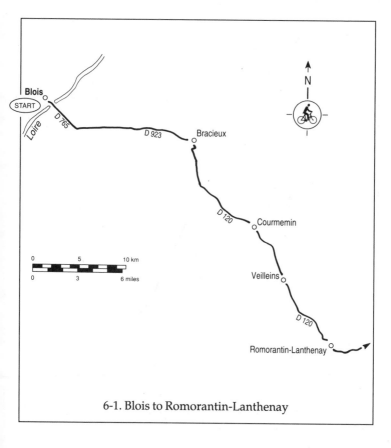

6-1. Blois to Romorantin-Lanthenay

Romorantin-Lanthenay to Bourges
66.5 km (41 miles)

Exit Romorantin on D75; go to INT with D60, 21 km.

Turn right onto D60; go to Theillay, then on D60 to Orçay, 10.5 km.

Turn right onto D126, which becomes D29; go through the forest of Vierzon to INT with D926, 4.5 km.

Turn left onto D926; go to INT with D104, 3 km.

Bear right onto D104; go to Bourges, 27.5 km.

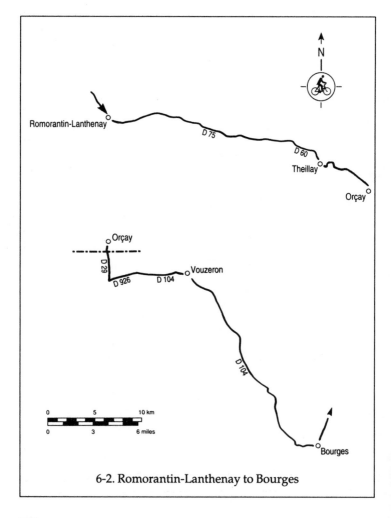

6-2. Romorantin-Lanthenay to Bourges

Bourges to Cosne-sur-Loire
65 km (40.5 miles)

Exit Bourges on ave. du 11 Novembre, which becomes D940; go to INT with D11, 7 km (from downtown Bourges).

Bear right onto D11; go to Henrichemont, 21 km.

Swing around to the right, then turn right onto D22; go to INT with D955, 22 km.

Turn left onto D955; go through Sancerre (famous wine town; fine restaurants) to Cosne-sur-Loire, 15 km.

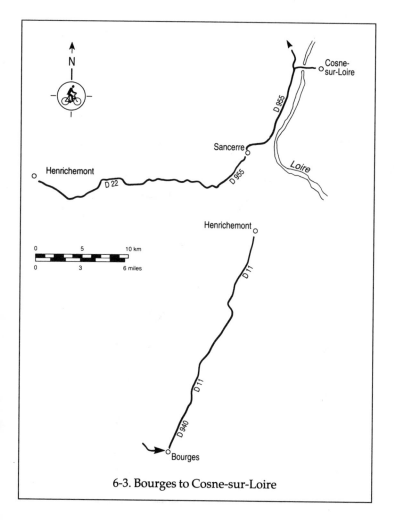

6-3. Bourges to Cosne-sur-Loire

Cosne-sur-Loire to Gien
41 km (25.48 miles)

Exit Cosne on D955 the same way you came into town; go to INT with D751, 2 km.

Turn right onto D751, which becomes D951 at boundary; go to Gien, 39 km.

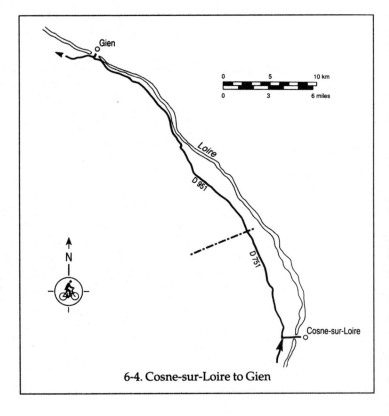

6-4. Cosne-sur-Loire to Gien

Gien to Orléans
76.5 km (47.5 miles)

Exit Gien on the same bridge across the Loire you took into town, and turn right onto D951; go to Sully-sur-Loire, 23 km. (**Note:** Don't miss viewing the château here.)

Exit Sully on D948; go to INT with D601, 1 km.

Turn left onto D60; go to Châteauneuf-sur-Loire, 18 km. (**Note:** in St. Benoît, D60 turns left. Watch for signs.)

Entering Châteauneuf, go up the hill and proceed into D952; go to INT with D11, 1 km.

Turn left onto D11; cross the Loire and go to Tigy, 8 km.

Turn right onto D14; go to Orléans, 33 km. (In Orléans, D14 intersects D15, which goes across the bridge and into downtown.)

Note: In St. Cyr-en-Val, after passing the church on your left, stay on D14; do not take D126 despite the sign. Where the two routes fork, bear left. You should pass a cemetery and a water tower on your left.

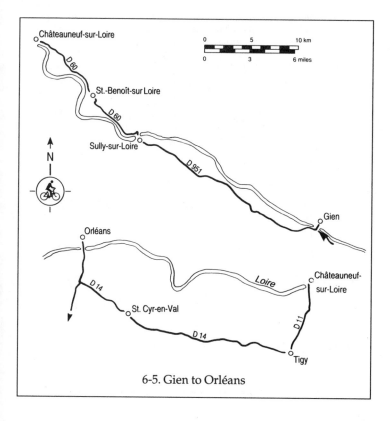

6-5. Gien to Orléans

Orléans to Blois via Beaugency
76.5 km (47.5 miles)

Exit Orléans on the street you took into town (D14); to to INT with D168, 5 km (south of downtown Orléans).

At the fork, bear left onto D168; go to Ardon, 9 km.

Turn right onto D7; go to Jouy-le-Potier, 6 km.

In Jouy, you will pass a cemetery on your right. When you get to the church, turn right onto D103; go to INT with D19, 6.5 km.

Turn right onto D19; go to Beaugency, 8.5 km.

Exit Beaugency on D917; go to Josnes, 9 km.

Turn left onto D70A; go to Mauvoy, 9.5 km via Concriers and Château Talcy.

At Mauvoy, turn left onto D50; go to Blois, 23 km.

Note: D50 bends to the right 1 km south of La Chapelle-St.Martin-en-Plaine; don't miss it

Note: At Mulsans, see the 12th century church: the porch roof-beams are very fine.

Entering Blois, go all the way down to N152 before turning right. This entrance becomes ave. Manoury which becomes rue d'Angleterre, which goes into downtown Blois.

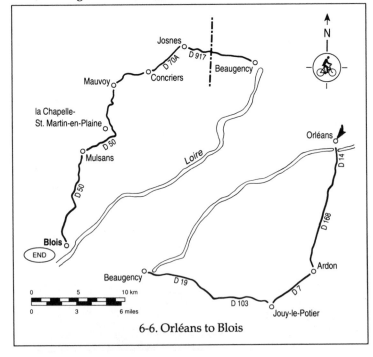

6-6. Orléans to Blois

Tour 7: The Loire Valley II

Blois to Chinon with optional loop to
Richelieu and Montsoreau in five stages
Total Distance 210 km (130 miles)
Terrain: Mainly flat, with occasional rolling
hills
Michelin maps 64 and 67

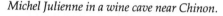

The optional three stage loop Chinon to Riche-
lieu allows you to see the largest and most colorful open-air market
in this part of France (held on Mondays); Montsoreau, a small river-
port on the Loire with a castle once occupied by a robber-baron; then
back to Chinon via Fontevrault Abbey.

This route includes seven of the Valley's most famous châteaux (Blois,
Chaumont, Amboise, Clos Lucé, Chenonceaux, Langeais, and Ussé),
the castle ruins at Chinon, the abbey at Fontevrault, the cathedral at
Tours, plus extensive vineyards and wine caves open to visitors.

Note: Any of the three Loire Valley tours can be combined with any
of the other.

Michel Julienne in a wine cave near Chinon.

Blois to Amboise
38 km (24 miles)

Exit Blois on Pont Jacques-Ange Gabriel; turn right at end of bridge onto D751; go to INT with D173, 6 km (from end of bridge).

Continue straight onto D173 (D751 veers left uphill); go to Candé-sur-Beuvron, 8.5 km.

Turn right onto D751; go to Chaumont-sur-Loire, 6.5 km.

Continue on D751 to Amboise, 17 km.

Optional extension to Chenonceaux:
Exit Amboise following signs to Chenonceaux on D81; go across long hill to Civray-de-Touraine, 10.5 km.

Turn left onto D40; go to Château Chenonceaux, 1 km.

Return by the same route, 11.5 km.

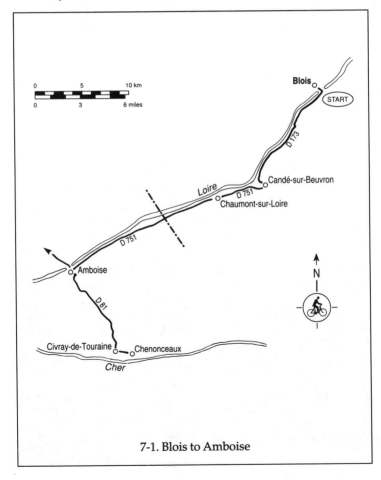

7-1. Blois to Amboise

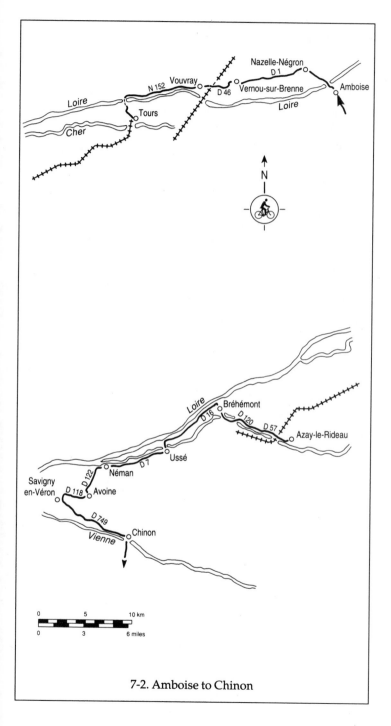

7-2. Amboise to Chinon

Amboise to Chinon via Tours and Azay-le-Rideau
71.5 km (44 miles)

Exit Amboise: cross bridge; bear left onto route de Nazelles-Négron; go to Nazelles, 3 km.

Turn left onto D1; go to Vernou-sur-Brenne, 9.5 km.

In Vernou, D1 swings first to the right then back to the left, crosses the Brenne (a small creek, not a river), and intersects D46.

Turn left onto D46; go to Vouvray, 4 km. (**Note:** Vouvray is a well-known wine town.)

In downtown, turn left, go two blocks to INT with N152; turn right onto N152; go to Tours, 12.5 km.

Approaching Tours, look across the Loire at the cathedral spires. When you judge the cathedral (no longer visible) should be exactly 90 degree to your left, look for a small suspension bridge for pedestrians and cyclists only on your left.

Turn left (carefully) onto this bridge; go past the cathedral (worth looking into) to blvd. Heurteloup. Turn right. Go one block and turn left; there is the train station, 1 km from where you left N152.

Take the 12:26 train to Azay-le-Rideau, 35 minutes. (Put bike into baggage area behind the motorman's compartment.)

At Azay, turn left onto D57 to go to *Château*, 1.5 km.

Exiting Azay, go back on D57 past station to INT with D120, 3 km.

Bear left onto D120; go to INT with D7, 3 km.

Turn left onto D7; go to INT with D119, 1.5 km.

Turn right onto D119; go to Bréhémont, 2 km.

At Bréhémont, get onto the dike road, D16, and turn left; go to Château Ussé, 8 km. (Turn left off D16 to go to château when it is directly to your left.)

At the château, turn right onto D7; go to Néman, 6.5 km.

Turn left onto D122; go to Avoine, 3.5 km.

In Avoine, just after passing the church, turn right onto D118; go to Savigny-en-Véron, 3 km.

At INT with D418, turn left to *Centre Ville* and go to the village square, 0.5 km.

At village square, turn left, keeping the square and the church on your left.

Take this vineyard road to INT with D749, 4 km.

Proceed onto D749; go to Chinon, 5 km.

Note: At traffic circle on D749, turn right to enter the circle, then go counter-clockwise 180 degrees; turn left and procede to Chinon.

Chinon to Richelieu
21 km (13 miles)

Exit Chinon: Cross bridge; continue straight to INT with D751, where D749 (which you are on) turns left, 2 km.

Turn left, staying on D749; go to INT with D26, 4 km.

Turn right onto D26; go to Champigny-sur-Veude, 9 kms. (The chapel here is famous for its architecture and windows.)

Turn right onto D749; go to Richelieu, 6 km.

Note: Continue straight into the center of town; there you will find the open-air market—provided it's Monday.

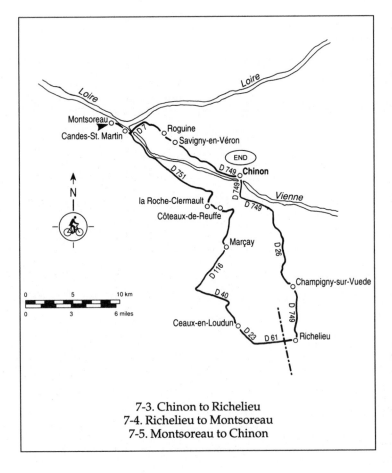

7-3. Chinon to Richelieu
7-4. Richelieu to Montsoreau
7-5. Montsoreau to Chinon

Richelieu to Montsoreau
41.5 km (26 miles)

Exit Richelieu on D61 (route de Loudun); go to INT with D23, 5 km. Turn right onto D23; go to Ceaux-en-Loudun, 2.5 km.

Exiting Ceaux, turn right off D23 onto D40; go to INT with D 1l6, 6 km.

Turn right onto D116; go through Marçay (The road bends first to the left then to the right and goes up a hill at the top of which you'll see a château on your right) to C-road marked *La Roche-Clermault*, 10.5 km. (4 km past the château).

Turn left; go past Côteaux-de-Reuffe (now a goat farm and goat cheese maker, visitors welcome), to INT with D759, 3 km.

Turn right onto D759; go to INT with D751, 1.5 km.

Turn left onto D751; go to Montsoreau, 13 km.

Note: Angevin-Gothic church in Candes-St. Martin at the confluence of the Vienne and Loire rivers is architecturally interesting inside. The view from the promontory above the village is outstanding. Candes and Montsoreau are contiguous villages.

Montsoreau to Chinon
16 km (10 miles)

Go back on D751 through Candes to Pont St. Martin; turn left onto bridge and D7; go to Roguine, 2 km. (The view to your left from the bridge is superb.)

At Roguinet, leave D118 and turn right onto the C-road to Savigny-en-Véron; go through Savigny to INT with D749, 5 km.

Proceed onto D749; go to Chinon, 5 km.

Tour 8: The Loire Valley III

From Tours to the Atlantic coast in five stages
Terrain: Essentially flat
Total Distance: 317 km (197 miles), excluding options
Michelin maps No. 63, 64 and 67

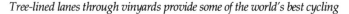

This third Loire Valley tour leads from Tours to the Atlantic coast in five stages, along the western Loire to where it flows into the sea.

Angers is the ancient capital of Anjou and has a medieval castle that pre-dates the Plantagenet Dynasty. (Henry Plantagenet, Count of Anjou and Duke of Normandy, became King of England. With the estates of his famous wife, the celebrated Eleanor of Aquitaine, he ruled the western half of France from the English Channel to the Pyrénées, a much larger domain than that ruled by the King of France. This region is famous for its white wines, notably those of Saumur and Muscadet.

Note: Any of the three Loire Valley tours can be combined with any of the other.

Tree-lined lanes through vinyards provide some of the world's best cycling

Tours to Montsoreau
60 km (37 miles)

Exit Tours: go west on blvd. Beranger to its end; turn left onto rue Giraudeau; go to its end; turn left onto rue Fromentel; go two blocks; turn right onto Rue Auguste Chevallier; cross the Cher river; turn right onto route de Savonnières (D7), 3km (from the center of Tours).

Take D7 to Villandry, 15.5 km. (**Note:** The Renaissance gardens at Château Villandry are well worth seeing.)

In the village of Villandry, watch for the Hôtel Cheval Rouge front on D7. Opposite is a tree-lined lane. Turn right onto this lane; go to D16 on the dike, 0.5 km.

Turn left on D16; go to Château Ussé, 21 km.

Note: shortly after accessing D16, you will come to a stretch of cobblestones. Either ride on the dirt path beside the cobbles or walk the bicycle. The cobbled section is about 250 meters long.

At Château Ussé, turn right onto D7; go to Néman, 7 km.

Turn left onto D122; go to Avoine, 3 km.

Turn right onto D118; go to INT with D7, 6.5 km.

Bear left onto D7; go to Candes-St. Martin, 2 km.

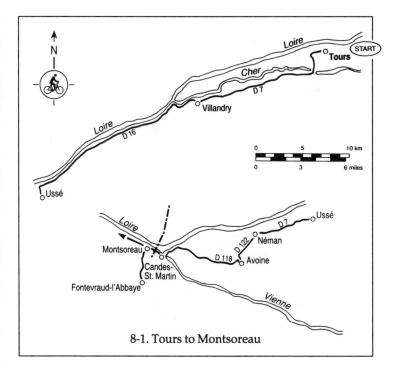

8-1. Tours to Montsoreau

Cross Pont St. Martin at the confluence of the Vienne and Loire rivers; turn right onto D751: go to Montsoreau, 1.5 km.

Optional extension to Fontevraud Abbey: Turn left onto D947; to to Fontevraud, 4.5 km (uphill all the way). In the abbey chapel are the Plantagenet tombs of Henry II of England; Eleanor of Aquitaine, and Richard the Lion-Heart.

Return to Montsoreau on the same road, coasting downhill.

Montsoreau to Angers
60 km (37 miles)

Exit Montsoreau on D947 westward; go to bridge (D952); turn right; cross the bridge; turn right onto E60 (E is correct). From the Château de Montsoreau to the far side of the bridge is 2 km.

Take E60 to Saumur, 10 km.

Exit Saumur on D229; go to Boumois; swing left under the railway to INT with D952, 9 km.

Turn right onto D952; go to Angers, 39 km.

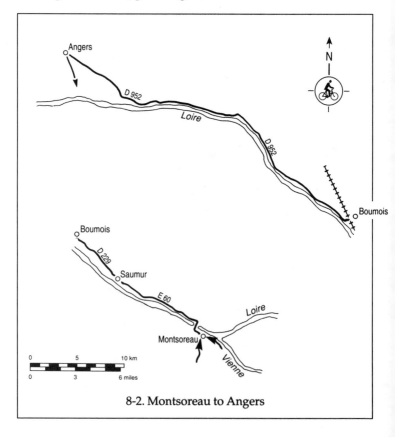

8-2. Montsoreau to Angers

Angers to Ancenis
67 km (42 miles)

Exit Angers on route de Cholet, N160 southward; go to Mûrs-Érigné, 8 km.

Turn right onto D751; go to Montjean-sur-Loire, 30 km.

Turn right onto D15, then left onto D210; go to St. Florent-le-Vieil, 13 km.

Exit St. Florent on D751 westward; go to Liré, 13 km.

Turn right onto D763; go to Ancenis, 3 km.

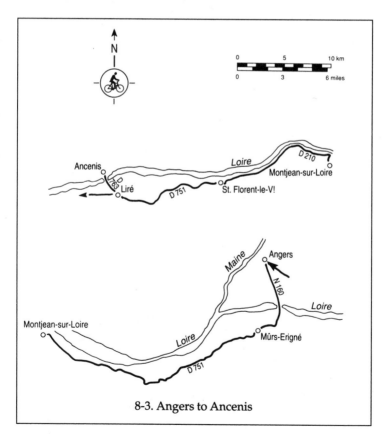

8-3. Angers to Ancenis

Ancenis to le Pellerin (avoiding Nantes)
72.5 km (45 miles)

Exit Ancenis on D763 (the same road you took into town); go to D751, 3 km.

Turn right onto D751; go to INT with D7, 16 km.

Turn left onto D7; go through la Chapelle-Basse-Mer to INT with D115, 6.5 km.

Turn right onto D115; go through Vertou to INT with D937, 21 km.

Turn left onto D937; go to INT with D11, slightly less than 1 km.

Turn right onto D11 (which bends sharply to the right at Viais); go through Font-St. Martin to INT with D751, 12 km.

Bear left onto D751; go to Bouaye, 2 km.

Exit Bouaye on D11; go through Brains to Le Pellerin, 11 km.

Note: In Brains, after you pass the church on your left, D11 bends left; after you pass the cemetery on your right, it bends right. When you intersect D723 approaching Brains, turn left onto the highway, then turn right off it onto D11 again.

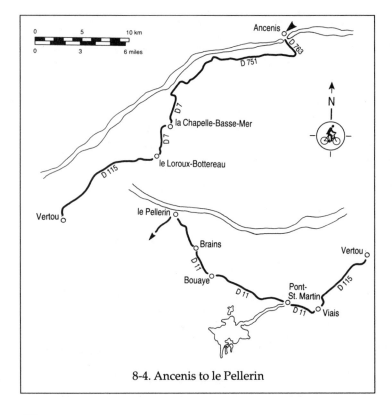

8-4. Ancenis to le Pellerin

Le Pellerin to la Baule
57.5 km (36 miles)

Exit Le Pellerin on D80; go to INT with D723, 2.5 km.

Turn right onto D723; to to INT with D58, 10 km.

Turn left onto D58; bypass St. Père-en-Retz; go to INT with D 213 at St-Brevin, 23.5 km.

Now, unless you wish to risk the expressway, either hitch a ride with a trucker, or take a taxi across the Loire Estuary to St. Nazaire.

In St. Nazaire, get onto rue Henri Gautier, the street that goes southward to the church of St. Nazaire and the *Sub-Prefecture*.

Go south on this street past the Sub-prefecture (which faces the rue de Croisic) and turn right onto blvd. President Wilson which becomes rue Albert I; go westward to INT with D292, 6.5 km (from top of rue Henri Gautier).

Turn left onto D292; go through Fornichet to la Baule, 15 km (to the center of town).

Note: If you spend an extra night in la Baule, take the D45 loop along the ocean-front to le Croisic and back, 27.5 km. Extremely scenic if you like the water and watching ocean-going vessels putting out to sea.

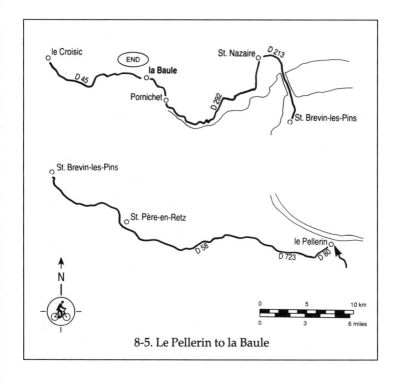

8-5. Le Pellerin to la Baule

Tour 9: By the Sea in Normandy

From Caen to Calais in seven stages
Terrain: Occasionally flat, but much hillier
than you think.
Total distance: 384 km (239 miles)
Michelin maps No. 51, 52 and 55

Splendid views of the sea from the bluffs;
exquisite fishing towns; historic beaches; and
an abundance of seafood everywhere. Honfleur, a fishing port, is one
of the loveliest towns in northern France. Fécamp, in addittion to
being a port city, is where the Benedictine Abbey that makes the
famous liqueur is located.

*Violaine Livry-Level prepares to enjoy a lunch of raw oysters, a favorite
dish in France.*

Caen to Honfleur
54 km (28 miles)

Exit Caen on quai Admiral Hamelin on the south bank of the Orne river, which becomes D513; go to INT with D27, 17.5 km from the center of Caen.

Take D27 to Deauville, 20 km.

Exit Deauville through Trouville on D5l3; go to Honfleur, 16.5 km. (**Note:** The beautiful part of Honfleur is around the Vieux Bassin.)

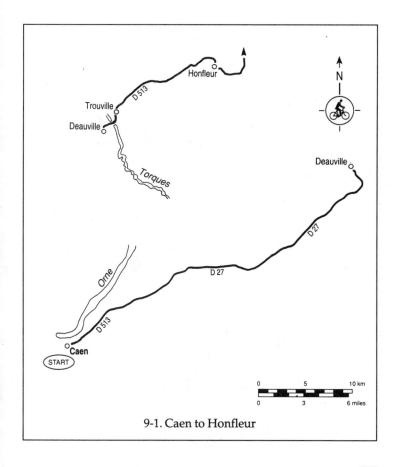

9-1. Caen to Honfleur

Honfleur via Etretat to Fécamp
62 km (39 miles)

Exit Honfleur on the Quai de la Quarantine, which becomes rue Jean Revel, then D180; cross to Le Havre on the new Pont de Normandie and go to the center of town, 19 km.

Exit le Havre on rue Georges Braque, which becomes rue d'Etretat, which becomes rue Ste. Adresse; go through the Ste. Adresse suburb and to the airport on D940, 8 km. (You do not actually go to the airport proper; just to one edge of it.)

Continue on D940 to Etretat, 23 km (from the edge of the airport.)

Exit Etretat on D11; go to Bénouville, 4 km.

Take D211 out of Bénouville to Yport, 8 km.

Exit Yport on D211; after curving around to the left and going up a hill, bear left onto the small road to Criquebeuf-en-Caux; go to Fécamp, 5.5 km.

Note: To visit the Benedictine Abbey Liqueur Museum, turn right onto rue Georges Cuvier, then left onto ave. President Coty, then right onto rue Boufart, and you'll come to the museum on your left.

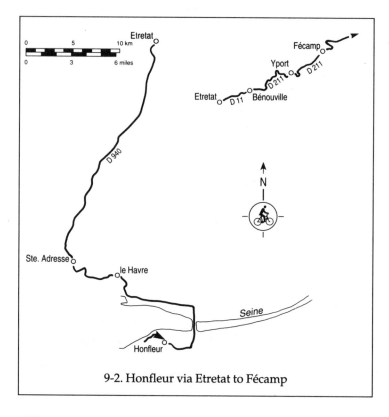

9-2. Honfleur via Etretat to Fécamp

Fécamp to Dieppe
62 km (39)

Exit Fécamp on D79; go to St. Valery-en-Caux, 28 km.

Exit St. Valery on D925; go to Veules-les-Roses, 8 km. Turn left onto D68; go to St. Aubin-sur-Mer, 7.5 km. Exit St. Aubin on D75; go to Dieppe, 18.5 km.

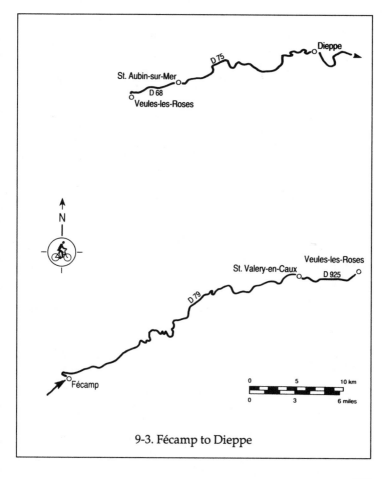

9-3. Fécamp to Dieppe

Dieppe to Abbeville
84.5 km (52.5 miles)

Exit Dieppe on ave. Général Leclerc (D925) to INT with D920, 3 km.

Turn right onto D920; go to Envermeu, 12 km.

When you pass the church on your left, bear right onto D149; go through Bailly-en-Rivière and Fresnay-Foiny to Grandcourt, 20 km.

In Grandcourt, turn left onto D16; go to INT with D126, 0.5 km.

Turn right onto D126; go to INT with D78, 7.5 km.

Turn right onto D78; go to Guerville and INT with D14, 1 km.

Turn left onto D14; go to Gamaches, 5.5 km.

Turn right, then left, and exit Gamaches on D22 (sign says *Abbeville*); go to Tours-en-Vimeu, 11 km.

In Tours-en-Vireu, turn right, then left, and go past the water tower on your right to INT with D86 at Ercourt, 4 km.

Turn left onto D86; go through Miannay to INT with D3, 11.5 km.

Turn right onto D3; go to Cambron, 3.5 km.

Turn left onto D925; go to Abbeville, 5 km. (**Note:** The reason for going around Robin Hood's barn is because these roads are better for cycling than the direct route.)

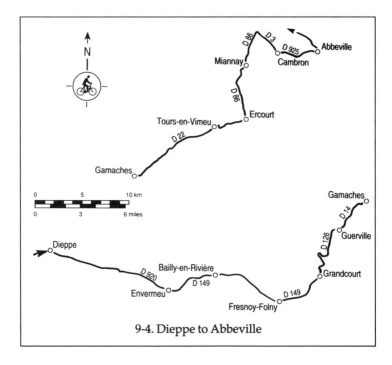

9-4. Dieppe to Abbeville

Abbeville to Berck-Plage
73 km (45 miles)

Exit Abbeville on D40; go to Noyelles-sur-Mer, 12.5 km. (Do not bear left onto the bypass; go straight into *Centre Ville*.)

In Noyelles, turn right onto D111; go through Nouvion (turn right, then back to the left) and through Crécy-en-Fonthieu to INT with D119, 24.5 km.

Turn left onto D119; go to Roussent, 13.5 km.

In Roussent, D119 bends right at the church, then left; turn right onto D139E; go to Boisjean, 4.5 km.

In Boisjean, turn left onto D142; go to INT with D140, 6.5 km.

At this junction, D140 veers right (NW); D142 becomes D142 E; take D142 E to INT with D940, 6 km.

Turn right onto D940; cross D917 D [cq] and go to D9l7, 2.5 km.

Turn left onto D917; go to Berck-Plage, 3 km (to the beach).

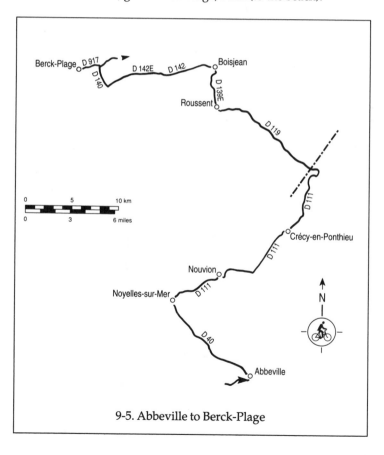

9-5. Abbeville to Berck-Plage

Berck-Plage to Boulogne-sur-Mer
60.5 km (38 miles)

Exit Berck-Flage on D917; go to Montreuil, 17.5 km.

Turn left onto N1; go to INT with D127, 2.5 km.

Turn right onto D127; go to Desvres, 22.5 km.

Turn left onto D341; go to Boulogne, 18 km.

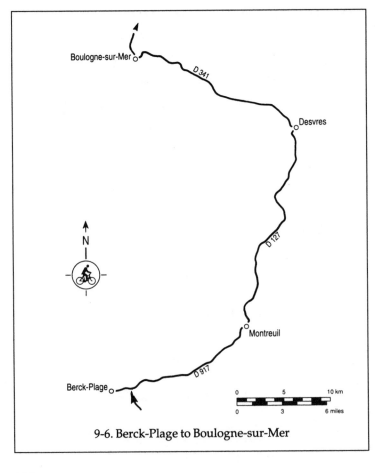

9-6. Berck-Plage to Boulogne-sur-Mer

Boulogne-sur-Mer to Calais
42 km (26 miles)

Exit Boulogne on D940 northeastward, go to Calais, 42 km.

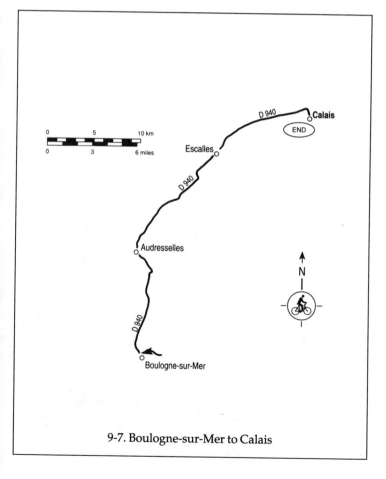

9-7. Boulogne-sur-Mer to Calais

Tour 10: Brittany—The Western Edge of France

Brest to le Mans in seven stages
Terrain: Extremely hilly.
Total Distance: 558.5 km (347 miles)
Michelin maps No. 58, 59 and 60

The Duchy of Brittany became part of France when Anne of Brittany married Charles XIII in 1491. When Charles died from an accident in 1498, his successor, a cousin, Louis XII, quickly married Charles's widow to keep Brittany a part of France. The Bretons have their own language which is closer to Gaelic than French. Mont-St. Michel is, of course, one of the half-dozen or so most famous churches in the world.

The terrain on this ride is surprisingly hilly, and there is an almost constant wind off the ocean, but by starting from Brest, the wind will usually be at the rider's back.

From le Mans, it's a quick trip back to Paris by train, via Chartres and Versailles, at either of which one can get off the train to have a look (at the cathedral of Chartres; at the château of Versailles) then continue on the next train; trains are frequent on this line.

The weather in France is not always sunny and warm, but these cyclists came prepared.

Brest to Morlaix
81.5 km (51 miles)

Exit Brest either by commuter train to le Relecq-Kerhoun, then get on D233, or cycle eastward on N165/E-60 (heavy truck traffic), cross over N165 and get on D233 (near the le Relecq train station), 10.5 km from the center of Brest, if you cycle.

Take D233 eastward to Landerneau, 11.5 km.

Turn left onto rue de la Fontaine-Blanche, then bear right onto rue Fengam, which becomes D29.

Go north on D29 through Plounéventer, Lanhouarneau and Plounévez-Lochrist to INT with D10, 25 km.

Turn right onto D10; go to Plouescat, 3.5 km.

In Plouescat, turn left at the church, go about 300 meters, then turn right onto D330.

Go to the ocean, where D330 bends to the right; follow D330 along the coast and down to Kérouzézé-Sibiril, 13.5 km.

Turn left onto D10; go to le Croissant-de-Plougoulm, 1.5 km.

Turn right onto D69; go to Plouénan, 8 km.

At Plouénan, turn sharp left onto D75, then turn right onto P65; go to INT with D769, 1.5 km.

Turn right onto D769; go to Morlaix, 16.5 km.

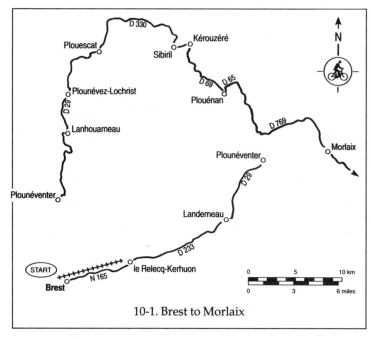

10-1. Brest to Morlaix

185

Morlaix to St. Brieuc
102.5 km (64 miles)

Exit Morlaix on D9 (towards Plougonven), which becomes D28 at the departmental boundary.

Go southeastward on D9/D28 through Callac (where you cross D787 and go under the railroad tracks) to INT with D31, 51.5 km.

Turn left onto D31; go to Bulat-Pestivien, 5.5 km.

Go left onto D24 A; go to Pont-Melvez, 4 km.

Just before you get into the village, turn right onto D24; go to Bourbriac, 10.5 km.

Turn right onto D22; go to St. Gildas, 18 km.

Turn left onto D45; go to St. Brieuc, 13 km.

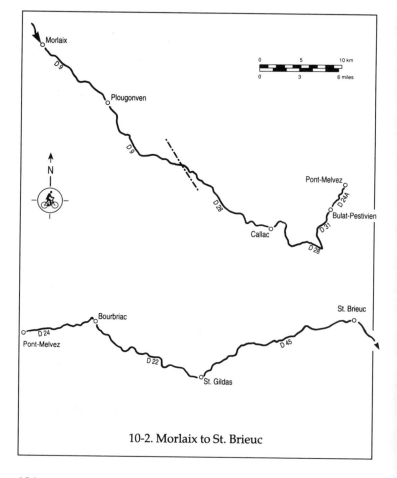

10-2. Morlaix to St. Brieuc

St. Brieuc to Dinan
60 km (37 miles)

Exit St. Brieuc on D1 (going under D790) to Quessoy, 13 km.

At Quessoy, circle around the church and turn left onto D28; go through Lamballe to Pléven, 23 km.

At Pléven, just after you pass the church on your left, the road forks. Bear right onto D68; go to INT with D794, 13 km.

Turn right onto D794; go through Corseul to INT with D68, 5 km.

Turn left onto D68; go to Dinan, 6 km.

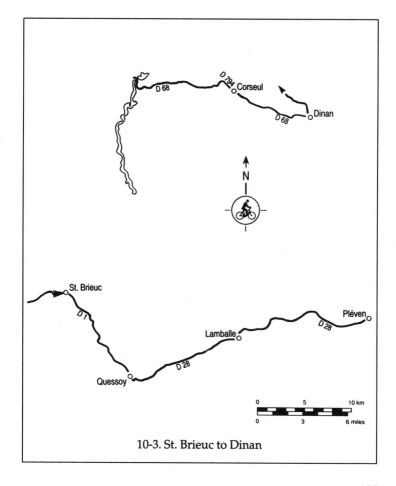

10-3. St. Brieuc to Dinan

Dinan to le Mont St. Michel
81.5 km (51 miles)

Exit Dinan on D2, direction Ploubalay; go to INT with D26, 2.5 km. (See castle ruins on your right.)

Turn left onto D26; go to Languenan, 8 km.

As soon as you pass the village church on your left, turn right onto D28; go to Pleslin, 6.5 km.

At Pleslin, after you cross the railway tracks, D28 turns northward. Do not turn: go straight on D366 through Plouer-sur-Rance to Châteauneuf, 16 km.

At Châteauneuf, you will briefly be on D74, which will take you over N137. As soon as you go over this highwaý, turn right onto D7; go to INT with D155, 11.5 km.

Turn right onto D155; go to le Vivier-sur-Mer, 6 km.

At le Vivier, go straight out of town on D797 through St.Broladre to Pontorson, 22 km.

Turn left onto D976; go to le Mont St. Michel, 9 km.

Note: 2.5 km north of Pontorson, turn right off D976; go a few meters to Moidrey and up to Beauvoir, then get back on D976. This is a pretty little road.

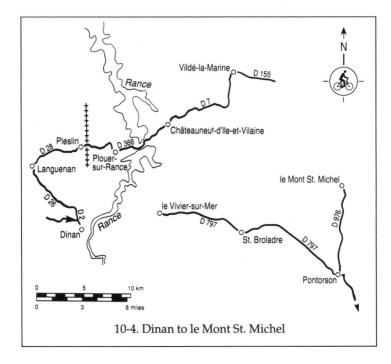

10-4. Dinan to le Mont St. Michel

Le Mont St. Michel to Fougères
58.5 km (36 miles)

Go back on D976 to Pontorson (indeed, you may have to spend the night there), 9 km.

Exit Pontorson on blvd. du Général de Gaulle; turn left onto rue de la Libération (N176) then turn right onto D30; go to St. James, 15 km.

Turn right onto D998; go to INT with D212, 2 km.

Turn right onto D212, which becomes D102; go through St. Brice-en-Coglès to INT with D113, 19.5 km.

Note: 5.5 km from where you leave D998, D102 turns right and for 1 km is combined with D15; then D102 turns left and continues south to St. Brice. Watch for the road signs.

Turn left onto D113; go to Fougères, 13 km.

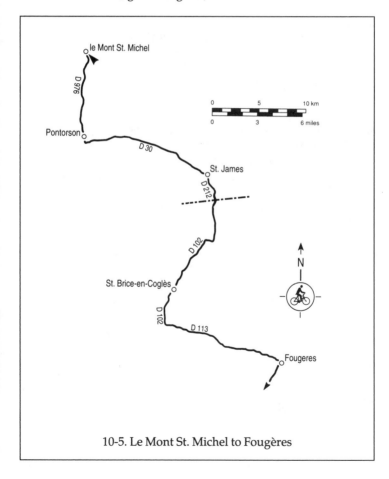

10-5. Le Mont St. Michel to Fougères

Fougères to Mayenne
79 km (49 miles)

Exit Fougères on D17; go to St. Christophe-des-Bois, 16 km.

Turn left onto D26; go to Châtillon-en-Vendelais, 5 km. (This seems like the wrong direction. But trust me.)

In Châtillon, cross the railway tracks and go past the church on your right. At the cemetery, turn left, then immediately back to the right onto D209.

Take D209 to Princé, 7.5 km.

At Princé, turn right onto D30; go to Croixille, 2.5 km.

At Croixille, turn left onto D29; go to Juvigné, 4 km.

In Juvigné, just when you get to the cemetery on your left, turn right onto D165; go through St. Hilaire-du-Maine; cross D31; and continue to Chailland, 13 km.

In Chailland, turn left at the church onto D248, the road through the forest of Mayenne. (Immediately after you pass the church you'll go over a hill and bend right, passing Château la Forge on your right just as you enter the forest.)

Take D248 through the forest, across N12, and to Châtillon-sur-Colmont, 17 km.

Note: On no account should you take N12 into Mayenne: The hills are even worse than on the small roads, and the traffic is fearsome. That road is extremely dangerous.

At Châtillon, you'll go up a hill into town and see the church right in front of you. Go around to the right of the church and turn right onto D138; go to Oisseau, 6 km.

At Oisseau, when you get to the church, turn sharp right onto D132; go to Mayenne, 8 km.

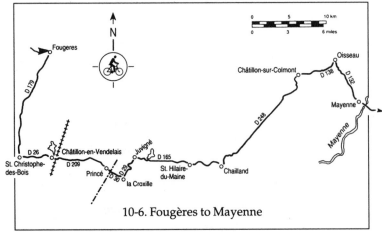

10-6. Fougères to Mayenne

Mayenne to Le Mans
95.5 km (59 miles)

Exit Mayenne on D35, direction le Mans. Go to INT with D113, 2 km.

Turn left onto D113; go to Villaines-la-Juhel, 26 km.

After you pass the church on your right, go about 250 meters and turn right onto D13; go to Courcité, 5.5 km.

Continue south on D13 to St. Pierre-sur-Orthe, 14 km.

Turn left onto D35; go to Sillé-le-Guillaume, 6.5 km.

In Sillé, turn right onto D5 eastward; go through St. Rémy to Segrie, 12 km.

At Segrie, just before you get to the church, turn right onto D21; go to INT with D82, 4 km.

Bear left onto D82; go to INT with D304, 15.5 km.

Proceed onto D304; go to le Mans, 10 km.

Note: This is the least trafficky way into Le Mans, but there will still be considerable traffic, so ride carefully.

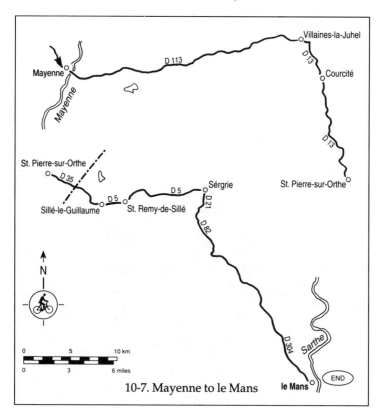

10-7. Mayenne to le Mans

Tour 11: Champagne Country

Reims to Melun in five stages
Terrain: Moderately hilly but a few severe
hills and a few perfectly flat roads
Total Distance: 319 km (198 miles) including
option
Michelin maps No. 56 and 61

The golden hills of Champagne are as heady
as the wine they produce. Five stages (but six nights): Spend the day
and the first night in Reims.

Reims, in addition to having miles and miles of wine cellars in
limestone caves, where Champagne is blended and stored, also has
one of France's greatest cathedrals, plus an outstanding museum of
art. Épernay also has great wine cellars and fine restaurants. In the
Middle Ages, Troyes had the greatest market in Western Europe and
its medieval quarter (for pedestrians only) is well-preserved. It
abounds with splendid churches and museums and is well worth an
additional day for sightseeing.

The first of the great Gothic cathedrals is located in Sens. In Fontainebleau, the château is where Francis I began the book collection
that is now the core of the French National Library, and it was here,
on the front steps, that the deposed Emperor Napoleon bade farewell
to his troops. Just outside of Melun is the château Vaux-le-Vicomte,
the splendor of which prompted the young Louis XIV to build Versailles. From here back to Paris is a quick commuter train trip.

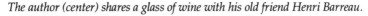

The author (center) shares a glass of wine with his old friend Henri Barreau.

Reims to Fère-Champenoise
90 km (56 miles)

Exit Reims: Go two blocks north of the cathedral and turn left on rue de Vesle which becomes rue Col. Fabien. At the three-pronged fork, angle right onto D226; go to INT with D26, 9 km from the cathedral.

Turn left onto D26; go to Gueux, 2.5 km.

Turn right onto D227; go to Poilly, 9.5 km.

At Poilly, turn left onto RD386; go to Épernay, 23 km.

To exit Épernay: Go south on rue Chandon to the Église St. Pierre et St. Paul. Turn right; go two blocks to ave. Marechal Foch; turn left. This becomes RD51; go to INT with D40, 3 km from the center of town.

After 1 km, you'll come to a fork. What looks like (and is) the main road is actually D10. Be careful to turn right, thus staying on D40.

Take D40 to Chaltrait, 12.5 km from where you left RD51.

At Chaltrait, turn right onto D38; go to INT with D18, 2 km. Turn left onto D18; go to Étoges, 5.5 km. (Both the church and château here are worth a look.)

In front of the church, turn right onto D343; go to Congy, 3.5 km.

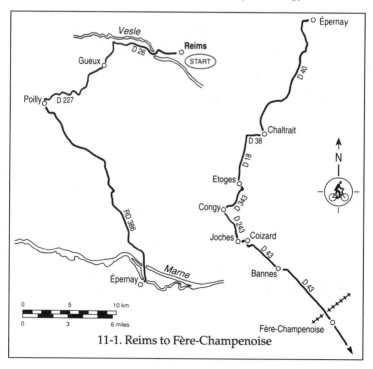

11-1. Reims to Fère-Champenoise

In Congy, make two left turns and exit on D243; go to INT with D43, 5 km.

Turn left onto D43; go to Croizard-Joches, 1 km.

Here, D43 turns right in front of the church, then left, then bends to the right. Take D43 to Bannes, 4.5 km from the church.

Continue on D43 to Fère-Champenoise, 9 km. (**Note:** After you cross the railway tracks, you'll go down a hill. Be cautious: you'll be getting into traffic.)

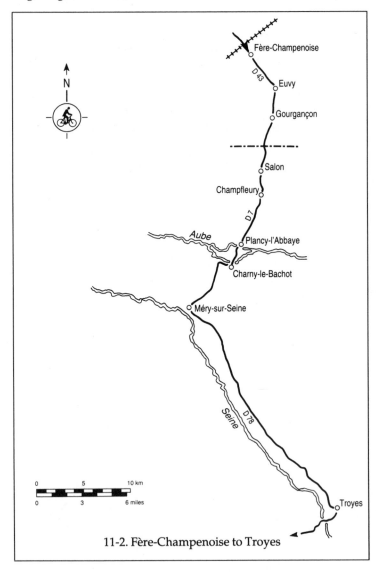

11-2. Fère-Champenoise to Troyes

Fère-Champenoise to Troyes
63 km (39 miles)

Take D43 southward out of Fère; it becomes D7 at the boundary. Go through Euvy, Gourgançon, Salon, Champfleury, and Plancy l'Abbaye to Charny-le-Bachot, 24.5 km.

At Charny, turn right. The road is now both D7 and D8. Go to where D7 turns left, 1.5 km.

Continue on D7 to Méry-sur-Seine, 6 km.

At Méry, turn left onto D78; go to Troyes, 31 km.

Troyes to Sens
76 km (47 miles)

Exit Troyes on ave. Général Gallieni, which becomes ave. Général Leclerc, which becomes N60. Go to INT with D141, 6.5 km from the Troyes train station.

Turn right onto D141; go through Montgueux (which is on a hill: enjoy the views) to INT with D60, 5 km.

Turn left onto D60; go to Dierrey-St. Pierre, 12.5 km.

At Dierrey, go north on D33 0.5 km to where D60 turns off to the left. continue on D60 to Faux-Villecerf, 7 km.

Turn right onto D23; go to INT with D29, 2 km.

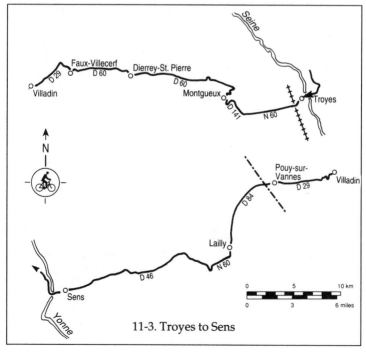

11-3. Troyes to Sens

195

Turn left onto D29; go to Villadin, 4 km.

In Villadin, turn left onto D374; go 1.5 km then turn right onto D29; go to Pouy-sur-Vannes, 7 km.

Just a few meters beyond Pouy, D29 crosses the boundary and becomes D84. Take D84 to Lailly and INT with N60/E-511, 10 km.

Turn right onto N60; go to INT with D46, 3 km.

Turn right onto D46; go to Sens, 17.5 km.

Sens to Fontainebleau
55 km (34 miles)

Exit Sens: Go west on Grande Rue; cross the Yonne river (both bridges) and watch for right turn onto D426.

Take D426 to INT with D26 at St. Martin-du-Tertre, 3 km from the cathedral in Sens.

Stay on D26 to Vallery, 16.5 km.

In Vallery, turn left, then right, and exit on D26 which becomes D219 bis; go to Voulx, 8 km.

Exit Voulx on D22; go through Flagy and Villecerf (where D22 turns sharp left) to Épisy, 16.5 km.

At Épisy, turn right onto D148; go through the famous forest to Fontainebleau, 11 km.

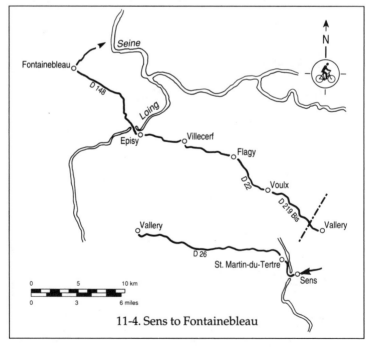

11-4. Sens to Fontainebleau

Fontainebleau to Melun
24 km (15 miles), plus 24 km (15 miles) option

Exit Fontainebleau on D210 to Vulaines-sur-Seine, 5.5 km.

Turn left onto D39; go to Melun, 18.5 km.

Note: The purpose of this short right is to see the château and chur-ches at Melun, but more importantly, château Vaux-le-Vicomte and its gardens, 5.5 outside Melun via N36 and D215. This is the château built by Louis XIV's finance minister Fouquet, with embez-zled money. Louis was so furious he banished Fouquet (he wanted to kill him), hired his architect and garden designer, and built Ver-sailles to show the world *real* splendor

Return to Paris by train. The train station (*Gare S.N.C.F.*) is on ave. Georges Clemenceaux.

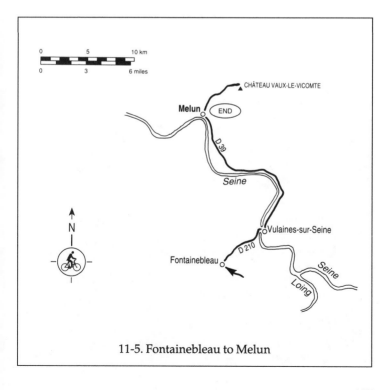

11-5. Fontainebleau to Melun

Tour 12: Burgundy—The Golden Slopes

From Dijon to Lyon in five stages
Michelin maps No. 65, 70, and 74
Terrain: Very hilly at first, then flat.
Distance: 267.5 km (166 miles)

This tour through the Burgundy wine country consists of five short but hilly stages. All the great red-wine vineyards are found between Dijon (famous for its mustard among other things) and Beaune, the wine capital of the region.

The famous white wines—the greatest white wines in the world—are produced from vineyards located between Beaune and Chalon. The wines from around Mâcon are now highly esteemed. The poultry from Bourg-en-Bresse is almost as famous as the regional wines: a coded tag is attached to each fowl. Lyon is a pre-Roman city, one of the largest in France, and Lyon, not Paris, is the culinary capital of the world. Stage distances on this route are short to allow ample time to visit famous vineyards, wine cellars, and wine museums.

Wine country. Photo courtesy Henri Maire.

Dijon to Beaune
43 km (27 miles)

Exit Dijon on ave. Jean-Jaurès and bear right onto D122; go to Clos-de-Vougeot, 20 km.

Proceed onto N74 for 1 km.

Turn right at the sign to Vosne-Romanée; go 1 km and back onto N74; turn right and go to Nuits-St. Georges, 2 km.

At Nuits-St. Georges, turn right then bear left; at the church, turn right and ascend steep hill on D8; go through Chaux and Marey-les-Fussey to INT with D18, 7 km.

Turn left onto D18; go to Beaune, 12 km.

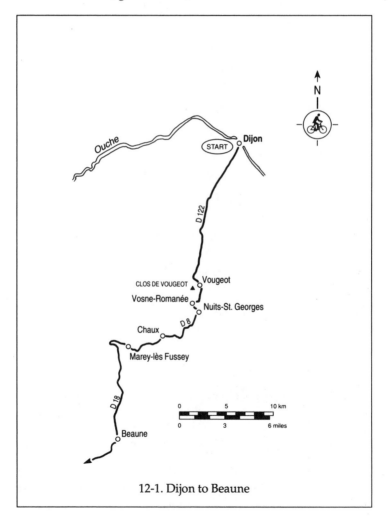

12-1. Dijon to Beaune

Beaune to Chalon sur Saône
47 km (29 miles)

Exit Beaune on ave. Charles de Gaulle (N73 and 74); take N73 to Pommard, 4 km.

From Pommard go south on D973 to INT with D11l B, 3 km.

Bear left onto D111B; go to Meursault, 1.5 km.

Exit Meursault on D113B; go to Puligny-Montrachet, 4 km.

Turn right onto D113A; cross N6 and go to Chassagne- Montrachet, 2 km.

Continue on D113A to Santenay, 4 km.

Turn right onto D113; go to INT with D974, 1 km.

Proceed onto D974; go to Rémigny, 0.5 km.

Turn sharp right onto D109; go to INT with D978, 8.5 km.

Proceed onto D970; go through Mercurey to INT with D981, 6.5 km.

Turn right onto D981; go to Givry, 4 km.

Turn left onto D69; go to Chalon-sur-Saône, 8 km.

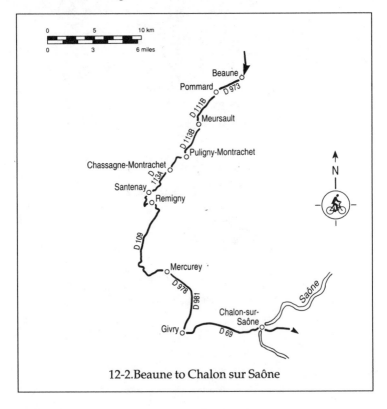

12-2.Beaune to Chalon sur Saône

Chalon-sur-Saône to Mâcon
71.5 km (45 miles)

Exit Chalon by crossing the Saône river and taking ave. de Verdun (N73) to St. Marcel, 4 km from downtown Chalon.

In St. Marcel, bear right onto D978; go to INT with D933, 9.5 km.

Bear right onto D933; go through Cuisery to Pont-de-Vaux, 35 km.

At the southern edge of Pont-de-Vaux, bear left onto D58; go to Bâgé-le-Châtel, 15 km.

Entering Bâgé, as soon as you go around the bend to the left and see the water tower, turn sharp right onto D68A; go to Mâcon, 8 km.

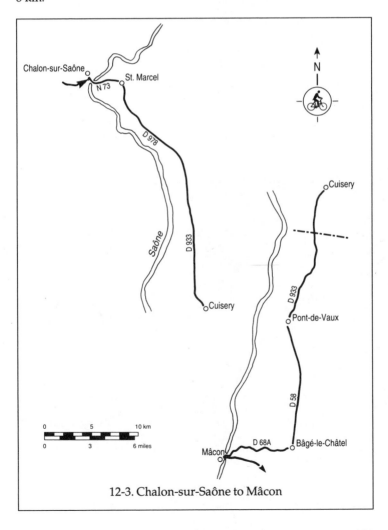

12-3. Chalon-sur-Saône to Mâcon

Mâcon to Bourg-en-Bresse
36 km (22 miles)

Exit Mâcon on N79 eastward, crossing the Saône river again, and go to INT with D80, 10 km.

Turn right onto D80; go to Vonnas, 8 km.

When you get to the church in Vonnas, turn left onto D96; go to Vandeins, 6.5 km.

At Vandeins, D96 becomes D45. Take it to INT with D936 at Corgenon, 6.5 km.

Turn right onto D936; go to Bourg-en-Bresse, 5 km.

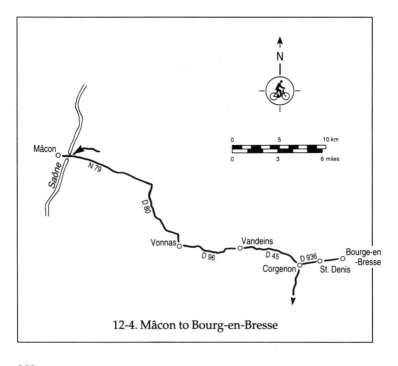

12-4. Mâcon to Bourg-en-Bresse

Bourg-en-Bresse to Lyon
70 km (44 miles)

Exit Bourg-en-Bresse on D936; go to St. Denis, 5 km.

Turn left onto D45 which becomes D67C; go to St-André-sur-Vieux-Jonc, 4.5 km.

D67 here becomes D67; take it to St. André-le-Bouchoux, 7 km.

Exit on D26 southward; go 0.5 km and bear right onto D67; go to St. Georges-sur-Renon, 4 km.

At St. Georges, turn left onto D80; go to la Chapelle-du-Châtelard, 4 km.

As soon as you pass the church on your left, turn right onto D27; go through Sandrans (swinging around the water tower, then you'll see a cemetery on your right) to INT with D82, 6 km.

Turn left onto D82; go to Amberieux-en-Dombes, 8 km. (**Note:** Don't miss the castle ruins and the view from up there.)

Exit Amberieux on D66, which becomes D16 at the boundary (1 km); go to Neuville-sur-Saône, 4.5 km.

Turn right, so the the swimming pool is on your right and the water tower is on your left, and cross the Saône.

As soon as you cross the river, turn left on D51; follow it (along the river) into the heart of Lyon, 16 km.

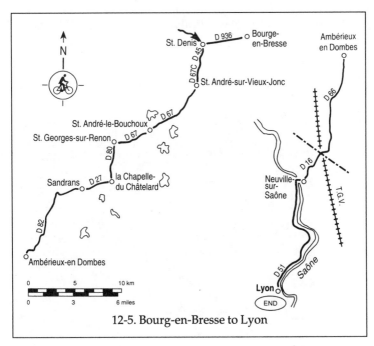

12-5. Bourg-en-Bresse to Lyon

Tour 13: The Jura—Foothills and Easy Mountains

From Dijon to Besançon and back in five stages
Michelin maps 66 and 70
Terrain: Hilly to mountainous.
Distance: 278.5 km (173 miles)

This tour through the Jura mountains leads from Dijon to Besançon and back in five short stages. This route can be a prelude to the Wine Tour No. 12. Hilly all the way (Besançon is only 25 miles from Switzerland). Dôle is beautiful town through which courses the Doubs river. Arbois is where Louis Pasteur conducted the experiments that gave his name to the process called 'pasteurization' (his home and laboratory are now a museum). Arbois, a small town of exquisite charm, is also the home of France's most unusual wine, akin to sherry in flavor and color. Rustic inns here serve Swiss-style fondues accompanied by the local sparkling wine.

Besançon, prior to the advent of digital watches, was the watch and clock making capital of France. Its astronomical clock has 30,000 moving parts and the 70 dials display a parade of mechanical figures six times daily. The city has three other outstanding museums: Fine Arts; History; and Folklore. The town surrounds a loop in the Doubs river. Gray is a town of less than 9,000 inhabitants on the Saône river, with fine medieval buildings and pervaded by an air of tranquility.

Note: Despite the hard terrain, the short daily distances and superb scenery make this a circuit within almost anyone's capabilities.

The famous wine grower, shipper, and connoisseur Henri Maire sampling a vin jaune.

Dijon to Dôle
61.5 km (38 miles)

Exit Dijon on ave. Raymond Poincaré (D70) to Arc-sur-Tille, 12 km.

When you see the church steeple down the street on your right, turn right, go past the church and out of town on D34 through Remilly-sur-Tille to Cessey-sur-Tille, 9 km.

Go straight out of Cessey on D24 through Labergemont-Foigney, Longchamp, Magny-Montarlot and Athée to Auxonne, 19.5 km.

In Auxonne, go east on N5 through downtown Auxonne, then turn right onto D24 (later D354) and go to St. Seine-en-Bâche, 9.5 km.

Turn left onto D31, which becomes D6 at the boundary, and go to Dôle, 11.5 km.

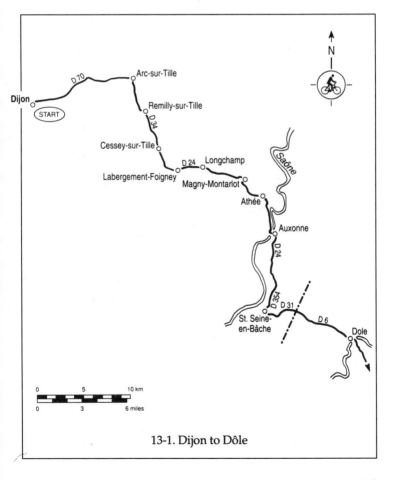

13-1. Dijon to Dôle

Dôle to Arbois
38 km (24 miles)

Start out of Dôle on D405 (direction Poligny). Right after you pass the train station on your right, you'll come to a church, also on your right. Here you bear left onto D7.

Take D7 through a succession of villages: Goux, La Loye, Belmont, Montbarrey, Santans and Germigney, to INT with D53, just south of Châtelay, 21.5 km.

Turn right onto D53; go through Chamblay, crossing D472, and through St. Cyr, where D53 bends to the left, to Villette-les Arbois, 11.5 km.

At Villette, turn right, cross the Cuisance river, and go to INT with D469, 1 km.

Turn left onto D469; go to Arbois, 4 km.

Note: The Cuisance is a small stream. If you take the footpath along one bank and back the other, it's beautiful, especially on an October afternoon.

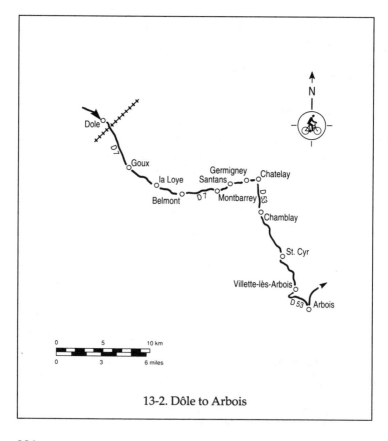

13-2. Dôle to Arbois

Arbois to Besançon
65 km (41 km)

From the Eglise St. Just, go northeastward on rue Delort (D107 E) to Montigny-les-Arsures, 3 km.

Take D249 out of Montigny to INT with D105, 2.5 km.

Turn right onto D105 to Salins-les-Bains, 9 km.

Turn sharp left onto D492; go through Nans-sur-Ste. Anne (where the road makes two left turns) to INT with D492, 17.5 km.

Turn left onto D9 and go to Besançon via Armancey and Cléron, 33 km. (You'll enter town on N83, which D9 merges into.)

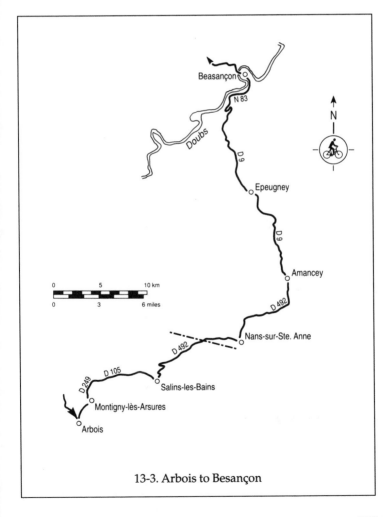

13-3. Arbois to Besançon

Besançon to Gray
55.5 km (35 miles)

Exit Besançon on the Grande Rue northwestward to rue Voirin (D67); go to Recologne, 17 km.

Turn left onto D149; go to INT with D459, 4 km.

Bear left onto D459; go to Ougney, 9 km.

When you come to the church, turn right onto D12, which becomes D21 at the boundary; go through Chaumercenne, Valay and Noiron to Gray, 25.5 km.

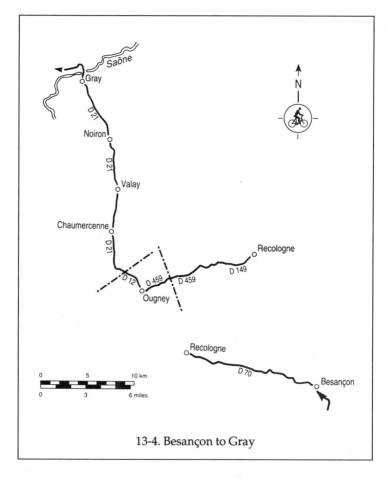

13-4. Besançon to Gray

Gray to Dijon
58.5 km (36 miles)

Go north out of Gray on D67 to Arc-lès-Gray, 1 km.

Turn left onto D2; go to Autrey-lès-Gray, 10.5 km.

In Autrey, turn left onto D176; go to Broye-lès-Loups-et-Verfontaine (a very large name for a village you could put on your coffee table), 6 km.

Go past the church on your left and out on D268 to Loeuilly, 2.5 km.

Turn right onto D38; go to Dampierre-et-Flée, 2.5 km.

Just after you pass the church on your right, the road forks. Bear left onto D27; go to Beaumont-sur-Vingeanne, 1 km. See the château.

Continue south on D27 to Mirebeau, 8.5 km.

At Mirebeau, go west on D112 to Tanay, 3.5 km.

At the fork as you get to Tanay, bear left onto D112E; go to Petit Beire, 6.5 km.

Go 100 meters north on D960, then turn left onto D28A; go to St. Julien, 5.5 km.

From St. Julien go southwestward on D28 to Dijon, 11 km.

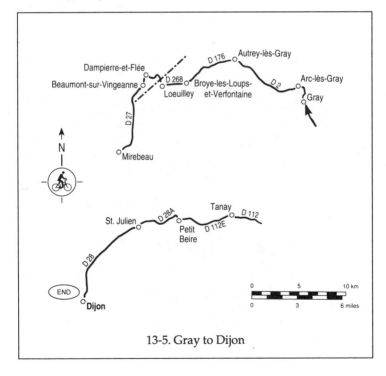

13-5. Gray to Dijon

Tour 14: Alsace-Lorraine—Where the Quiche Came From

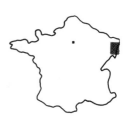

Strasbourg to Mulhouse in three stages
Terrain: Mountainous.
Distance: 161 km (100 miles)
Michelin map No. 87

This tour leads through mountainside vine-yards and medieval towns: Three stages in the Vosges mountains and along the Rhine river. Extremely hilly. Alsace has been Franco-Germanic since prehistoric times. It has its own language, its own architecture, its own cuisine (Quiche, the cheese and onion custard pie originated here), its own distinctive wines, and its own distinguished sons such as the world-famous physician-musician-philosopher Dr. Albert Schweitzer.

Riquewihr, one of the four best-known wine towns, is so beautifully preserved that the whole town has been declared a national monument. There are wine firms here that have been in the same family for more than three-and-a-half centuries. Nearby Ribeauvillé and Kayserberg are almost equally charming and steeped in vinous tradition. Colmar, with backdoors opening onto the river, and its many museums, is among the most picturesque towns in France. The ride along the river down to Mulhouse has few equals for scenic aplendor.

Note: An optional 30-mile extension (an additional stage) on scenic roads permits a visit to Basel, Switzerland.

French faces reveal a hardy character tempered with kindness.

Strasbourg to Sélestat
61 km (38 miles)

Exit Strasbourg on rue de Koenigshafen (N4) toward Saverne; go to D45, 4.5 km west of Strasbourg cathedral.

Turn left onto D45; go to Ergersheim, 13.5 km.

Turn left onto D30; go to INT with D127, 1 km.

Turn left onto D127; go to Bischoffscheim, 10 km.

Cross D422 and take D435 to Rosheim, 2 km.

Exiting Rosheim southwestward, turn left onto D35; go to Barr, 11 km.

In these hilly villages, D35 wiggles and squirms; but stay on it to INT with N59, 19 km.

Turn left on N59; go to Sélestat, 4.5 km.

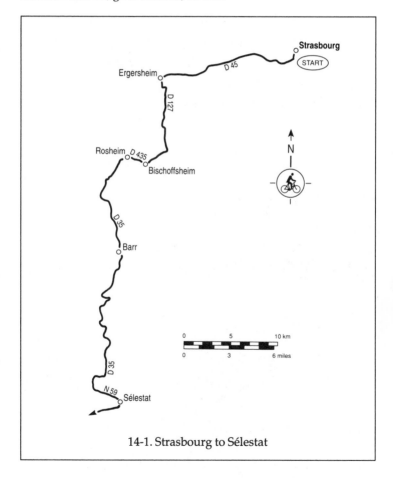

14-1. Strasbourg to Sélestat

Sélestat to Colmar
37.5 km (23 miles)

Exit Sélestat on D159; go to Kintzheim, 4.5 km.

Turn left onto D35, which becomes D1 bis; go to Ribeauvillé, 11.5 km.

Take D1B out of Ribeauvillé; it becomes D3A; go to Riquewihr, 4.5 km.

Take D3 from Riquewihr to INT with D1-bis, 5 km.

D1 bis (it is also D4); D3 becomes D10.

Take D10 to Turckheim, 6 km.

From Turckheim, take D11 eastward to Colmar, 6 km.

Colmar to Mulhouse
62.5km (39 miles)

Exit Colmar on N415 eastward; go to INT with D12, 7 km.

Turn left onto D12; go to INT with D52, 10.5 km.

Turn right onto D52; go to Ottmarsheim, 32 km.

Turn right onto D108; go to N66 at Rixheim, 8 km.

Bear right onto N66; go to Mulhouse, 5 km.

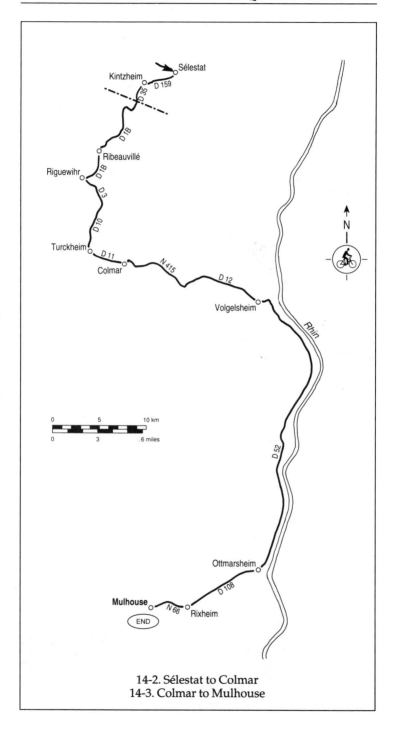

14-2. Sélestat to Colmar
14-3. Colmar to Mulhouse

Tour 15: Castles and Cathedrals

A loop from Meulan to Chantilly in seven stages
Terrain: Moderately hilly.
Total Distance: 466 km (290 miles)
Michelin maps No. 52, 55 and 56

This route leads past castles and cathedrals from St. Germain to Chantilly, in seven stages over varied terrain.

This circuit, which begins and ends a short commuter-train ride from Paris (to escape heavy traffic), is especially for those who love French art, architecture, and history. Along the way is Monet's home at Giverny, with its restored gardens; the awesome ruins of Château Gaillard, Richard the Lion-Heart's supposedly impregnable castle; the cathedral of Rouen, of which Monet painted more than 30 pictures in different light; the highest cathedral in the world at Beauvais; the largest Gothic cathedral in the world at Amiens; the cathedral at Noyon, whose bishop helped Saint Radegonde escape from her cruel Merovingian husband, king of the Franks, in the 6th Century; the graceful cathedral at Soissons; the walled town of Senlis, with its small but beautiful cathedral; and the château at Chantilly with its gallery of portraits of famous persons.

Note: By cycling 35 miles from Soissons to Reims instead of down to Senlis and Chantilly, this route can be combined with the Champagne route for a total of 426 miles in 12 rides, essentially a two-week trip, allowing for an extra day sightseeing in Rheims.

Riverside roads are abundant in France.

Meulan to les Andelys
61.6 km (38 miles)

Exit Meulan: Go out the front of the train station; turn right; go a few meters, then turn right onto D911 (go under the RR tracks) and go to Gasny (watch for the bend to the right at La Roche Guyon), 29 km.

At Gasny, turn left onto D5; go to Giverny (near which are Claude Monet's gardens (restored with a grant from Mrs. Dewitt Wallace, wife of the founder of Reader's Digest magazine), 6.5 km.

Continue on D5 to INT with D313, 4 km.

Go northwestward on D313 to Les Andelys, 22 km.

Note: Just as you come to Les Andelys, you'll see the ruins of Richard the Lion-Heart's 'impregnable' fortress, Château Gaillard, on a promontory overlooking the Seine. It was finally taken by Philippe Auguste during his war with King John after Richard's death.

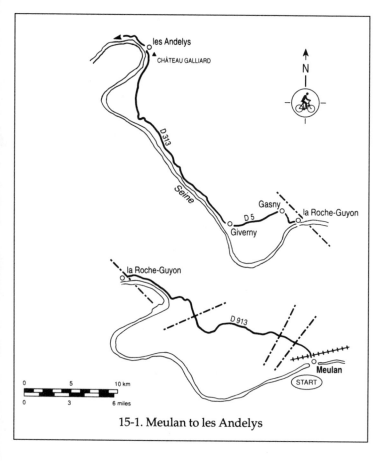

15-1. Meulan to les Andelys

Les Andelys to Rouen
47 km (29 miles)

Exit les Andelys on D313; go to Muids, 10 km.

Turn right onto D65; go to Herqueville, 3.5 km.

Turn right onto D19; go to Pîtres, 9.5 km.

Cross D231 and take D20, which becomes D95, to Franqueville, 10.5 km.

Turn left on N14, then right onto D7; go to St. Aubin, 4 km.

Turn left onto D42; go to INT with N31, 3.5 km.

Proceed onto N31; go to N138 in the north suburbs of Rouen.

Turn left and go into Rouen.

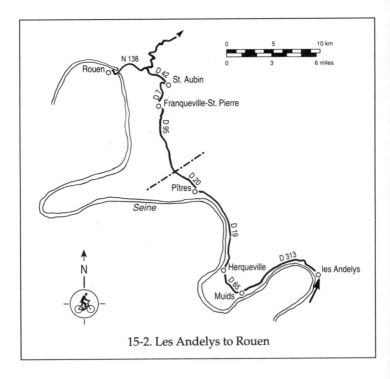

15-2. Les Andelys to Rouen

Rouen to Beauvais
93.5 km (58 miles)

Exit Rouen the same way you came in, but where N31 intersects D42, bear left on N31 and go to D15, 6.5 km from the center of Rouen.

Turn left on D15; go to Morgny, 13.5 km.

Turn right onto D12; go to Ry, 8.5 km.

Turn left onto D93; go 0.5 km, then turn right onto D62; go to Elbeuf-sur-Andelle, 4 km.

Turn left onto D87; go 1 km north, then turn right onto D62, which becomes D262; go to Nolleval, 6.5 km.

Take D262 out of Nolleval; go to where the road forks, 2.5 km.

Bear right onto D128; go to INT with D84, 1 km.

Turn left onto D84; go to INT with D57, 4 km.

Go through les Acres and Beauvoir-en-Lyons to Merval, 5 km.

At Merval, take D145 eastward; go to INT with D21, 2 km.

Turn right onto D21; go to Gournay-en-Bray, 8.5 km.

Exit Gournay on D21, which becomes D1 at the boundary; go to Beauvais, 30 km.

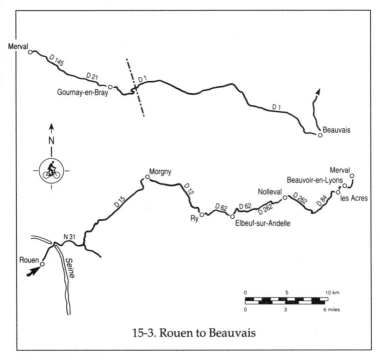

15-3. Rouen to Beauvais

Beauvais to Amiens
54 km (34 miles)

Exit Beauvais on D149 and D11; go to Monsures, 30 km. (D11 becomes D210 when you cross the boundary at Monsures, but it's the same road.)

Take D210 to Amiens, 24 km.

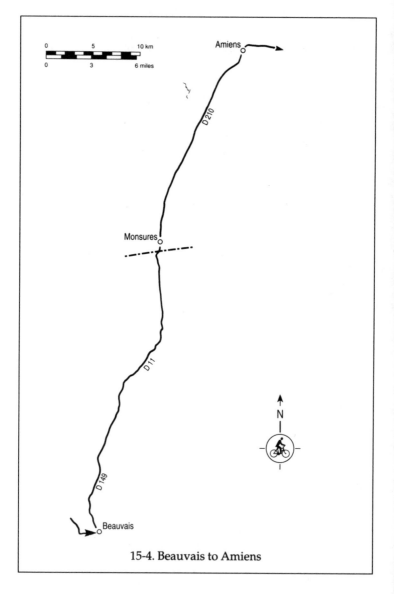

15-4. Beauvais to Amiens

Amiens to Noyon
81.5 km (51 miles)

Exit Amiens on D1 and go to Corbie, 10 km.

At Corbie, turn right onto D233 which becomes D42E and, later, D1E, but is always the 'river road' along the Somme, and go to Bray, 19 km.

Take D1 out of Bray through Herbécourt, over the *autoroute*, to INT with D148 at Flaucourt, 10 km.

Turn right onto D148; go to Villers-Carbonnel, 6 km.

From Villers, take D35 to Nesle, 15 km.

At Nesle, take D15 south to Ercheu, 7.5 km.

Turn right onto D154, which becomes D545; go to Campagne, 6 km.

Here, cross the canal, pass the church on your left, and go up a hill as you leave Campagne on D103.

Take D103 to Genvry, 4 km.

Turn right onto D558; go to Noyon, 4 km.

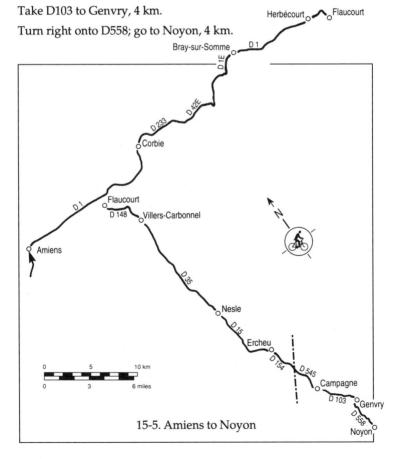

15-5. Amiens to Noyon

Noyon to Soissons
45 km (28 miles)

Exit Noyon on N32; go to Pont l'Évèque, 1.5 km.

Turn left onto D145; go to Vic-sur-Aisne, 24.5 km. (The château here is worth a look.)

Turn left onto D91; go to Soissons, 19 km.

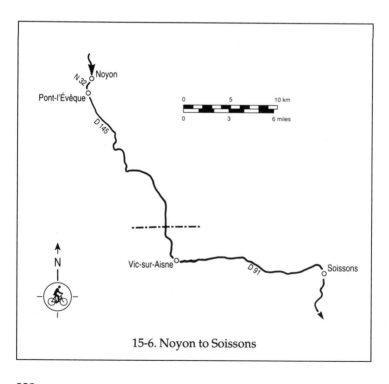

15-6. Noyon to Soissons

Soissons to Senlis and Chantilly
83.5 km (52 miles)

Exit Soissons on D1 south to INT with D805, 3.5 km.

Turn right onto D805; go to Longpont, 12 km.

From Longpont take D17 to la Ferté-Milon, 14.5 km. (The château ruins here are interesting.)

From la Ferté, take D396 to INT with D77, 2 km.

Turn right onto D77; go to Thury-en-Valois, 7 km.

When you pass the church on your left, turn left and go to D922, 0.5 km.

Take D922 to Nanteuil-le-Haudouin, 15.5 km.

From Nanteuil, take D330A, which turns into D330 after crossing N330, to Senlis, 19 km. (The cathedral is in the old inner city.)

Take D44 from Senlis to Chantilly, 9.5 km (to the château).

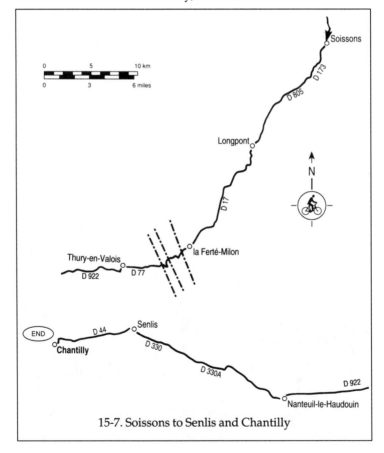

15-7. Soissons to Senlis and Chantilly

Tour 16: The Auvergne—Home of the Ancient Gauls

A loop through the Auvergne mountains in seven stages
Terrain: Extremely mountainous.
Total Distance: 435 km (270 miles), including optional extension
Michelin maps No, 73 and 76

This tour covers the Auvergne in seven stages, all of them hilly to mountainous, starting and ending in Clermont-Ferrand, accessed by train from Paris. This is a circuit for strong riders who love the hauntingly beautiful appeal of small villages nestled in old mountains. This region in southeastern France is famous for its dairy products, especially its butter and a blue cheese similar to Roquefort called Bleu d'Auvergne, and perhaps even more famous for its poignantly wistful folk songs, originated by lonely cowherds tending their flocks on isolated but lovely mountainside pastures.

Le Puy is famous for its church perched precariously on the point of a needle-like rock, several other churches dating back to the 10th Century, and three excellent museums.

The longest stage is 52 miles; the average is just under 40, but each is breathtakingly panoramic, as well as being an aerobic workout.

Morning sunlight illuminates a village in the mountains.

Clermont-Ferrand to Ambert
81 km (50 miles)

Exit Clermont: Go east on rue Maréchal Joffre, which becomes ave. Carnot, to blvd. Fleury; turn right onto blvd. Fleury; go to rue de l'-Oradou (D8 E); go to Le Cendre, 11 km on D765 and D772.

Before you go under the RR tracks and to the church; bear left onto D8; go to Martres-de-Veyre, 5 km.

Turn left onto D225; go to INT with D996 (formerly N496); 41 km.

Turn right onto D996; go to Ambert, 24 km.

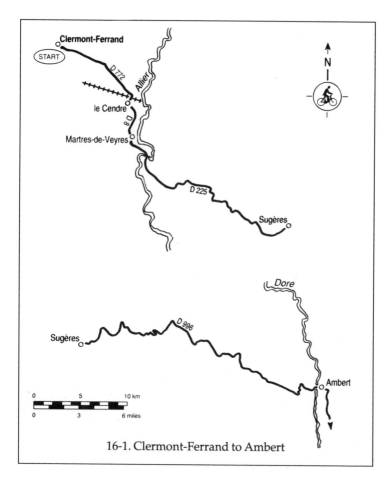

16-1. Clermont-Ferrand to Ambert

Ambert to Le Puy-en-Valey
84 km (52 miles)

Leave downtown Ambert on D996 (formerly N496), direction St. Athème and Montbrison; turn right onto D38 (still in Ambert); go to INT with D205, 10 km.

Turn left onto D205; go to INT with D251 (formerly D111E), 2 km.

Turn right onto D251, which turns into D111 shortly before reaching La Rayolle: go to INT with D202, 15 km.

Turn left onto D202, which becomes D9; go through Craponne and around St. Georges-Lagricol to INT with D29, 24 km.

Turn right onto D29; go to INT with D103, 8.5 km.

Turn right onto D103, which runs along you'll never guess what river: the Loire. Go to Le Puy, 24.5 km.

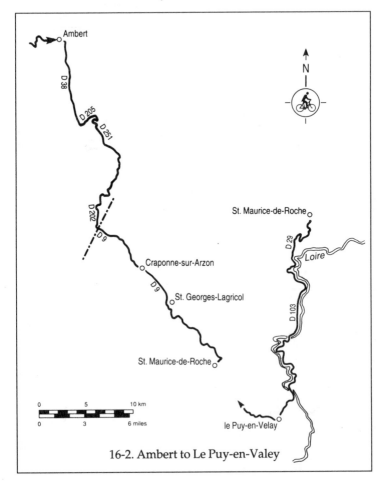

16-2. Ambert to Le Puy-en-Valey

Le Puy-en-Valey to Langeac
41 km (25 miles)

Exit Le Puy on D590; go to Langeac, 41 km.

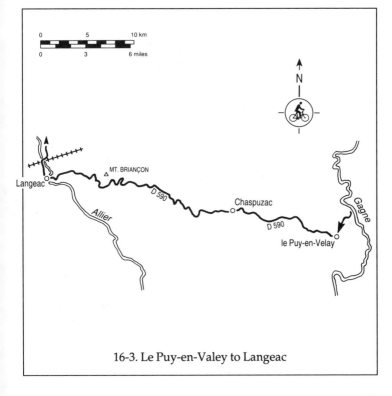

16-3. Le Puy-en-Valey to Langeac

Langeac to St. Flour
64.5 km (40 miles)

Exit Langeac on D56; go under the RR tracks and a little farther to INT with D585, 2 km from the center of Langeac, D56 continues northward; you turn left onto D585

Take D585 to INT with D4, 10.5 km.

Turn left onto D4; go to INT with D990, 17 km. (Just before you get to D990, D4 becomes D602.)

Turn right onto D990; go to INT with D13; 6 km.

Turn left onto D13; go through Ruynes where D13 bends to the right at the church and continue to Viaduc de Garabit, 17.5 km.

Turn right onto N9; go to St. Flour, 11.5 km.

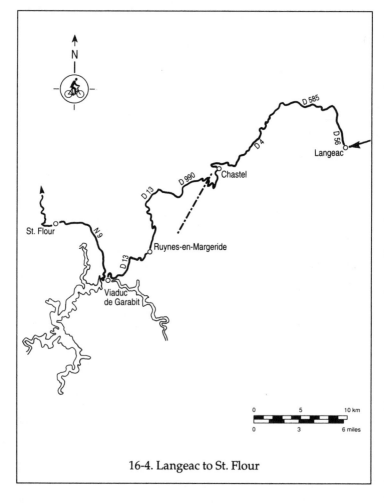

16-4. Langeac to St. Flour

St. Flour to Condat
67 km (42 miles)

Exit St. Flour on D926; turn right onto D679 (still in town); go to Neussargues-Moissac and INT with N122 (formerly N588), 23 km.

Turn left onto N122 (N588); go to Murat, 10 km.

Turn right onto D680; go to INT with D3, 7.5 km.

Turn right onto D3; go to INT with D16, 9 km.

Turn right onto D16; go to Condat, 19 km.

(**Note:** The abbey ruins where D16 joins D679, 3 km south of Condat, are worth a look.)

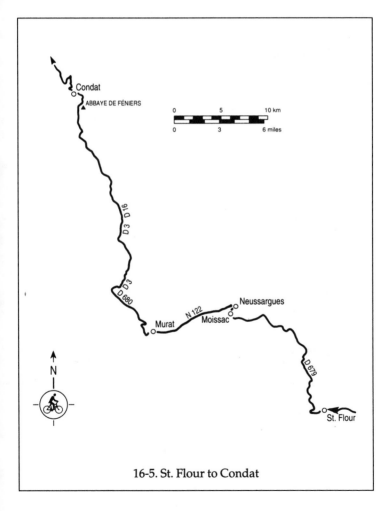

16-5. St. Flour to Condat

Condat to La Tour-d'Auvergne
30.5 km (19 miles)

Exit Condat on D678; turn left onto D62, which becomes D88; go to INT with D203, 23.5 km.

Proceed onto D203; go to La Tour-d'Auvergne, 7 km.

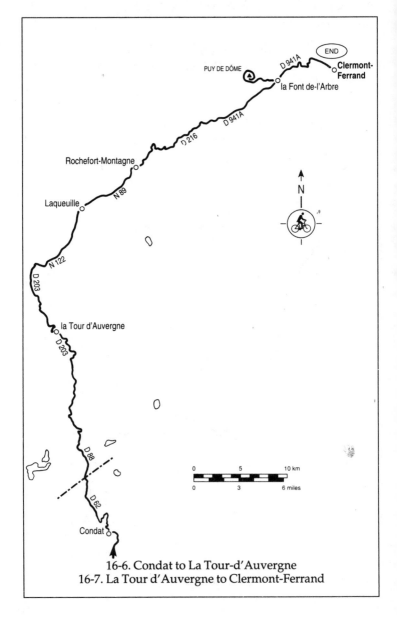

16-6. Condat to La Tour-d'Auvergne
16-7. La Tour d'Auvergne to Clermont-Ferrand

La Tour d'Auvergne to Clermont-Ferrand
67.5 km (42 miles)

Exit La Tour on D203 north; go to INT with D922 (formerly N122), 8.5 km.

Turn right onto D922 (N122); go to Laqueuille, 8.5 km.

Exit Laqueuille on N89, direction Rochefort-Montagne; go to Rochefort, 9 km.

At Rochefort, turn right onto D216; go to N891 10.5 km.

Cross N89. D216 now becomes D941A; go to la Font-de-l'Arbre, 10 km.

Now, if you want to see the famous Puy de Dome and the temple ruins, pay the toll and … good luck. It's 6 km to the top and an awesome ascent, but worth it.

Coast back to D941A (6 km) and go to Clermont-Ferrand, 9 km.

Tour 17: From the Mountains to the Sea

Clermont-Ferrand to the Mediterranean in
nine stages
Terrain: mountains, hills, and flatlands.
Total Distance: 496.5 km (309 miles)
Michelin maps No. 76, 80, 83, and 91

Like the Auvergne Circuit, this trip starts in
Clermont, and involves hilly roads and
several mountains, but striking scenery, and flattens out when it gets
to the Camargue marshland bordering the Mediterranean in this part
of the crescent. Nîmes has wellpreserved Roman temples and other
buildings of extraordinary interest; Avignon has the palace in which
Popes resided for three centuries; Arles is where Vincent van Gogh
did some of his most remarkable painting while hospitalized there.
Alès has a fine museum with two paintings by Pieter Brueghel the
Elder. All the towns along the way have medieval houses plus superb
churches in both Romanesque and Gothic style.

Note: This route can be combined with the Auvergne Circuit by
heading south from St. Flour instead of continuing the circuit. This
would make it a route of 388 miles in 11 stages.

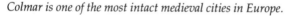

Colmar is one of the most intact medieval cities in Europe.

Clermont-Ferrand to Lempdes
68 km (42 miles)

Exit Clermont: Take rue Marechal Joffre/ave. Carnot to rue Sablon; turn right onto rue Sablon; go to blvd. de la Fayette; turn left onto this blvd. Go to the 4-way intersection and angle right onto ave. Léon Blum which is also D69; take D69 to Aubière, 3.5 km (from the center of Clermont).

Skirt around the church and make two right turns onto D21; go to Romagnat, 2 km.

Turn left onto D3 which becomes D786; go through Veyre-Monton to INT with N9.

Cross N9; get onto D225; go through Vic-le-Comte to INT with D996 (formerly N496), 23 km.

Turn right onto D996; go to Sauxillanges, 8 km.

When N496 turns right, keep going straight on D214 to INT D34: turn left to Jumeaux, 12 km.

In Jumeaux, turn right, cross the Allier river and turn left onto D76; go to Brassac-Les-Mines, 2 km.

Here the road swings to the right and you'll pass two churches on your right. Go to Ste. Florine, 1.5 km.

Take D651 out of Ste. Florine and go down the hill to Lempdes, 6 km.

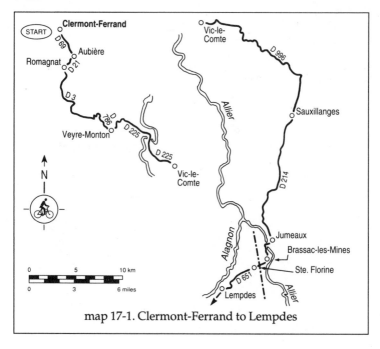

map 17-1. Clermont-Ferrand to Lempdes

Lempdes to St. Flour
57 km (35 miles)

Exit Lempdes on D653; go to Grenier-Montgon, 14.5 km.

At Grenier, turn left onto N9; go to Massiac, 4 km.

At Massiac, turn right onto N122 (formerly N588); go to Molompize, 6.5 km. (Just before you get to Molompize, you'll see castle ruins on your right.)

At Molompise, after you pass the church on your right, turn left onto D44. (You'll see an old sign saying *Gare S.N.C.F.*)

Take D44 through Rézentières to INT with D679, 20.5 km.

Turn left onto D679; go to St. Flour, 11.5 km.

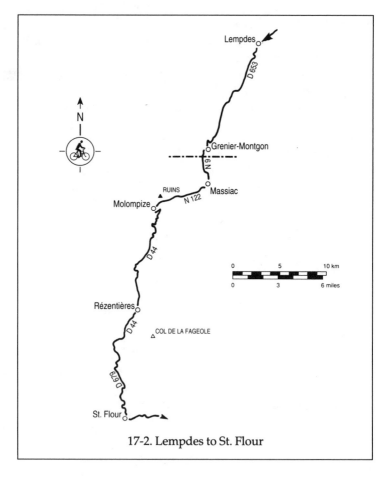

17-2. Lempdes to St. Flour

St. Flour to Mende
83 km (52 miles)

Exit St. Flour on N9 south; go to St. Chély-d'Apcher, 35 km.

Going up the hill out of St. Chély, the road forks. Bear left onto N106 (formerly N107); go to Mende, 48 km.

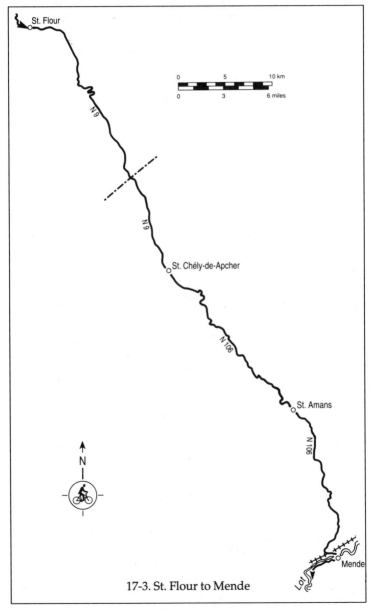

17-3. St. Flour to Mende

Mende to Florac
39.5 km (25 miles)

Exit Mende: Go past the train station on your left; turn right; cross the Lot river; go around the church and out of town on N88 to Balsieges, 7.5 km.

At Balsieges, just after you pass the train station on your left, the road forks; bear right, cross the river and turn left onto N106; go to Florac, 32 km.

Note: When you crest Col de Montmirat, elevation 1,048 meters, you have a great view.

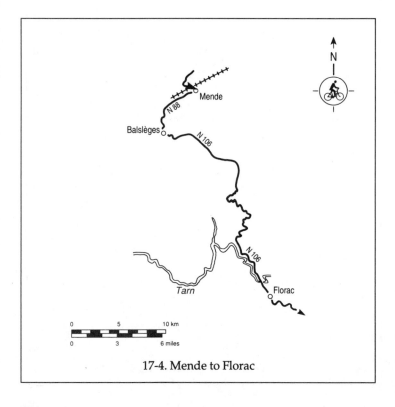

17-4. Mende to Florac

Florac to Alès
71 km (44 miles)

Exit Florac on N106 southeastward; go to Alès, 71 km.

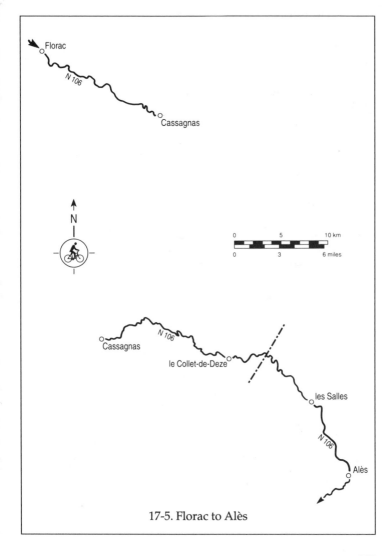

17-5. Florac to Alès

Alès to Nîmes
41 km (26 miles)

Exit Alès: Go west on rue Jules Cazot; cross the Pont de Rochebelle and turn left onto the Quai Ferréol.

At the 3-way intersection, the quai stays beside the river (naturally); ave. Marcel goes straight; route de St-Jean-du-Pin veers off to the right. This is the road you want, D50.

Take D50 down to Anduze, 14.5 km. (Both the château and the old château ruins here are interesting.)

At Anduze, turn right, then left, then right again, then left again; go past the château on your right; cross the RR tracks, and out of town on D907.

Take D907 through Lézan, Lédignan, Fons, and around Gajan to INT with N106, 34 km.

Turn right onto N106; go to Nîmes, 7 km. (Nîmes is one of the most handsome old Roman towns in the Provence. Don't miss La Maison Carrée, the well-preserved Roman temple.)

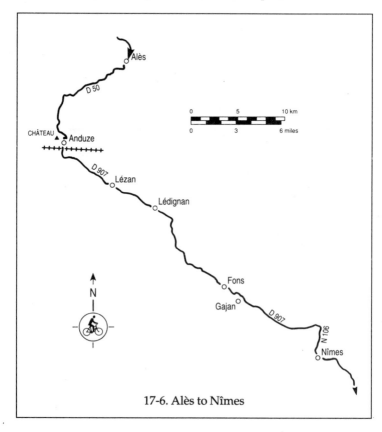

17-6. Alès to Nîmes

Nîmes to les Saintes-Maries-de-la-Mer (at the Mediterranean)

Exit Nîmes: From the Roman Arena, go southwest on the rue de la République to rue St. Gilles; turn left onto this street which is also D42. (You'll see a sign saying this is the way to the *Aeroport*.)

Take D42 to St. -Gilles, 19 km.

Going into St. Gilles, you go under the Canal du Bas-Rhône. Going out of St. Gilles, on N572, you cross over the Canal du Rhône.

Take N572 to D37, 3 km.

Turn right onto D37; go to INT with D570, 11 km.

Turn right onto D570; go to Les Saintes-Maries-de-la-Mer, 23 km.

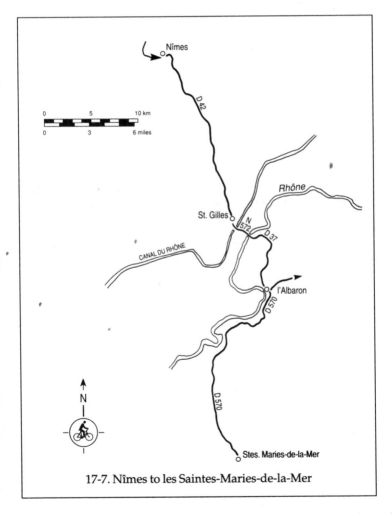

17-7. Nîmes to les Saintes-Maries-de-la-Mer

Les Saintes-Maries-de-la-Mer to Arles
56 km (35 miles)

Take D570 northeast until you have crossed the Rhône river and see the right turn to Fourques, 38 km.

Turn right; go to Fourques (0.5 km) and turn right onto D15.

Take D15 back across the Rhône, go under the RR tracks and into Arles, 3 km. (This is the easiest way into town.)

Note: You'll come into Arles from the suburb called Trinquetaille on the bridge by the same name. Keep going straight on the rue de la République and at rue Balze, you'll see the Arlatan Museum of Art, Decorative Arts, and Folklore, endowed by Frédéric Mistral with Nobel Prize money he won in 1904 for literature.

Arles to Avignon
39.5 km (25 miles)

Take D35 north out of Arles to Tarascon, 15 km from the Roman arena in Arles to the château in Tarascon.

Exit Tarascon on D35; go to the bridge, 12 km.

Turn left; cross the Rhône river and go to INT with D2, 1 km.

Turn right onto D2; go along the Rhône, under the RR tracks, under N100, to D900 (also D980), 9.5 km.

Turn right; recross the Rhône, and go into Avignon, 2 km to the center of the city.

Return to Paris by train; to get to the station, go south on rue de la République and Cours Jean-Jaurès, cross the blvd. St. Roch, and there it is, straight in front of you.

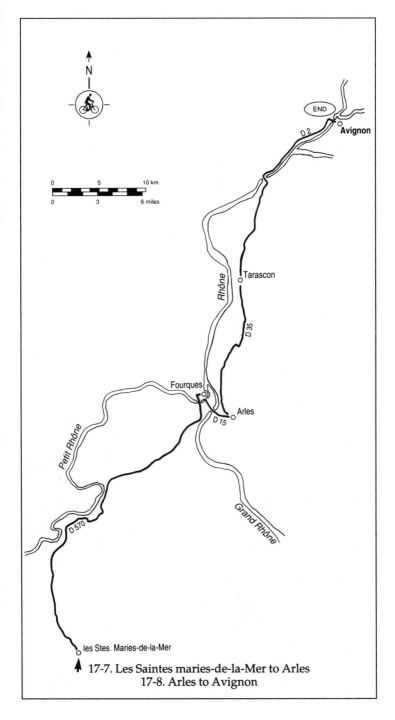

N

0   5   10 km
0   3   6 miles

Rhône

Tarascon

D 35

Fourques

Arles

D 15

Petit Rhône

Grand Rhône

D 570

END

Avignon

D 2

les Stes. Maries-de-la-Mer

17-7. Les Saintes maries-de-la-Mer to Arles
17-8. Arles to Avignon

Tour 18: The Glory That Was Rome

A circuit through famous old Roman cities
in seven stages
Terrain: predominantly hilly, but flat in the
Camargue marshland.
Total Distance: (all seven stages): 330 km
(205 miles); six stages: 277.5 km (172 miles)
Michelin maps 80 and 83

The *Provence* is so named because it was once a Roman province.
The route can be shortened by going directly from Arles to Nîmes.

This tour is a seven-stage zig-zag that begins and ends in Nîmes,
with short and relatively easy rides, for the cyclist primarily interested in history and sightseeing. First go to Nîmes by train, and
devote either the first or the final day to exploring this splendid old
city.

Note: In addition to combining this with the preceding route, the
ride to LesSaintes-Maries-de-la-Mer can be omitted by going directly from Arles to Nîmes. Total distance as outlined: 205 miles in
seven stages.

Pont-du-Gard has the famous three-tiered Roman aqueduct still in
use today after almost 2,000 years, irrefutable witness to the genius
of Roman engineering. Châteauneuf-du-Pape is the town that gives
its name to the sturdy red wine made from the Petit Syrah grape,
reportedly brought to France by the Crusaders.

Bullfights are common in Southern France. The arena at St. Cricq

Nîmes to Alès
57.5 km (36 miles)

Exit northwestward on N106 to INT with D907, 5 km (from the Roman arena in Nîmes).

Turn left onto D907; go through Lédignan and Lézan to Anduze, 38 km.

At Anduze, start out of town on D910, directon St. Christol-lès-Alès, but after less than half a kilometer turn left onto D129 and go to Générargues, 3.5 km (measured from the junction of D907 and D910 in Anduze).

At Générargues, go straight north; the road is now D50. Take D50 to Alès, 11 km.

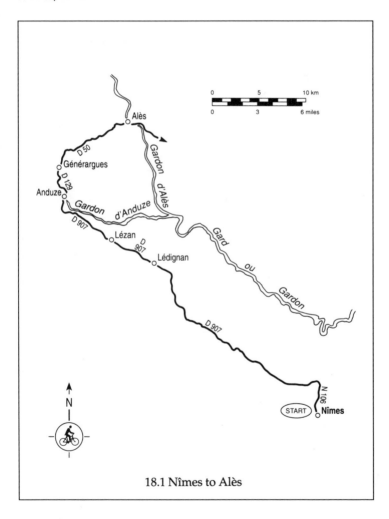

18.1 Nîmes to Alès

Alès to Pont-du-Gard
54 km (34 miles)

Exit Alès going south; go to INT with D981, 2 km.

Turn left onto D981; go to INT with D114, 20 km.

Turn right onto D114; go to Collorgues, 6.5 km.

At Collorgues, just after you pass the church on your left, turn left onto D120 which merges into D982; go to Uzès, 11.5 km. (The château and the church here are worth a look.)

Exit Uzès on D981 southeastward; to to Pont-du-Gard, 14 km.

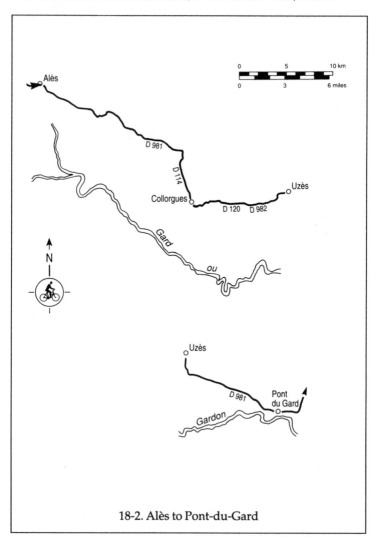

18-2. Alès to Pont-du-Gard

Pont du-Gard to Orange
48.3 km (30 miles)

From Pont du Gard take D19A to N861, 3 km.

Turn left onto N86; go to Pouzilhac, 12 km.

You will go up a steep hill; when you get up it, turn right onto D101 just before you get into the village proper, where you see a cross on a stone pedestal.

Take D101 to St. Victor-la-Coste, 8 km. (See the castle ruins.)

In St. Victor, D101 goes off to the right; do not turn; go north on D240 to Laudun, 4 km.

Exit Laudun north on D12l; go to Orsan, 4 km.

At Orsan, take D765 east and south (the road bends) to INT with D976, 7.5 km.

Turn left onto D976; go to Orange, 6 km.

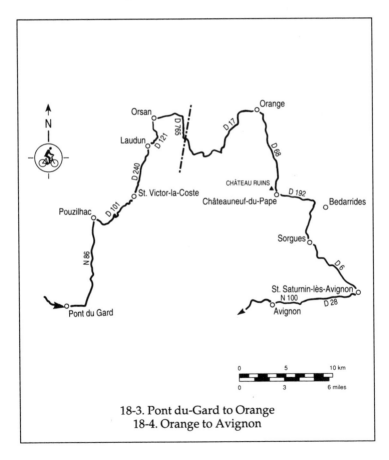

18-3. Pont du-Gard to Orange
18-4. Orange to Avignon

Orange to Avignon
32 km (20 miles)

Exit Orange on D68; go to Châteauneuf-du-Pape, 10 km. (See the château ruins).

At Châteauneuf, turn left onto D192 toward Bédarrides; go past the swimming pool on your left and turn right onto D17; go to Sorques, 7 km.

At Sorques, go under the RR tracks, past another swimming pool (on your right, this time) and follow D6 to St. Saturnin-lès-Avignon, 9 km.

(Incidentally, if you think there is something grammatically screwy about using a plural article, *les*, with a singular noun, Avignon in this case but there have been others, you should know this is not really the plural article: it has a grave accent over the *e* and means *by* or *near*.)

At St. Saturnin, turn right on D28 and N100, go to Avignon, 7 km.

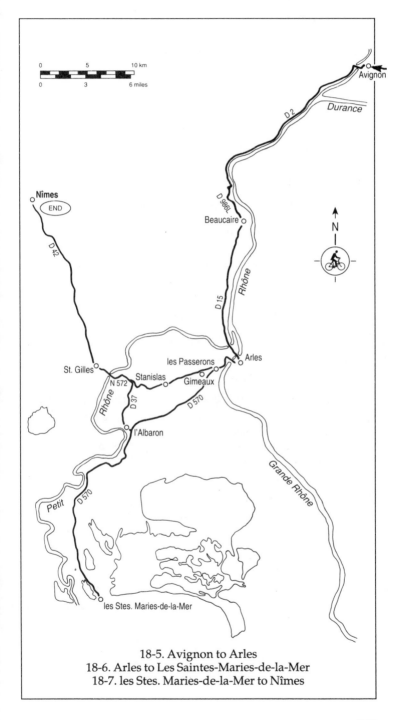

0 5 10 km
0 3 6 miles

Avignon

Durance

D 2

Nîmes
END

D 986L

Beaucaire

N

D 42

Rhône

D 15

les Passerons

St. Gilles

Arles

Stanislas

N 572

Gimeaux

D 37

D 570

l'Albaron

Rhône

D 570

Petit

Grande Rhône

les Stes. Maries-de-la-Mer

18-5. Avignon to Arles
18-6. Arles to Les Saintes-Maries-de-la-Mer
18-7. les Stes. Maries-de-la-Mer to Nîmes

Avignon to Arles
45 km (28 miles)

Exit Avignon on D900; cross the Rhône and go to D2, 1.5 km from the château in Avignon.

Turn left onto D2; go to INT with D986L, 23 km.

Turn left onto D986L; go to Beaucaire, 4.5 km.

Exit Beaucaire on D15; go to Arles, 16 km.

Arles to Les Saintes-Maries-de-la-Mer
40 km (25 miles)

Exit Arles on N572; go to D570, 2 km.

Turn left onto D570; go to Les Saintes-Maries-de-la-Mer, 38 km.

Les Saintes-Maries-de-la-Mer to Nîmes
53 km (33 miles)

Exit Les Saintes-Maries-de-la-Mer on D570; go to INT with D37, 23 km.

Turn left onto D37; go to INT with N572, 8 km.

Turn left onto N572; go to St. Gilles, 3 km.

Exit St. Gilles on D42; go to Nîmes, 19 km.

If You Go from Arles to Nîmes:

Exit Arles on D15 north to Fourques, 3 km.

Turn left; get on N113; turn left and go south to les Passerons, 4 km.

At les Passerons—a cluster of farm houses and outbuildings— turn right, then immediately back to the left; take this very small road through the marshlands and the farms named Gimeaux and Stanislas to the INT with D37, 10 km.

Proceed onto D37; go to N572, 1.5 km.

Turn left onto N572; go to St. Gilles, 3 km.

Exit St. Gilles on D42 north; go to Nîmes, 19 km.

Tour 19: Languedoc—The Land of Dreams

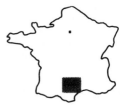

A circuit starting and finishing in Toulouse in eight stages
Terrain: Hilly to mountainous.
Total Distance: 607.5 km (378 miles)
Michelin maps No. 80, 82, and 83

This tour constists of eight stages, starting and ending in Toulouse. Although the average stage is just 47 miles, this is extremely hilly and sometimes mountainous country.

Toulouse, inhabited by Gauls (Celts) long before the Roman and Visigothic incursions, is today a modern city on the Garonne river (which runs all the way across France to Bordeaux) and abounds with architectural marvels, great churches and museums. The caves at Roquefort-sur-Soulzon (not to be confused with the city named Roquefort in southwestern France) is where the world's most famous cheese is aged. From Denmark to South Carolina, efforts to duplicate the flavor have been attempted; all have failed. It is well worth a visit to see how it acquires its unique flavor. It was famous in ancient Rome and is mentioned by Pliny the Elder; it was the favorite cheese of the Emperor Charlemagne (AD 742–814).

Albi was the seat of the Albigensian heresy, brutally suppressed in the 13th Century by the cruel Simon de Montfort. Béziers has fine churches and museums. Lodève is a mysterious little town of dark, narrow, twisting streets and wrought-iron balconies, with a river on one side and forests on the other.

But apart from Roquefort's cheeses, the greatest attraction on this route is Carcasonne, the most perfectly preserved medieval walled city in the world. The outer defensive wall was built by Louis IX (Saint Louis) in the 13th Century. Inside these walls, virtually nothing has changed during the passage of more than 700 years. It is truly a dream-world, a time-warp.

Toulouse to Albi
88.5 km (55 miles)

Exit Toulouse on D112 (allée Marengo) which is a block south of the train station; go to Lavaur, 37 km.

Exit Lavaur on D49 east; go to INT with D47, 4.5 km.

Turn left onto D47; go to Cabanès, 6.5 km.

In Cabanès, D47 turns right. Make a slight dogleg, first on the right then to the left, and continue north on D43 to INT with D631, 6 km.

Turn right onto D631; go to Graulhet, 2 km.

In Graulhet, turn left onto D664; go north to D43, 1.5 km.

Exit Graulhet on D43, passing the small airport on your right, and ride along the Agros river (more like a creek) to INT with D 30, 6.5 km.

Turn left onto D30; go to INT with D84, 2 km.

Turn right onto D84; go to Albi, 17 km.

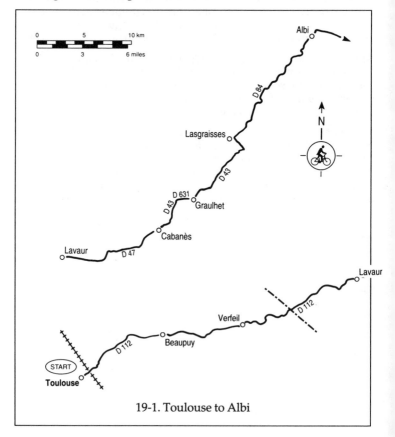

19-1. Toulouse to Albi

Albi to St. Sernin-sur-Rance
68 km (42 miles)

Exit Albi on Ave, Teyssier, D81 to the lake and INT with D59, 27 km. (The old castle ruins here are romantic.)

Turn left onto D59; go to INT with D57, 4 km.

Turn left onto D57; go to INT with D79, 2 km.

Turn right onto D79; ~o to INT with D53, 6 km.

Turn sharp left onto D53, go downhill and watch for the castle ruins on your left; go to INT with D86, 6 km.

Go straight onto D86 and to INT with D999, 2 km.

Turn right onto D999; go to St. Sernin-sur-Rance, 21 km.

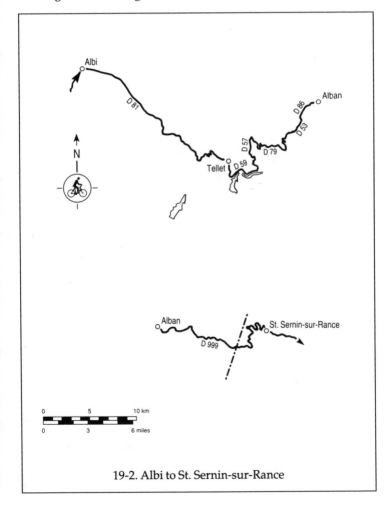

19-2. Albi to St. Sernin-sur-Rance

St. Sernin-sur-Rance to Millau
86 km (53 miles)

Exit St. Sernin on D999 east; go through St. Affrique to Lauras, 42 km.

Go north out of Lauras on D999 to INT with D23 east, 0.5 km.

Turn right onto D23; go to Roquefort-sur-Soulzon, 3.5 km.

Note: This is where the most famous cheese in the world comes from. The cheeses themselves can come from anywhere, provided they are made from sheep's milk, but only the mold and the atmospheric conditions in the caves here give it the distinctive flavor. Supermarket Roquefort has been aged the minimum 60 days. Try some that has been aged a year. It's fantastic!

Return on D23 to D999, 3.5 km.

Turn right on D999; go to St. Rome-de-Cernon, 3.5 km.

Angle left onto D31, which intersects D993; go to St. Rome-de-Tarn, 6 km.

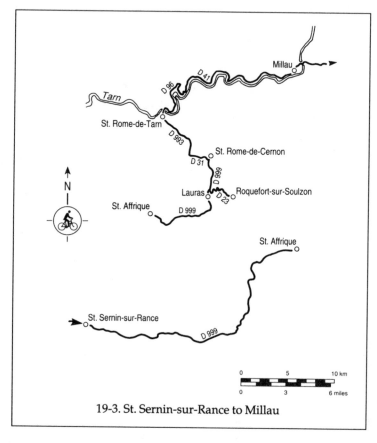

19-3. St. Sernin-sur-Rance to Millau

Exit on D993 north; go down the hill and cross the Tarn river and immediately turn right onto D96, 1 km. See the château ruins on your right.

Take D96 to INT with D41, 4 km.

Turn right onto D41 and go along the Tarn to Millau, 19 km.

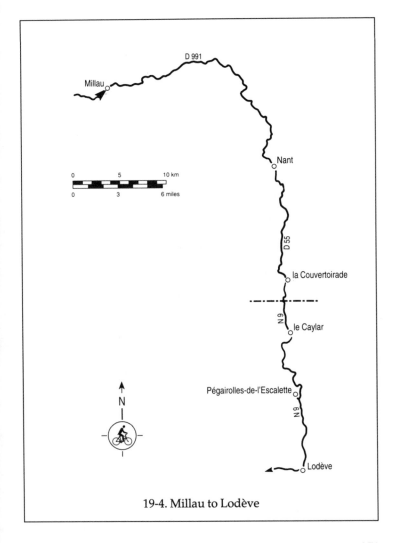

19-4. Millau to Lodève

Millau to Lodève
75 km (47 miles)

Exit Millau on D991 east, the Dourbie river Gorge Road; go to Nant, 32 km.

Exit Nant on D991 south; go to INT with D55, 1 km.

Go south on D55 to N9, 21 km.

Proceed onto N9; go through Le Caylar to Lodève, 21 km.

Note: You might wish to dodge off N9 at Pegairolles-de l'Escallette, 10 km south of Le Caylar, to see the château.

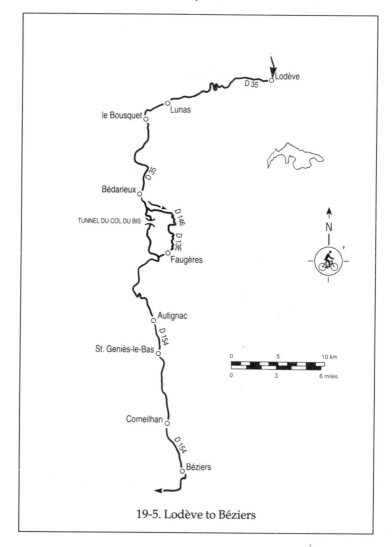

19-5. Lodève to Béziers

Lodève to Béziers
72 km (45 miles)

Exit Lodève on D35 west; go through Lunas and le Bousquet to Bédarieux, 29 km.

Exit Bédarieux on D909; go to INT with D146, 1.5 km.

Turn left onto D146 and circle around the Col du Buis tunnel which is off-limits to cyclists. This is a very pretty little road, but very confusing. Go east 3 km then turn right. (Straight on is D146E.)

You are still on D146, heading south. Go 1.5 km.

Now you come to an intersection with...yes, D146. Turn right onto D146E and go west to INT with D13 E, 1 km.

Turn left onto D13 E; go to Faugères, 5 km.

At Faugères, make a dogleg, first right then left, keeping the church on your right, and go to D909, making the left turn little loop that takes you across the RR tracks and to D909 so that when you cross it, you're on D154, 1.5 km.

Get onto D154 and go all the way to Béziers, 29.5 km. This road wanders somewhat, so watch for the road signs.

Béziers to Carcassonne
77 km (48 miles)

Exit Béziers on D11 west.

You will cross several départemental boundaries. D11 lasts 18.5 km, then becomes D5 for the next 18.5 km, then becomes D11 again, but this time combined with D610 (D11 goes a ways then angles off to the northwest). Stay on D610 to Trèbes.

The total distance from Béziers to Trèbes is 69.5 kms.

At Trèbes, turn right onto N113; go to Carcassonne, 7.5 km.

Note: The Carcassonne you see in books is just a small (but beautifully preserved) part of a very large city. The old walled Carcassonne is called *La Cité*. It is just a few blocks south of N113, depending on where you turn off. The great view is from D104 south of town where it crosses over the A-16 autoroute—a toll road similar to an American interstate. Unfortunately, the noise on the highway detracts from the romance of the view.

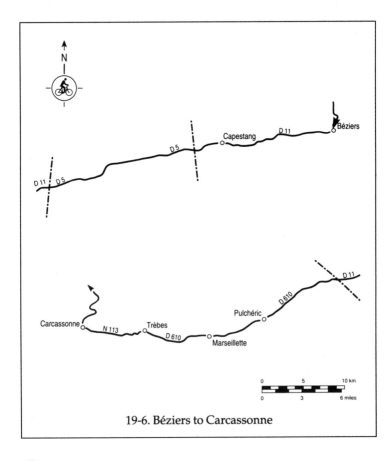

19-6. Béziers to Carcassonne

Carcassonne to Castres
65 km (40 miles)

Exit Carcassonne on D118 north; go to Mazamet, 47 km.

Exit Mazamet on N112; go to Castres, 18 km.

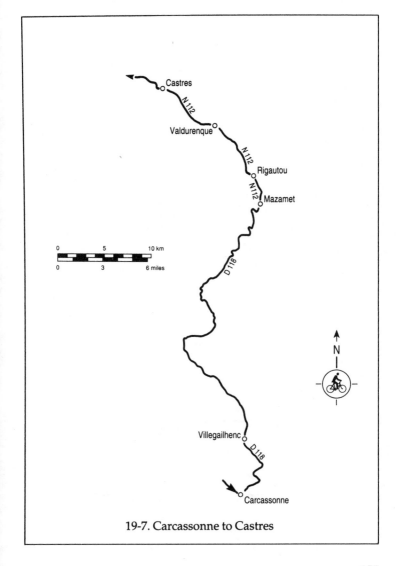

19-7. Carcassonne to Castres

Castres to Toulouse
76 km (47 miles)

Exit Castres on D112 west; go to Lavaur, 39 km.

In Lavaur, D112 makes a left turn and go out past the hospital on your left.

Stay on D112 to Toulouse, 37 km.

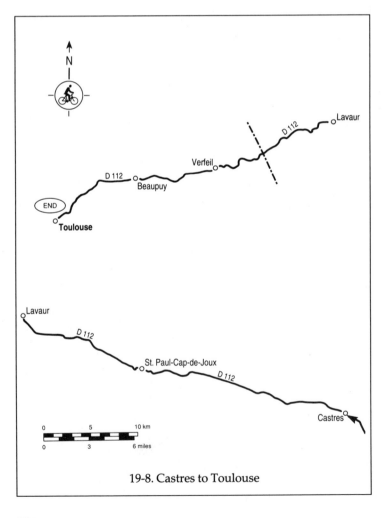

19-8. Castres to Toulouse

Tour 20: The Mediterranean Crescent

Montpellier to Spain and back to Perpignan
in seven stages
Terrain: Four flat rides; two mountain rides;
one half-and-half.
Distance: 330 km (205 km)
Michelin maps 83 and 86

This seven-stage ride starts in Montpellier and
ends in Perpignan with an extension down the coast to Spain just for
the sake of touching foot in another country. The rides are short and
the terrain is easy; the scenery consists of sea and coastal towns
(fishing villages as well as beach resorts). This is among the most
relaxing and undemanding of cycling routes in France.

Montpellier is a university town; France's foremost medical school is
there. Sète, in addition to being a picturesque fishing port, is where
one takes the boat to Tangier (Come weez me to ze Casbah!). Canet-
Plage is an attractive beach resort. Banyuls is a town perfumed with
orange trees and the home of a sweet wine almost like a liqueur
(sometimes taken as an aperitif; more often as a dessert wine). Visitors
are welcome to the cellars to see an audiovisual display and to taste.
It's approximately 6.5 miles down to Port Bou in Spain. You can ride
down there, have lunch in Spain, then spend a second night in
Banyuls —or ride on to Perpignan (36 miles) after lunch.

Architecture in southern France shows the Mediterranean influence.

Montpellier to Sète
34.5 km (21 miles)

Exit Montpellier: From the Place de la Comedie at the south end of the Esplanade, go one block west then turn left onto the Grande Rue J. Moulin; go down to the church and turn right onto Cours Gambette; go four blocks and turn left onto rue Chaptal which is also D5.

Follow D5 to Montbazin, 19.5 km.

At Montbazin, D5 turns sharp right; stay on it to INT with D2, 3 km.

Turn left onto D2; go through Poussan, under A9, over N113 and around Balaruc-le-Vieux to Sète, 15 km (to the waterfront).

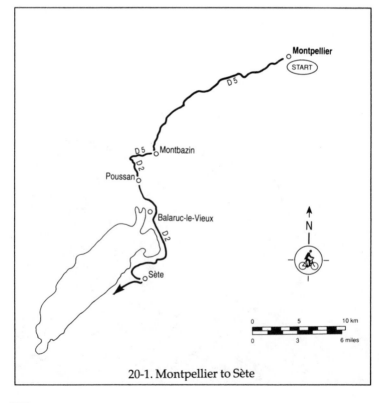

20-1. Montpellier to Sète

Sète to Béziers
55 km (34 miles)

Exit Sète on N112; go to Agde, 23 km.

From Agde, follow D32E to Le Cap d'Agde and back, 4km each way.

Exit Agde on D13; go to Bessan, 6 km.

Exit Bessan on D28 west; go to Béziers, 18 km.

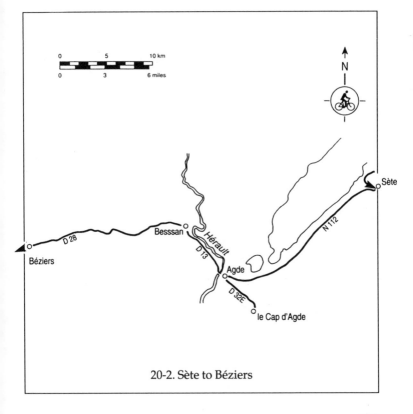

20-2. Sète to Béziers

Béziers to Port-la-Nouvelle
69 km (43 miles)

Exit Béziers on N113 southwest; go to INT with D14, 3 km.

Take D14 through Lespignan, under the Autoroute where D14 crosses the boundary and becomes D618, to Fleury, 12 km.

Exit Fleury on D1118; go to Narbonne-Plage, 12 km.

Go one more kilometer to INT with D168; turn right; go to Narbonne, 14 km.

Exit Narbonne on N9; go to Sigean, 18 km.

Exit Sigean on N139; go to Port-la-Nouvelle, 9 km.

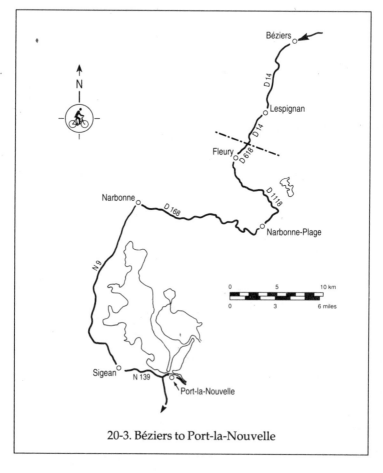

20-3. Béziers to Port-la-Nouvelle

Port-la-Nouvelle to Canet-Plage
56.5 km (35 miles)

Exit Port-la-Nouvelle on D139; go to INT with D709, 1 km.

Turn left onto D709; go to N9, 9 km.

Go around the traffic circle and south on N9 to the exit onto D627, 3 km.

Get off N9 and onto D627 east; go to Port-Leucate, 14 km. (Do not confuse this with Leucate or Leucate-Plage.)

At Port-Leucate, get on the coast road, D90; go to St. Laurentde-la-Salanque, 17.5 km.

Exit St. Laurent on D111 south; go to Canet-en-Roussillon, 9 km.

Turn left onto D617; go to Canet-Plage, 3 km.

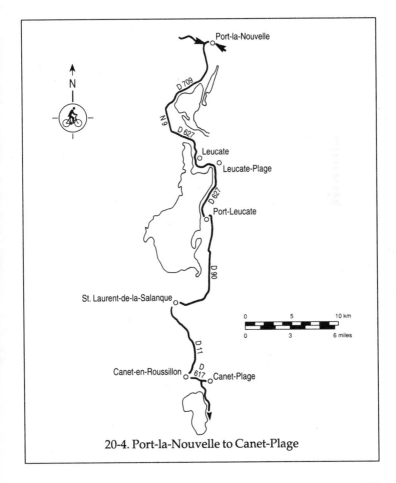

20-4. Port-la-Nouvelle to Canet-Plage

Canet-Plage to Banyuls-sur-Mer
42 km (26 miles)

Exit Canet-Plage on D81 south; go to Argèles-sur-Mer, 18 km.

In Argèles, turn left onto D114; go to N114, 1 km.

Turn left onto N114; go to INT with D86, 3 km.

Turn right onto D86; go to Banyuls-sur-Mer, 20 km.

Note: This stretch of D86 is mountainous but beautiful; the views are terrific. Don't miss Notre Dame de Consolation and the Tour Madeloc.

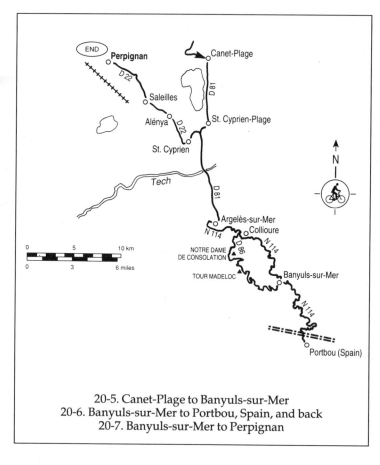

20-5. Canet-Plage to Banyuls-sur-Mer
20-6. Banyuls-sur-Mer to Portbou, Spain, and back
20-7. Banyuls-sur-Mer to Perpignan

Banyuls-sur-Mer to Portbou, Spain, and back
30 km (19 miles)

Exit Banyuls on N114; go to Portbou, 15 km.

Return by the same route. (This, too, is mountainous.)

Banyuls-sur-Mer to Perpignan
43 km (27 miles)

Exit Banyuls on N114 north; go to Argèles-sur-Mer, 18 km.

Exit Argèles on D81; go to St. Cyprien, 10 km.

Exit St. Cyprien on D22; go through Alénya and Saleilles to Perpignan, 15 km.

Note: The train station in Perpignan is on blvd. du Conflent at the end of ave. Général de Gaulle.

Tour 21: Porcelain, Cognac, and Seafood

Limoges to La Rochelle in five stages
Terrain: Hilly at first, but flattening out
toward the end
Total Distance: 283.5 km (176 miles)
Michelin maps 71 and 72

Limoges porcelain is among the most famous
in the world. The manufacturers welcome visitors, and the museum traces the history of the industry. Châlus is the site of the castle whence Richard the Lion-Heart received his fatal wound while quarreling over buried treasure that didn't exist. Nontron is an attractive town with red-tiled roofs and steep streets.

The cathedral at Angoulême is one of the three finest examples of Romaneque architecture in France, and also has an excellent museum of fine art. As for Cognac, … you detect the scent from miles away. In the warehouses of Cognac, the finest brandy in the world reposes, some of it a century old. The value of this velvety liquid in this one town is estimated in the billions of dollars. The famous *houses* welcome visitors.

Saintes is an ancient Roman town with a large amphitheatre. Surgères has a castle that dates back to the 11th Century, the usual complement of fine old churches, but also has something you'll find nowhere else: an insect museum. La Rochelle is an historic port city; the inner city is closed to motor traffic, and has a plethora of restaurants specializing in seafood.

Cyclists stop at a grocery store for picnic supplies

Limoges to Nontron
67 km (42 miles)

Exit Limoges: From the Orsay Gardens near the center of town, take rue Armand Dutreix a short block and bear left onto rue François Perrin which becomes D79; go to Aixe-sur-Vienne, Il km. (**Note:** after 7 km, D79 becomes D20 for no apparent reason.)

Exit Aixe on D20; go to INT with D15, 15.5 km. (**Note:** At les Cars, 2 km before you get to D15, there are interesting castle ruins on your right.)

Turn right onto D15; go to Chalûs, 6.5 km. (see the castle ruins here. From the parapet of this castle, on March 25, AD 1199, a crossbowman shot a bolt that struck Richard the Lion-Heart, King of England, in the left shoulder. The wound became infected and Richard died of the infection at 7 pm. Tuesday, April 6, 1199, at age 42. His blood, brains and intestines were buried at Chalûs. His heart was sent to Rouen, capital of Normandy of which he was the hereditary duke, as well as being duke of Aquitaine. The rest of him is buried in Fontevrault Abbey. [see Tour 7.])

Exit Chalûs on D6 bis which becomes D85 at the boundary; go to INT with D707, 30 km.

Turn right onto D707; go to Nontron, 4 km.

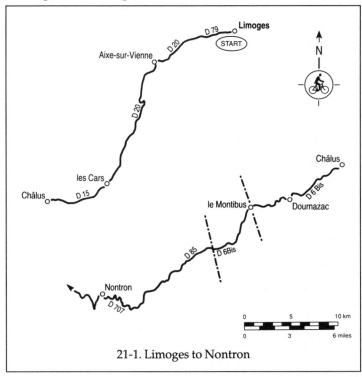

21-1. Limoges to Nontron

Nontron to Angoulême
47 km (29 miles)

Exit Nontron on D75 west; it becomes D4 at the boundary; go to INT with D939, 39.5 km. (See the castle ruins at Marthon and the Château la Tranchade at the INT with D939.)

Proceed straight onto D939; go to Angoulême, 7.5 km.

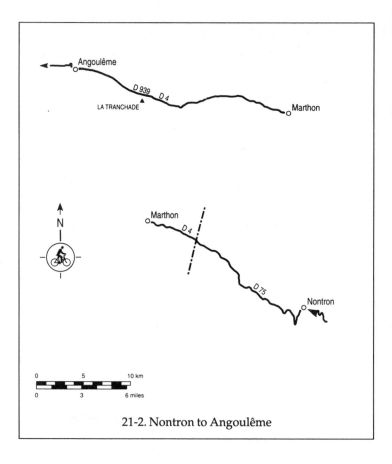

21-2. Nontron to Angoulême

Angoulême via Cognac to Saintes
72 km (45 miles)

Exit Angoulême: From the promenande around the ramparts, take D72 west out of the city; go to Vibrac, 19.5 km.

At Vibrac, turn left onto D63; go to the church; turn right at the corner of the cemetery (on your right) onto D22; go to INT with N141, 11 km.

Turn left onto N141; go to Jarnac, 2 km.

Exit Jarnac on D157 (you'll pass a cemetery on your left); go to Cognac, 13 km.

Note: Francis I, the king who brought the Renaissance to France — and Leonardo da Vinci along with it—was born in this town. It is also where the world's foremost brandy is made and stored. Every year, millions of dollars worth evaporates through the pores of the oak casks in which it ages.

Exit Cognac through the suburb of Crouin on D83 west; go to INT with N141, 6.5 km.

Turn left onto N141; go 0.5 km (600 meters, actually) and turn left onto D83 again which becomes D24 at the boundary.

Take D24 to Saintes; 21.5 km from where you left N141.

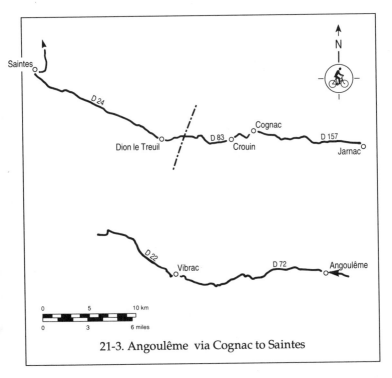

21-3. Angoulême via Cognac to Saintes

Saintes to Surgères
53.5 km (33 miles)

Exit Saintes on D114; go through Taillebourg (see the castle ruins here) and St. Savinien to Tonnay-Boutonne, 30 km.

Start out of Tonnay on D114 but turn right, then back to the left, onto D107E2; go to INT with D212, 8 km.

Turn left onto D212; go to INT with D107, 2 km.

Turn left onto D107; go to Vandré, 7 km.

At Vandré, turn right onto Dll4; go to Surgères, 6.5 km.

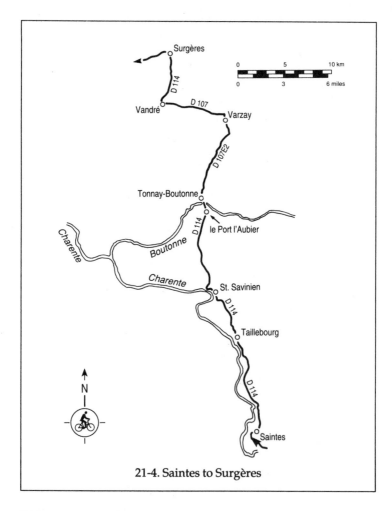

21-4. Saintes to Surgères

Surgères to La Rochelle
44 km (27 miles)

Exit Surgères on D209 west; go to INT with D208, 10 km.

(After you cross Dll7, go 1 km to le Cher. Turn left. You'll see a chapel on your right and a cemetery on your left. Now turn right and go 1 km to the junction with D208.)

Turn left onto D208; go to Ardillières, 5 km.

Turn right onto D111; go to Mortagne 12 km.

Turn left onto Dll3; go to Châtelaillon-Plage, 5 km.

At Châtelaillon, turn right onto D202; go through Angoulins and Aytré to La Rochelle, 12 km. (**Note:** At St. Jean-des-Sables, D202 veers right. Don't follow it but stay on the shore road.)

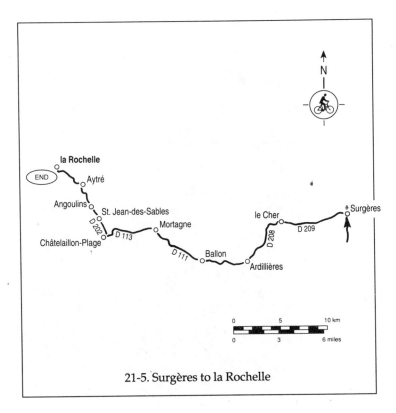

21-5. Surgères to la Rochelle

269

Tour 22: Serious Cycling

Versailles to Poitiers in 9 stages with one optional side-trip
Terrain: Moderately to very hilly with a few flat stretches
Total Distance: 466.5 km (290 miles) including the optional longer route.
Michelin maps No. 60, 64 and 67

This route can be subdivided: one can return to Paris by train from every town along the way except Loudun.

The route starts from Versailles to get away from Paris traffic. Versailles is 20 minutes from Paris by frequent commuter trains, and five minutes from the station, one is out in the country. However, Versailles is worth a visit: the royal château there, built by Louis XIV, is the largest in the world, and the 8,000-acre park is incredibly beautiful.

Chartres has the most famous of all great Gothic Cathedrals. It was started in the 8th Century; the present cathedral dates back to 1233.

A street in the medieval section of Chartres. Photo courtesy Office de Tourisme de Chartres.

Its stained glass windows have no equal. Châteaudun's castle is remarkable for its transitional architecture: part medieval fortress; part early Renaissance château.

Vendôme's abbey church is France's finest example of 'Flamboyant Gothic' architecture. The wood'caricature' carvings under the choir seats, called 'misericords', are the best example of that peculiar art-form in France. The city is built on islands in the river and is virtually one huge flower garden. Blois is a royal residence town on the Loire river; the François I wing of the château with Italian loggias is unique in France.

Amboise is another royal residence town and is also where Leonardo da Vinci spent his last three years and is buried. The optional side-trip to Chenonceaux (16 miles round trip) permits a visit to the most photographed château in France, the one that extends out over the (Cher) river. Tours is the hub of the Loire Valley château-and-wine country with a great cathedral and many excellent museums.

En route to Chinon one can see the magnificent Franco-Italian Renaissance gardens at Villandry, actually five gardens covering 17 acres first planted in 1534. Chinon is an ancient castle town where Joan of Arc first met the dauphin and future king of France, Charles VII. En route to Loudun one visits Richelieu, the first planned town in Europe, laid out in squares and rectangles surrounded by a wall and moat. Loudun dates back to pre-Roman times and was fortified by Philippe-Auguste, the grandfather of Saint Louis.

Poitiers is the former capital of Aquitaine where Eleanor held her famous'Courts of Love'. She financed the city's cathedral, but more renowned is the church of Notre Dame, the foremost Romanesque church in France. Here, too, is the Baptistry of Saint John, built in AD 357, the oldest Christian edifice in Western Europe. The museum here, combining art and history, is one of the best provincial museums in all of France.

Versailles to Chartres
81 km (50 miles)

Exit Versailles: From the Quartier St. Louis, take the rue de Satory (D91) up the long hill and out of town to INT with N306, 31.5 km. (**Note:** Approaching Dampierre you go down a steep descent on a twisting road; be careful.)

Proceed onto N306; go to Rambouillet, 10 km.

Exit Rambouillet on N10 south; go to INT with D150, 1.5 km.

Turn right onto D150; go to Orphin, 8.5 km.

Exit Orphin on D176 west; go 0.5 km and turn left onto D150 which becomes D32 at the boundary.

Continue through Ecrosnes, Gallardon and Coltainville to INT with D105-3, 21 km (from Orphin).

Turn right onto D105-3 (sign says *Gasville*; go through Champhol to Chartres, 8 km. (**Note:** by taking this little road into Chartres, you see the greatest of all Gothic cathedrals seeming to rise out of a sea of wheat-fields and float on the top of the wheat. In town, the best view is from down along the river.)

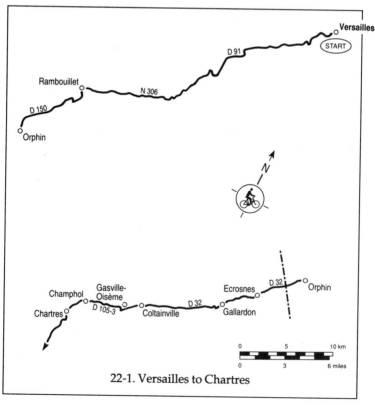

22-1. Versailles to Chartres

Chartres to Châteaudun
47 km (29 miles)

Exit Chartres on D935 south to Dammarie, 9 km.

At Dammarie, D935 bends to the left. Continue straight on Dl27 through Le Gault-St. Denis to INT with D123, 21 km.

Turn right onto D123 (sign says *Godonville* and *Villiers-St. Orien*); go to Villiers, 2.5 km.

In Villiers, just past the church, turn right onto Dlll.

Take D111 to Châteaudun, 14.5 km.

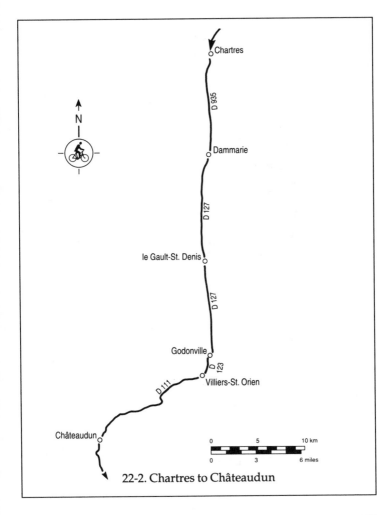

22-2. Chartres to Châteaudun

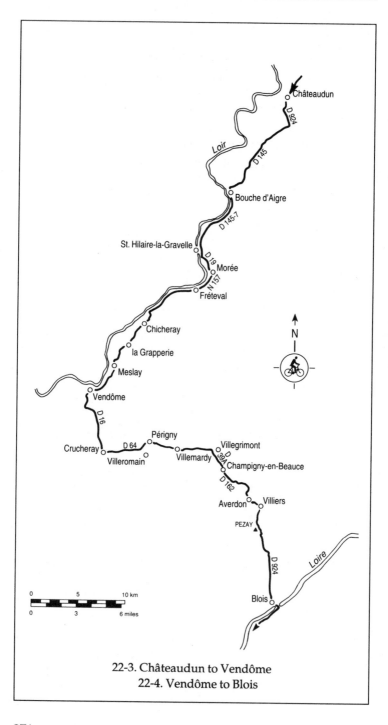

22-3. Châteaudun to Vendôme
22-4. Vendôme to Blois

Châteaudun to Vendôme
45 km (28 miles)

Exit Châteaudun on N10; go to INT with D924, 1.5 km.

Turn left onto D924; go to INT with D145, 2 km. (This road is easy to miss so watch for it.)

Turn right onto D145; go to Bouche d'Aigre, 10.5 km.

At Bouche d'Aigre (a small village), bear left onto D145-7; go along the Loir [cq] to St. Hilaire-la-Gravelle, 9 km.

At St. Hilaire, turn left onto D19; go to Morée, 2 km.

Exit Morée on N157 southwest; go to INT with bridge to Fréteval and D2, 3 km.

Do not turn either way; continue straight, with the river on your right, to INT with D341, 6 km.

Turn left onto D34; go up the hill 11 km to the small road to Chicheray and la Grapperie.

Turn right onto this road and go to la Grapperie, 3.5 km.

At la Grapperie, turn left, then back to the right; go to Meslay, 3.5 km.

At Meslay, turn left; go to the church; turn right and go out past the cemetery through Areines to INT with D917, 2.5 km (from the church in Meslay).

Turn right onto D917; go to Vendôme, 1.5 km.

Vendôme to Blois
40 km (25 miles)

Exit Vendôme on N10 south. Go up the long hill to the turn-out (on your right, a half-moon circle) to cross Nl0 and get onto D16 A.

Cross N10 carefully; take D16 A to Dl6, 1 km.

Turn right onto D16; go to Crucheray, 4.5 km.

At Crucheray, just past the church on your left, turn left onto D64 (sign says *Villeromain*).

Take D64 crossing D957 to Périgny, 5.5 km.

In Périgny, at the bottom of the hill, turn right; go up the hill; turn left then immediately back to the right; go to Villemardy, 3.5 km.

You'll come into Villemardy passing a water tower on your left. Bend through the village to INT with D39 (sign says *Villegrimont*), 3.5 km.

Turn right onto D39A; go to Champigny-en-Beauce, 3 km.

In Champigny, turn right, then back to the left onto D162, direction Averdon.

Take D162 through Averdon to Villiers, 6 km.

At Villiers, the road bends to the right. Continue on D162 to the INT at Château Pezay, 3 km.

Approaching Château Pezay, you will pass large sheds on your right with huge farm machinery in them, such as reapers. Make a dogleg first to the right then to the left, onto D171 which is oposite the gateway to Château Pezay.

Take Dl71 to INT with D924, 2 km.

Turn right onto D924; go to Blois, 5.5 km (to the château in the heart of downtown Blois).

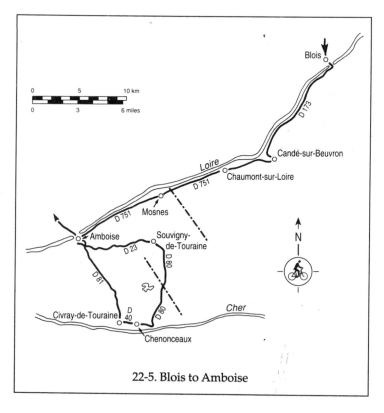

22-5. Blois to Amboise

Blois to Amboise
38.5 km (24 miles)

Exit Blois: Cross the Pont Jacques-Ange Gabriel; immediately turn right onto D751; go to INT with D173, 6 km from the bridge.

At D173, D751 goes left and up a hill; continue going straight on D175 to Candé-sur-Beuvron, 9 km.

At Candé, D173 bends sharp left and goes up a mild incline then intersects D751, turning right as it does so.

Exit Candé on D751; go through Chaumont-sur-Loire to Amboise, 23.5 km.

Note: At Chaumont, the view of the château from the Loire River Bridge is worth a look.

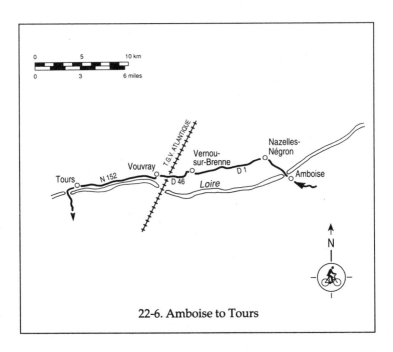

22-6. Amboise to Tours

Optional Ride to Chenonceaux and Back
23 km (14 miles) or 28.5 km (18 miles)

Exit Amboise straight up the hill on D81 (the route out of Amboise is marked with frequent signs); go to Civray-de-Touraine, 10.5 km. (You'll go uphill 8 km; undulating 0.5 km; then down a steep hill 2 km into Civray; be careful going down this hill because of traffic at the bottom.)

At Civray, turn left onto D40; go slightly more than 1 km to the entrance to the château, a road that turns off to your right and crosses the RR tracks.

Just after you cross the tracks, there is a fenced-in bicycle parking area on your left.

You can return to Amboise via the same roads, thus a 23 km roundtrip, or:

Go back to D40; turn right; go through the village of Chenonceaux to the INT with D80, 2.5 km.

Turn left onto D80; go up the long hill; cross D61; go to Souvigny-de-Touraine, 10 km.

Entering Souvigny, you'll pass a cemetery on your left, then a church on your right.

At the church, turn left onto D23 and go down to Amboise, 5.5 km.

Amboise to Tours
27.5 km (17 miles)

Exit Amboise: Cross the bridge and N152; angle left onto the Route de Nazelles-Négron (you'll see the sign pointing the direction). Go to Nazelles, 3 km.

At Nazelles, turn left onto D1; go to Vernou-sur-Brenne, 9.5 km.

At Vernou, D1 bends first to the right, then back to left; crosses a small bridge over the Brenne (a creek), and intersects D46.

Turn left onto D46 which bends to the right and goes under the TGV tracks. (If you're lucky, you'll see the blue-and-silver TGV streaking by at 260 km per hour.)

Take D46 to Vouvray, 4 km.

In Vouvray, turn left; go two blocks south to INT with N152.

Turn right onto Nl52; go to Tours, 11 km.

Note: As you approach Tours, look to your left across the Loire to the twin spires of the cathedral. When you judge the cathedral — no longer in sight—is directly on your left, you'll see a small suspension bridge on your left. This bridge is used by pedestrians and cyclists, and an occasional moped rider. Cross N152 carefully, with the traffic light, and get on this bridge. Go across the Loire and straight past the cathedral on your left—and worth a look inside—to the Blvd Heurteloup. Turn right onto the Blvd; go two blocks and you will be in front of City Hall, in the center of the city.

Tours to Chinon
54 km (34 miles)

When blvd. Heurteloup crosses rue Nationale at City Hall (there's a small garden here with a fountain in it) the boulevard becomes blvd. Beranger going west.

Go to the end and turn left onto rue Giraudeau. Go to the end of this street and turn left onto rue Fromentel.

Go two blocks on rue Fromentel and turn right onto rue Auguste Chevallier [cq].

Cross the Cher river. Go a few more meters then turn right onto Route de Savonnières, D7.

From the center of Tours to this junction with D7 is 3 km.

After 1.5 km, the road you are on, D7, flat as a pancake, straight as an arrow, and heavily trafficked, appears to go up a hill.

Actually, this uphill is D37. D7 angles off the the right. Take this right turn, direction Savonnières and Villandry.

From this turn continue on D7 through Savonnières (beside the Cher river) to Villandry, 12 km.

Note: The world-famous gardens at Château Villandry should not be missed.

Just past the château is the Hotel Cheval Rouge facing D7. Opposite the hotel is a small, tree-lined lane that goes north to the dike.

Turn right on this lane and go to the dike, 0.5 km.

Turn left onto the dike road (D16) beside the Cher which, at the RR bridge, flows into the Loire.

Take D16 to Château Ussé, 19.5 km.

Note: Soon after you get on the dike, you will come to a dip and a 250 m long stretch of road paved with cobblestones. The cobbled portion bends to the right then goes up a small incline to the smooth pavement again. Either ride on the dirt path beside the cobbles or walk the bike. Riding on cobblestones is tough on spokes and kidneys.

When you see Château Ussé directly on your left, turn left and go it, 1.5 km (included in the 19.5 km mentioned above).

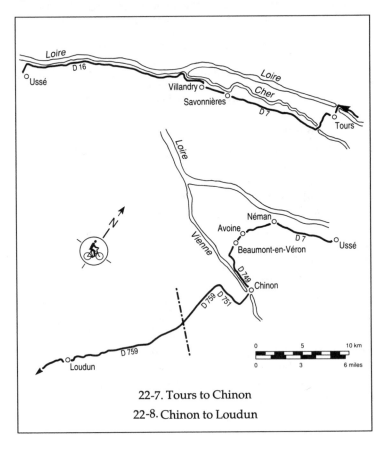

22-7. Tours to Chinon

22-8. Chinon to Loudun

At the base of the garden retaining wall you will intersect D7.

Turn right and go to Néman, 7 km.

You will cross five small hills. After the fifth one, the road will level out. When you get to the edge of Néman, you will see a small unmarked road turning to the left.

Turn onto it, then angle immediately to the right. Go to Avoine, 4 km. (On this very small road you will pass many enormous oak trees with mistletoe in their branches.)

In Avoine, go to the church and turn left onto D749.

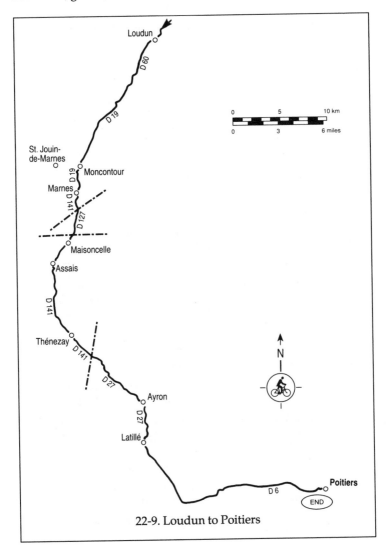

22-9. Loudun to Poitiers

Go south on D749 up the long hill past Beaumont-en-Véron and down the other side to the bend to the left and to the traffic circle, 3.5 km.

Go around this circle very carefully, watching for vehicles turning off to go to Loudun.

Go counter-clockwise 180 degrees and turn right onto D749 to Chinon.

Go to Chinon, 3 km. (The view from the castle is magnificent!)

Chinon to Loudun
25 km (16 miles)

Exit Chinon: Cross the bridge and go to INT with D751, 2 km.

Turn right onto D751; go to INT with D759, 3 km.

Turn left onto D759; go to Loudun, 20 km.

Note: Loudun is more than 2,000 years old. It was a Druid stronghold and place of worship, then a fortified Roman *castrum* in the time of Julius Caesar's conquest of Gaul. The Foulques Nerra Tower is nearly 1,000 years old. The deconsecrated Romanesque church, now a fish market, is almost 1,000 years old. The Martray Gate and town walls, built during the reign of PhilippeAuguste, are 800 years old. Loudun has a vélodrome—an oval bicycle racetrack. There is much to see here, thus the short ride.

Loudun to Poitiers
80 km (50 miles)

Take the loop road to the D60 turn-off and go southwest onto D 60 up the hill and carefully across N147.

Continue on D60 to INT with Dl9, 8.5 km from the center of Loudun.

Turn left onto Dl9. Go through Moncontour where D19 bends to the left. (If you miss this bend and go straight, you'll be on D46 to St. Jouin-de-Marnes. If you make the bend, you ll see the Gendarmerie on your left.)

Continue on D19 to INT with D37, 11 km.

Turn left onto D37; go to Marnes, 0.5 km.

Exit Marnes going up the hill and past the church on your right on D141 which becomes D127 at the boundary then D141 again.

At the top of the hill, just after you pass the church, there is an interesting panoramic view to your right. You can see the old donjon in Moncontour and also the St. Jouin Abbey.

Take D141 through Maisoncelle to Assais, 8.5 km.

The mayor of Assais, having nothing better to do, has made some of the village streets one-way. Ignore this nonsense, but be careful.

In Assais, D141 turns left and is briefly D60, then branches off to the right. Take D141 to Thénezay.

In Thénezay, D141 zig-sags through this small but attractive town; watch for the signs to Ayron.

Exit Thénezay on D141, direction Ayron.

D141 becomes D27 at the boundary. Continue to Ayron, 11.5 km from the center of Thénezay.

At Ayron, D27 intersects N119 and goes east for slightly less than a kilometer, then turns right toward Latillé.

Take D27 to Latillé, 5 km.

In Latillé, D27 bends to the left and goes up a steep hill.

Stay on D27 south; go to INT with D6, 8 km (from the center of Latillé).

Turn left onto D6; go through the Forest of Saint Hilaire into Poitiers, 18.5 km.

You'll go down a hill into Poitiers, cross RR tracks, and to a major intersection. Turn left when the light is green and go a block to where you see the train station on your left.

Take the street opposite the station up the long, steep hill, making an S-curve.

At the top of the hill you'll see the Préfecture on your right and a flowered traffic circle with a fountain in it on your right.

Go around the traffic circle counter-clockwise and turn right when you see City Hall down the street on your right.

Turn to the right; go toward City Hall and you will come to the square that is the center of the city.

Tour 23: *Really* Serious Cycling

Poitiers to Pamplona, Spain, in however
many stages you wish to make it (twelve are
detailed below, but of disparate distances)
Terrain: from flat to awesome mountains.
Total Distance: 627 km (390 miles)
Michelin maps No. 68, 72, 75, 78, 79, and 82

This tour leads from Poitiers to Pamplona
(Spain). The number of stages depends on the ability of the cyclist and
the amount of time at the cyclist's disposal. There are 22 enticing
overnight stopping places, but twelve overnight stops make it a
wholly practicable and enjoyable trip. The notable towns along the
way are listed in sequence. Over the course of eight times along this
route, the writer has stayed in all of these towns, but for reasons
subjective as well as practical, prefers the towns marked with an
asterisk. The accompanying maps show all the towns; the choice of
daily distances and thus of overnight stops is left to the reader.

In sequence: (Starting from Poitiers): l'Isle-Jourdain; Availles-Limou-
zine*; Confolens*; Rochechouart; Nontron*; Brantôme; Bourdeilles*;
Montpon-Ménéstérol;Castillon-la-Bataille*;Sauveterre-de-Guyenne;
La Réole; Bazas*; Captieux; Roquefort (*not* the cheese town!); St.
Sever*; Amou*; Orthez*; Sauveterre-de-Bearn; Saint-Palais*; Saint-
Jean-Pied-de-Port*; Arnéguy [this is the town on the frontier: half in
France, half in Spain. The following towns are in Spain]; Valcarlos;
Roncesvalles; Burguete*; Pamplona*.

The terrain includes everything from absolutely flat to rolling hills to
extremely tough ascents. The scenery is spectacular in the hills and
mountains. At one point, the route follows a mountain ridge with
breathtaking views. Tucked into the hills are Basque villages with
bull-fight rings. One traverses the vast pine forest as well as part of
the Bordeaux wine country. The route includes the region where
Armagnac is produced.

Roncesvalles is a collegium high in the Pyrénées where Masses are
chanted in a 12th Century church throughout the day and night, and
is also where Charlemagne's rear guard was ambushed and de-
stroyed by Basques in the 8th Century, giving rise to the famous
'Chanson de Roland.' Ernest Hemingway had a strong affection for
both Burguete, a Basque village straddling a Pyrénées ridgeline, and
Pamplona, the town famous for the 'running of the bulls.'

The cycling route does *not* follow the train route. To abort this ride,
one must detour to Perigueux, Mont-de-Marsan, or Dax. Although it
requires commitment and determination, it is not beyond the capabilities of any reasonably good cyclist. It has been accomplished by a
nine-year-old girl on a small three-speed bike, and by a 62-year-old
man on a heavily-loaded 10-speed touring bike. It is not, however, a
trip for the faint-hearted or for those accustomed to the psychological
comfort of a 'sagwagon.'

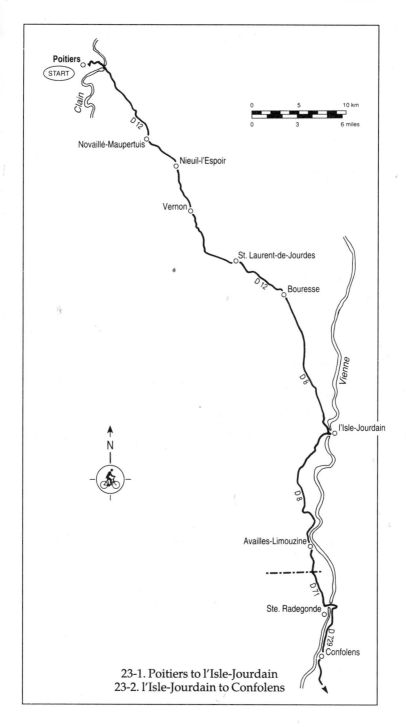

23-1. Poitiers to l'Isle-Jourdain
23-2. l'Isle-Jourdain to Confolens

Poitiers to l'Isle-Jourdain
47.5 km (30 miles)

Exit Poitiers: From behind City Hall (Hôtel de Ville) go down the hill on rue Jean-Jaurès; cross the Clain river on Pont Neuf; go up the hill on rue du Faubourg du Font Neuf which becomes Tour de Nouaille, to INT with D12, 6.5 km from City Hall.

Turn right onto D12; go to Nouaille-Maupertuis, 3 km.

Exit Nouaille on D12; go through Nieuil-l'Espoir, Vernon, and St. Laurent-de-Jourdes to Bouresse, 24.5 km.

When you get to the north edge of Bouresse, turn right onto D8.

Go through Bouresse on D8 and to l'Isle-Jourdain, 16.5 km.

l'Isle Jourain to Confolens
27 km (17 miles)

Exit l'Isle-Jourdain: Cross the Vienne river; go up the hill on D10 to INT with D8.

Turn left onto D8; go through Availles-Limouzine to Ste.Radegonde (D8 becomes D71 at the boundary) 22.5 km.

Turn left; cross the Vienne river and turn right onto D729; go to Confolens, 4.5 km.

Confolens to Nontron
74.5 km (46 miles)

Exit Confolens up the hill on D948 to INT with D59, slightly less than 2.5 km.

Turn right onto D59; go to Chabanais, 20 km.

Exit Chabanais: Cross the Vienne and N141; turn left at the church onto D29 south; go to Rochechouart, 10 km. (D29 becomes D54 at the boundary.)

Exit Rochechouart on D901; turn right onto D10 and left onto D675.

Take D675 to Nontron, 42 km.

Nontron to Tocane-St. Apre
45 km (28 miles)

Exit Nontron on D675 south; go to Brantôme, 22 km, keeping to the old road that leads through the town.

In Brantôme, turn right onto D78; go past the abbey on your right and along the river through Bourdeilles (a beautiful little castle-town) to Tocane-St. Apre, 23 km.

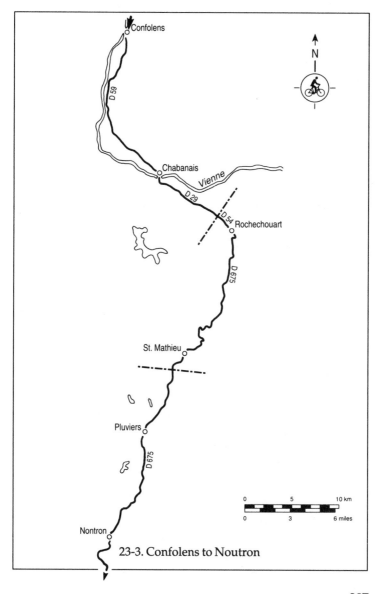

23-3. Confolens to Noutron

Tocane-St. Apre to Castillon-la-Bataille
75.5 km (47 miles)

Exit Tocane: Go west on D710 to INT with D103, 0.5 km.

Turn left on D103; go up the mountain to INT with D109, 6 km.

Turn sharp right onto D109; go along the ridgeline to D43, 6 km.

Turn right onto D43; go 1 km to where D109 branches off to the left.

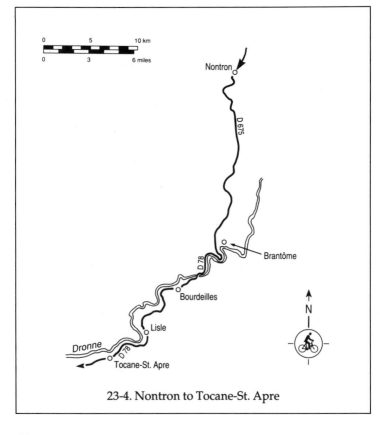

23-4. Nontron to Tocane-St. Apre

Turn left onto D109; go to St. Vincent-de-Connezac, 6 km.

At St. Vincent, cross D709; D109 becomes D41 E and, later, D 41.

Follow this road to INT with D13, 8.5 km.

Bear left onto D13; go to St. Michel-de-Double, 9 km.

Go south on D13 to the 5-way intersection, 3 km from the church in St. Michel.

Turn right; go to St. Laurent-des-Hommes, 3.5 km.

Exit St. Laurent on D3; go to Montpon-Ménéstérol, 9 km.

Exit Montpon on D9 south; go to Castillon-la-Bataille, 24 km.

Note: At Villefranche-de-Lonchat, D9 twists first to the right then sharply back to the left descending a very steep hill. Ride carefully. D9 becomes D21 at the boundary. Seven km before you get to Castillon, a cut-off to the left goes up a steep hill to the château where Michel de Montaigne wrote his famous essays. If you've read Montaigne, this is worth seeing. Just before you get to Castillon you will intersect D936, turn right, and go uphill into town. 'La Bataille' was added to the name because it was here the last battle of the Hundred Years' War was fought.

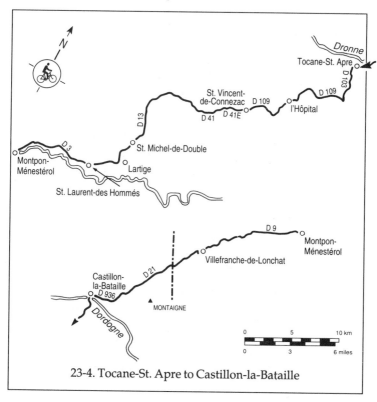

23-4. Tocane-St. Apre to Castillon-la-Bataille

Castillon-la-Bataille to Bazas
65 km (40 miles)

Exit Castillon: Cross the Dordogne river (there's a great view of the city behind you) and take D11 south to Sauveterre-de- Guyenne, 20 km.

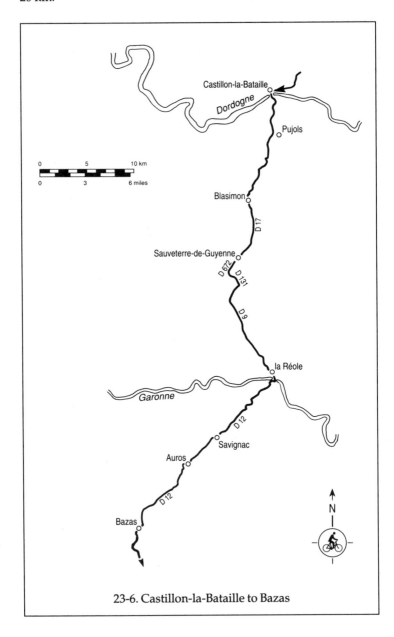

23-6. Castillon-la-Bataille to Bazas

Note: At Pujols, if you detour up the hill into the village and look into the church, the brass plate on the 19th Century organ will surprise you.

Go straight through Sauveterre; exit on D672 which you will have proceedd onto 2 km northeast of town.

From Sauveterre, go southwest on D672 to INT with D131, just a fraction less than 2 km from the exact center of Sauveterre.

Turn left onto D131; cross the Vignaque (a creek), then go up the hill to a junction with a very small road that branches off to the right, 2 km from where you turned left from D672 onto D131.

Turn right onto this road; go to INT with D9, 1.5 km.

Angle left onto D9; go to La Réole, slightly less than 10 km.

Exit La Réole: Cross N113 and D9; cross the Garonne river (look back at the view) and turn right onto D12. You will pass a small airport 2.5 km from the center of La Réole.

Continue on D12 through Auros, where you join Dl5 then turn sharp right onto D10 and, after 0.5 km, back to the left on D12; go to Bazas, 25 km from la Réole.

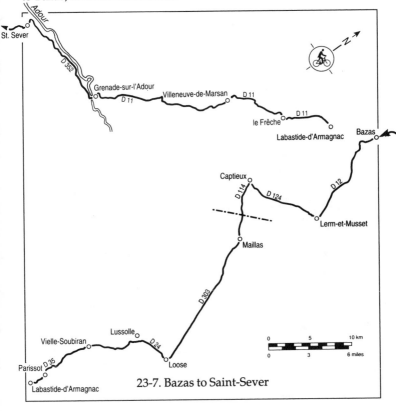

23-7. Bazas to Saint-Sever

Bazas to Saint-Sever
110 km (68 miles)

Exit Bazas up a mild incline on D932 south; go to INT with D12. (D932 goes to Captieux but D12 is prettier and has much less traffic.)

Turn left on D12; go to Lerm-et-Musset, 12 km.

At Lerm-et-Musset, turn right onto D124; go to Captieux, 10 km. (Incidentally, the name of this town is pronounced *cap-see-uh*.)

At Captieux, turn sharp left onto D114, which becomes D303 at the boundary; go to Losse, 26 km.

At Losse, D24 splits. After you pass the cemetery on your right, instead of going south past the church, turn right.

Just before you get to Lussolle, after riding 4 km west from Losse, you will see a very small road branching off to the left.

Take it, through Vielle-Soubin to INT with D933, 10.5 km.

Note: You will cross eight small creeks, dipping down then going back up each time.

Cross D933 and continue to D35, 2.5 km.

Turn left onto D35; go to Parissot, 0.5 km.

In Parrisot, a small hamlet, turn right; go to Labastide-d'Armagnac, 2 km.

Note: This is the center of the Armagnac-making country. Cognac is distilled twice; Armagnac is distilled once. It has more flavor

France has inspired painters for centuries.

than Cognac. Bas-Armagnac is more highly prized than plain Armagnac. The cheaper stuff is in a flagon-shaped bottle; The best is in a Bordeaux-wine-shaped bottle. Labastide, with its arcades flanking the town square and its architecture, is worth inspecting.

Exit Labastide-Armagnac on Dll southwest; go to Villeneuve-de-Marsan, 14 km.

Cross D934; go through town; exit on D11 which briefly conjoins D934 south, then turns off sharp right 2 km south of the center of Villeneuve.

Take D11 to INT with D30, 7 km from where D11 leaves D934.

Turn right onto D30 toward Mont-de-Marsan; go 0.5 km to where D11 turns off to the left.

Turn left onto D11; go to Grenade-sur-l'Adour, 8 km.

Exit Grenade on D11 south; go across the river and turn right onto D352 which more-or-less parallels the Adour now on your right.

Take D352 west to INT with D933, 12 km.

Turn left onto D933; go up the very steep hill into Saint-Sever, 1 km.

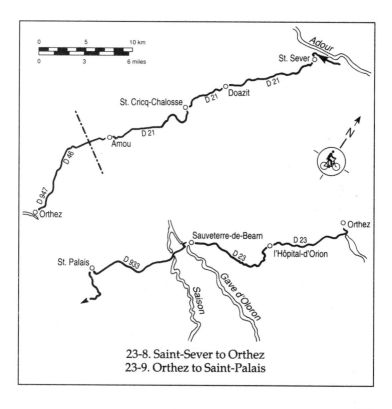

23-8. Saint-Sever to Orthez
23-9. Orthez to Saint-Palais

Saint-Sever to Orthez
42 km (26 miles)

Exit Saint-Sever on D933 south. As you go up the mild incline, just at the edge of town, turn right onto D21. (Incidentally, this is the classic medieval pilgrimage route to Santiago de Compostella.)

Take D21 through Doazit to St. Cricq, 16 km.

Note: The architecture in St. Cricq, a small village, is strikingly handsome. It is worthwhile to look around. There is also a small Plaza de Toros here. Bull-fighting is not legal in France so they pay the fine in advance and have the bull-fight anyway.

Exit St. Cricq on D2 southeast; go 0.5 km to where D21 branches off to the right. You are now in the mountains with spectacular views.

Follow D21 to Amou, 12 km. This is one of the most enchantingly beautiful towns I've ever seen.

Exit Amou on D21 which becomes D46 at the boundary; go to INT with D46, 5 km.

Turn left onto D46; go to INT with D947, 5 km.

You are now on a very high hill. Look south beyond Orthez; you can see the Pyrénées in the hazy distance. That's the mountain you're going to cross. Awesome.

Proceed onto D947; go down the hill (carefully) into Orthez, 3.5 km.

Orthez to Saint-Palais
36 km (22 miles)

Exit Orthez on D947 south.

After you go under A-64, 1.5 km south of town, turn right onto D23.

Take D23 to Sauveterre-de-Bearn, 21.5 km.

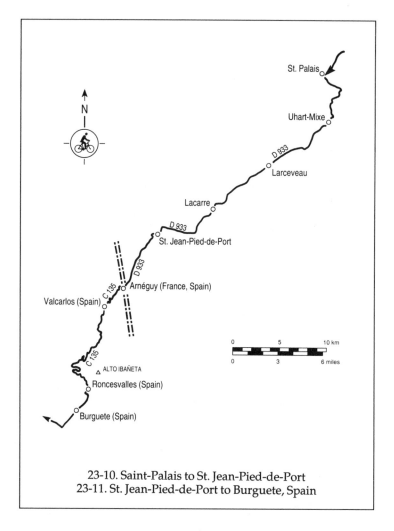

23-10. Saint-Palais to St. Jean-Pied-de-Port
23-11. St. Jean-Pied-de-Port to Burguete, Spain

Note: The Saint Andrew window in the village church is both interesting and unusual. The view across the Gave d'Oloron from the
wall behind the church is breathtakingly beautiful.

Exit Sauveterre-de-Bearn on D933; go to Saint-Palais, 13 km.

Note: Saint-Palais is an elegant town in the shadow of the high
mountains. It is lovely to sit at a sidewalk café here and enjoy the
passing parade and the changing colors on the buildings as the sun
nears the horizon then disappears behind the mountains.

Saint-Palais to St. Jean-Pied-de-Port
26.5 km (16 miles)

Exit Saint-Palais on D933 south; go along the Bidouze river to St.
Jean.

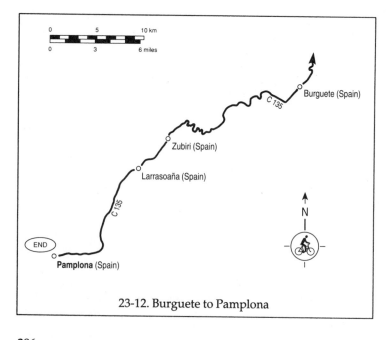

23-12. Burguete to Pamplona

St. Jean-Pied-de-Port to Burguete, Spain
36 km (22 miles)

Exit St. Jean on D933 south. Go to Arnéguy, a small town that strad-dles the frontier. Show your passport to the Spanish frontier guards.

Note: Approaching Arnéguy, you will ride up a long but gentle hill with the Petite Nive (river) on your right. Looking out to the right, you will see white Basque houses with red shutters perched on the green slopes of the mountains.

When you cross the frontier into Spain, you will be on C135. You are now going to ascend a real mountain with many switchbacks.

At 3 km up the mountain, you will come to Valcarlos. Just beyond, the view to your left is exceptionally beautiful.

Continue up C135 to the Alto de Ibañeta, 16 more km. This is where you cross and begin the long descent. It is classically known as the Roncevalles Pass. Somewhere near here is where Charlemagne's rear guard was attacked by the ferocious Basques and his nephew, Roland, was killed because he was too stubborn to summon aid. This gave rise to the famous medieval poem, the Chanson de Roland.

The altitude here is 1,057 meters. It seems much higher when you have ascended on a bicycle.

Descend to Roncesvalles, 2 km. In the old church here in this col-legium, a choir and three priests celebrate High Mass continuously, one after the other.

Descend to Burguete, 2.5 km. This 17th Century village high in the Pyrénées has magnificent views and interesting architecture. The Casa Garate, a tavern, is where Ernest Hemingway used to hang out. The proprietor assumes that all Americans were personally ac-quainted with Mr. Hemingway. Humor him (or her; it's a husband-and-wife team.)

Burguete to Pamplona
42 km (26 miles)

Exit Burguete on C135; go to Pamplona, 42 km.

Tour 24: Au Revoir!

Pamplona to Bordeaux in six stages
Terrain: Mountains; hills; flat roads; and
mild hills again
Total Distance: 324 km (201 miles)
Michelin maps No. 78, 86

This final route takes you from Pamplona, in
Spain, to Bordeaux in six stages. This is an
extension (or the termination) of route 24; it brings the cyclist back to
a major railroad line. It is also, however, a route with its own appeal
and charm.

The route starts in the Pyrénées mountains, then descends through
the foothills. After Montfort, it flattens out and remains flat the rest of
the way. En route to Bordeaux one traverses the Graves wine district
including several of the most famous-name wine châteaux and their
vineyards. Near Hasparren, a Basque town in the foothills, are visit-
able grottos and caves. The Basque church at Louhossoa is stunning
inside and should be seen. If you take the TGV from Bordeaux to Paris,
you'll arrive in three hours.

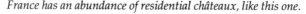

France has an abundance of residential châteaux, like this one.

Pamplona (Spain) to Burguete
44.5 km (28 miles)

Exit Pamplona on C135 north; climb to Burguete, 44.5 km.

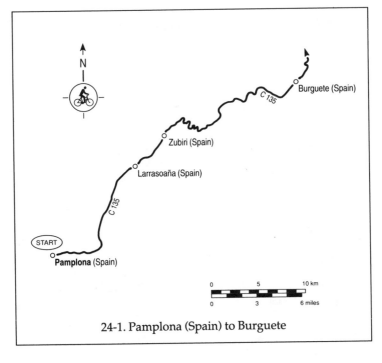

24-1. Pamplona (Spain) to Burguete

Burguete to Hasparren
71.5 km (44 miles)

Take C135 north, over the pass above Roncesvalles then down the mountain to Arnéguy, 31.5 km.

Note: Descending the mountain, control the bicycle by braking with one hand at a time, not both at once. This prevents getting cramps in the thumbs in both hands. You will come to one stretch where, although it's downhill, you have to pedal because of some peculiarity in the field of gravity.

Take D933 from Arnéguy to St. Jean-Pied-de-Port, 8 km.

Turn left onto D918; go through Uhart-Cize and along the Nive river to Louhossoa, 24 km.

Note: Look into the Basque church at the crossroads here. It's most unusual.

At Louhossoa, D918 bends left in front of the church. Go straight on D252 through Mendionde to INT with D22 at Ia Place, 9 km.

Turn left onto D22; go to Hasparren, 7 km.

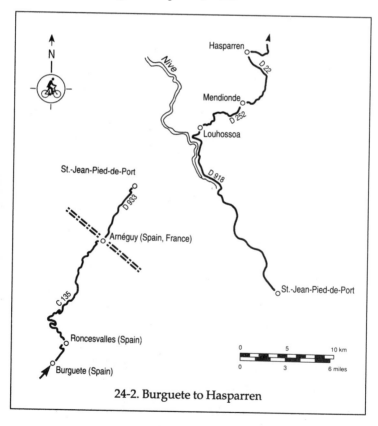

24-2. Burguete to Hasparren

Hasparren to Montfort-en-Chalosse
57 km (35 miles)

Exit Hasparren on D10 north; go to Labastide Clairence, 5 km.

Continue north on D10 to INT with D936, 5 km.

Turn right on D936; go to Bidache, 10 km.

Exit Bidache on D10 north which becomes D19; go to Peyrehorade, 9 km.

Cross N117 and exit Peyrehorade on D29; go to Cagnotte, 7.5 km.

Continue north on D29 out of Cagnotte to INT with D13, 1.5 km.

Turn right onto D13; go to Pouillon, 7 km.

Just as you get to Pouillon, when you pass a cemetery on your left, you'll intersect D61, making a left turn.

Exit Pouillon on D61, passing a swimming pool on your left; go to INT with D107, 8 km.

Turn sharp left onto D107 (later joing D7); cross D947; go to Montfort-en-Chalosse, 14 km.

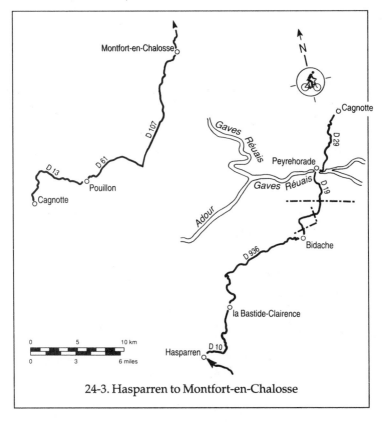

24-3. Hasparren to Montfort-en-Chalosse

Montfort-en-Chalosse to Sabres
54.5 km (34 miles)

Exit Montfort on D7 north; go to Tartas, 15 km.

You are now out of the hill-country and about to enter the great pine forest called the Landes.

Exit Tartas on D14; go through Arengosse, where you cross D38 by turning first to the right then back to the left, and continue on D14 to Luglon, 32 km.

At Luglon, less than half a kilometer toward les Basses, you'll see D327 turning off to the left with one of those wayside crosses in the point formed by the intersection.

Turn left onto D327; go to Sabres, 7.5 km.

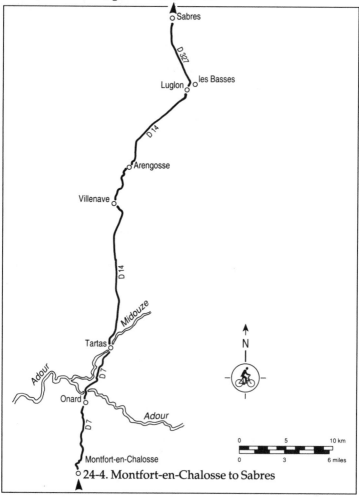

24-4. Montfort-en-Chalosse to Sabres

Sabres to Belin-Béliet
47.5 km (30 miles)

Exit Sabres on N134 north; go to INT with D626, 0.5 km.

Turn left onto D626; go to Commensacq, 10 km.

Exit Commensacq on D34 north; go to Pissos, 12 km.

Exit Pissos on N134; go to Moustey, 6 km.

Exit Moustey on D120; go to INT with D134, 2 km.

Turn left onto D134 (which becomes D110E5); go to INT with D110.

Turn right onto D110; go to Belin-Béliet, 5 km.

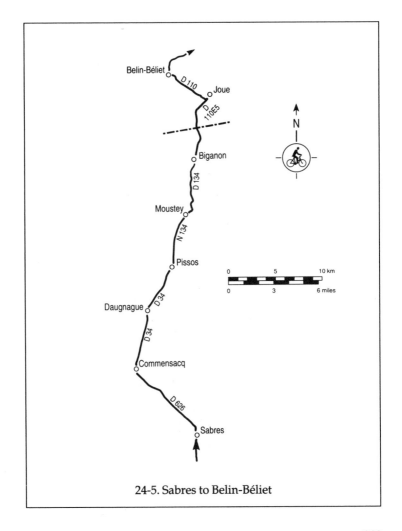

24-5. Sabres to Belin-Béliet

Belin-Béliet to Bordeaux
49 km (30 miles)

Exit Belin-Béliet on N10 north; go to INT D3: turn right on D3 to INT
D111.

Turn left onto D111; go through St. Magne where you cross D5 and
bend to the left, to INT with D651, 25 km.

Proceed onto D651; go through Saucats and Léognan (passing
several famous Graves wine châteaux) to Bordeaux, 22 km.

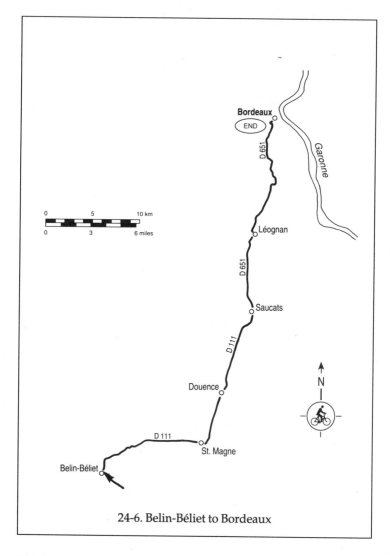

24-6. Belin-Béliet to Bordeaux

APPENDIX

On the following pages, you will find useful reference information that relates to the text of Parts I and II of the book.

Overview Map of France

Metric Conversion

US Customs Information

Dealing with the Postal Service
(includes list of postal codes)

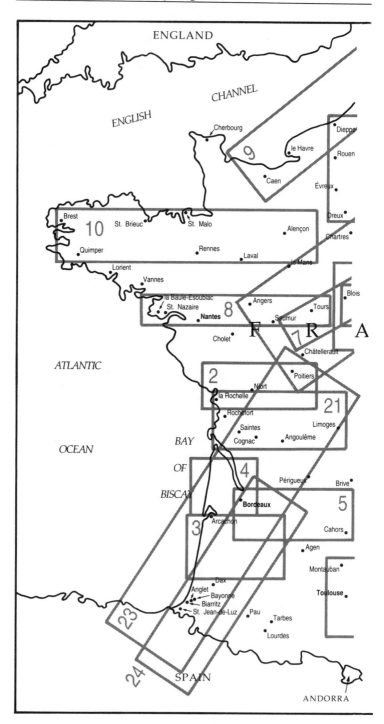

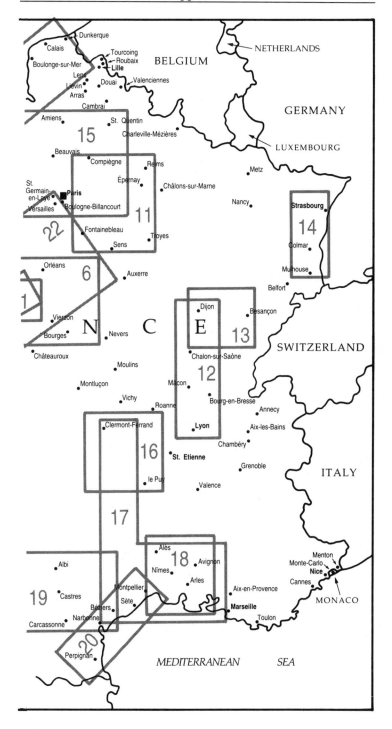

Appendix 1. Metric Conversion

In France, the metric system is used for all measurements: distance (dimensions), weight, and quantity. Because this is an integrated decimal system, based on multiples of ten, one hundred, one thousand, etc., it is far more logical than the archaic system still used in the US, which is based on things too ridiculous to mention. The most practical and sensible approach to the metric system is simply to accept it. But many American visitors to France cannot make the transition so easily. This appendix is for the benefit of those who cannot (or do not wish to) adjust from inches, yards, miles, quarts, and pounds to centimeters, meters, kilometers, liters, and kilograms.

Meters (along with multiples and fractions thereof) are used to measure distance or length; liters for volume; grams for weight. Latin prefixes indicate fractional portions of the unit; Greek prefixes indicate multiples. Thus a centimeter is a hundredth of a meter; a kilometer is one thousand meters.

Distances between crossroads, towns, villages, cities, etc., on France's superbly well-marked roads are given in kilometers. One kilometer equals 0.62 miles. One mile equals 1.61 km.

One foot equals 0.305 meter. One yard equals 0.914 meter. One meter equals 3.281 feet, or 1.09 yards.

One inch equals 2.54 centimeters. One centimeter is 0.39 inch.

Metric units are usually abbreviated. The most frequently encountered abbreviations are:

km	kilometer (also plural)	**g**	gram(s)	**cl**	centiliter(s)
kg	kilogram(s)	**l**	liter(s)	**m**	meter(s)
		cm	centimeter(s)		

Bike sizes in France are measured in centimeters. American frame sizes, measured in inches, have no exact equivalent in French frame sizes because frames are not made in fractions of a centimeter. Here are some approximate equivalent bike frame sizes:

Inches	cm	Inches	cm	Inches	cm
19	48	22	56	25	64
19½	50	22½	57	25½	65
20	51	23	58	26	66
20½	52	23½	60	26½	67
21	53	24	61	27	68
21½	55	24½	62		

Except in the best-stocked shops, it is unusual to find a bike with a frame larger than 64 centimeters because Europeans, especially Mediterranean Europeans, tend to be less tall than Americans. The 64-centimeter frame would fit a person with a 37-inch inseam, and a person with a leg that long would be about 6 feet tall or six feet plus an inch or two, which is unusually tall in France.

One pound equals 0.454 kilogram, ('kilo' for short, is the basic measurement of weight used in grocery stores). One kilogram equals 2.205 pounds. Thus, 500 grams is just slightly more than a pound. If your own weight is 150 pounds in America, you will weigh 68 kilograms in France.

As for liquid measurements, a standard glass of draft beer in France contains 25 centiliters. This is about eight and a half ounces. A wine bottle with a cork in it, the standard-sized wine bottle, contains 75 centiliters. This is 25 and a third ounces. Cheap wine is sold in liter (or 99 cl) bottles. One liter equals one quart plus slightly less than two more ounces, (33.813484 ounces).

Most French roads, especially the older ones, have markers spaced at precisely one kilometer intervals. This makes it easy to determine your speed in terms of kilometers per hour (km/h); you simply note how many minutes and seconds it takes to go from one marker to the next, then convert the total to seconds and divide 3,600 by that total. For example, if you take three minutes and 24 seconds from one marker to the next, that's 204 seconds. 3,600 divided by 204 equals 17.647 km/h. That's also 10.966 miles per hour. It's possible to do this with pencil and paper, but it's easier and quicker to buy a pocket calculator that does reciprocal metric conversions such as the Sharp *Elsi-Mate Metric Converter EL-339*.

Temperatures in France are given in degrees Celsius. This system is now widely used in the United States, but most Americans seem to be more accustomed to the Fahrenheit scale, which, like most of our other measurements, defies logic. On the Fahrenheit scale, plain water at sea level boils at 212 degrees and freezes at 32. On the Celsius scale, water boils at 100 degrees and freezes at 0 degrees.

Whether you are cold or cool or warm or hot, you can generally tell by 'feel.' But forecasts are sometimes handy to know—what the temperature is expected to be tomorrow or the day after, and the meteorological forecasts in French newspapers give these predictions in Celsius. The Paris newspaper *Le Figaro*, distributed throughout France, has the best weather forecast. It is indexed under the heading *Météo*.

To convert Celsius to Fahrenheit, multiple the number of degrees Celsius by 9; divide by 5, then add 32. That does it. To convert Fahrenheit to Celsius, subtract 32 from the number of degrees Fahrenheit, multiply by 5, then divide by 9. The calculator, of course, is quicker.

But again, If you know what the reading is and how you feel, you can relate and extrapolate and adjust your thinking to Celsius. If the forecast says it's going to get up to 40° tomorrow, cancel the ride. That's 104°F. Anything from 16°C up to 26°C (60.8°F to 78.8°F) is comfortable. Below 16°C is a bit chilly; below 10°C is cold. Going the other way, 27°C is hot; 33°C and up is *too* hot.

Appendix II. US Customs Information

Returning from France (or anywhere else), you must complete a Customs Declaration and sign it, whether or not you are a US citizen. Families returning together may prepare a joint declaration with children claiming the same exemption as adults except for alcoholic beverages.

You may declare orally every item acquired abroad and brought back with you (whether purchased or given to you) if the total value does not exceed $1,400. You must state the price in US dollars, or their equivalent in the currency of the country of acquisition. Repairs or alterations to articles taken abroad and returned (such as a bicycle or camera) must be declared, whether the work was paid for or was free of charge. You must state the fair retail value of items given to you.

You must declare in writing your acquisitions when:

☐ The total value exceeds $1,400

☐ You have exceeded the quantity of alcoholic beverage allowed

☐ You are bringing back something for someone else

☐ You are asked by the Customs Inspector to do so. (I have found it simplest to keep a record of everything I buy and the price paid, and to make a list regardless of total value. This simplifies matters.)

You are allowed $400 exemption on personal or household items you bring back, e.g. wine glasses, mayonnaise maker, decals, etc.

There's a tobacco exemption but I'm not going to discuss it because I feel cyclists shouldn't smoke. Nor should anyone else, for that matter.

If you are 21 years old or older, you may bring back duty-free and tax-free one liter (33.8 fluid ounces) of alcoholic beverages. Effectively, this means ONE bottle or wine or Cognac or Calvados or whatever. If you exceed the limit, you must pay duty, internal revenue tax, and possibly sales tax. On all alcoholic beverages, duty is ten percent of the retail sales price. Internal revenue tax is $10.50 per proof gallon on distilled spirits; 17 cents to $10.50 per proof gallon on wine, and 29 cents per gallon on beer. These rates are subject to change (upward).

The duty-free exemption on other items (clothing, books, souvenirs, and so forth) is $400. The duty on purchases or gifts worth up to $1,000 beyond the $400 is ten percent. If you exceed $1,400, the rate is usually 12 percent but can be whatever the Customs Officer decides to charge. (So don't be flippant or haughty. Be serious and courteous.)

Do not be misled by the term, 'Duty-Free' at airport shops whether they are abroad or in the US. Items purchased in these shops are subject to the same tariffs and taxes as items purchased anywhere else. However, once you pass through Passport Control at the airports in France, you do not have to pay the Value Added Tax (VAT) on items you purchase in duty-free shops beyond thse control points. The current VAT is about 18 percent, so that's a considerable savings. (If you buy a major item in France, such as a bicycle or a camera or anything else that costs a lot of money, get a sales receipt. If you take the item out of the country within 30 days of purchase, you can apply for a refund of the VAT. The airports have offices where you can apply for such a refund. It's time-consuming, but on a purchase of, say, a 3,000-franc bicycle, a refund of 540 francs, currently about $90, is worth the trouble. Ruesch International which has offices in several US cities can also help obtain this refund. Dial 1-800-424-2923 for information.)

Prohibited Items: Fresh or dried fruit; fresh or dehydrated vegetables; fresh or cured meats (such as those delicious saucissons secs); seeds of any kind; soil samples (such as a 'little piece of France'); cheese; yoghurt; and live animals of any sort.

If you conceal, fail to declare, or misrepresent any item, it is subject to confiscation and you are subject to a fine or even jail. So declare EVERTHING, even magazines, newspapers, postcards, things you may think are insignificant.

If you are the 'banker' for a large group (let's say ten couples traveling together and they have entrusted you with the money to pay hotel bills, trainfares, and whatnot) and the total amount comes to more than $10,000, even a penny more, no matter whether in traveler's checks or US or foreign currency, or letters of credit, you must fill out Customs Form 4790 (obtainable from a Customs Inspector). It's legal to carry as much money as you wish but you must fill out the form if the amount exceeds $10,000.

One final caveat: You are going to be cycling through the countryside. That's the whole point of the trip. You may be staying at a country inn, e.g. a farm house that has rooms to rent. Thus you will have been on a farm. Indeed, you will have been on a farm (or something like it) if you camp out, or even if you stop to smell the flowers.

The Customs Declaration form asks you whether you have been on a farm. The Customs Inspector may ask you orally the same questions. If you say yes, you will have to have your shoes disinfected and posibly other items as well.

I do not advise anyone to try to contravene the laws of the land. However, I have been visiting French friends who live out in the country, many of them farmers, wine growers, or orchardists, for thirty-seven years. And for the same thirty-seven years, I have let it be assumed that I spent the whole time abroad, whether it was three weeks or three years, in downtown Paris (which is probably a lot less sanitary than any farm: When you go for a stroll in Paris or any other city, watch where you step!).

Appendix III. Dealing with the Postal Service

Every hamlet, village, town and city in France has a five-digit postal code, similar to the US Zip code or British postal code, but placed before the place name instead of after it. Hamlets and small villages often are assigned the postal code of a larger, nearby village or town. For example, the postal code of Savigny-en-Véron is 37420, the postal code of its slightly larger neighbor Avoine. But every place where mail is delivered has a postal code and using the code is important because throughout France there are many little towns and villages with identical names, and many more with similar names.

When writing a French address, remember to put the postal code in front of the name of the town. Every town in France is located in a Département which has a name; Airvault, for example, is in the Deux-Sevres Département, but because of a sensible postal code system, it is not necessary to add the Département name. Remember, also, to add FRANCE to the address. Otherwise the US mail sorters will not know in which country the town is.

Paris is divided in twenty arrondissements, each of which has its postal code. The main number for Paris is 75000. That will suffice if you dont know the arrondissement. The good street guidebooks to Paris tell the arrondissement of each street and using the correct code is, of course, helpful. Lyon also has arrondissements but only nine of them. Again, use of the main postal code, 69000, will suffice.

Finally, remember to write (or rubber stamp, or use the stickers provided by the Post Office) AIR MAIL on the envelope; otherwise it will be sent surface mail and a lot of history will have transpired before it reaches France by boat. Air mail to France costs (early 1992) 50 cents for half an ounce, 95 cents for one ounce, and an additional 39 cents for each additional half ounce.

List of Postal Codes (of places mentioned in this book)

The French Postal Code, the equivalent of the American Zip Code, precedes the names of the town. Add FRANCE on the line below the one with the postal code and the town name when you are mailing from any other country but France.

80100	Abbeville	86150	Availles-	41000	Blois
81000	Albi		Limouzine	33000	Bordeaux
30100	Alès	84000	Avignon	62200	Boulogne
63600	Ambert	37190	Azay-le-Rideau	24310	Bourdeilles
37400	Amboise			01000	Bourg-en-Bresse
80000	Amiens	66650	Banyuls-sur-Mer	18000	Bourges
40330	Amou	44500	Baule (la)	24310	Brantôme
44150	Ancenis	33430	Bazas	29200	Brest
27700	Andelys (les)	45190	Beaugency	31100	Burguete
49000	Angers	21200	Beaune		(Navarra, ESPAÑA)
16000	Angoulême	60000	Beauvais		
39600	Arbois	33830	Belin-Béliet	33410	Cadillac
33740	Arès	62600	Berck-Plage	14000	Caen
13200	Arles	25000	Besançon	46000	Cahors
64220	Arnéguy	34500	Béziers	62100	Calais
		33390	Blaye	66140	Canet-Plage

34300	Cap-d'Adge	63680	la Tour	51100	Reims
33970	Cap-Ferret		d'Auvergne	33190	Réole (la)
33840	Captieux	76600	le Havre	37120	Richelieu
11000	Carcassonne	72000	le Mans	68340	Riquewihr
33350	Castillon-la-	50116	le Mont-St.	46500	Rocamador
	Bataille		Michel	87600	Rochechouart
81100	Castres	43410	Lempdes	17000	Rochelle (la)
71100	Chalon-sur-	44640	le Pellerin	41200	Romorantin-
	Saône	43000	le Puy		Lethenay
38122	Chalons	27700	les Andelys	40120	Roquefort
51000	Chalons-sur-	24620	les Éyzies	12250	Roquefort-sur-
	Marne	33340	Lesparre-Médoc		Soulson
87230	Châlus	13460	les Saintes-	76000	Rouen
60500	Chantilly		Maries-de-la-Mer	40630	Sabres
28000	Chartres	87000	Limoges	17100	Saintes
28200	Châteaudun	86150	L'Isle-Jourdain	13460	Saintes-Maries-
84230	Châteauneuf-	34700	Lodève		de-la-Mer (les)
	du-Pape	86200	Loudun	64220	Saint-Jean-Pied-
37150	Chenonceaux	69000	Lyon		de-Port
37500	Chinon	71000	Mâcon	64120	Saint-Palais
63000	Clermont-	72000	Mans (le)	18300	Sancerre
	Ferrand	53100	Mayenne	49400	Saumur
16100	Cognac	77000	Melun	64390	Sauveterre-de-
68000	Colmar	48000	Mende		Bearn
15190	Condat	12100	Millau	33540	Sauveterre-de-
16500	Confolens	40000	Mont-de-Marsan		Guyenne
41700	Contres	40380	Montfort-en-	67600	Selestat
58200	Cosne-sur-		Chalosse	60300	Senlis
	Loire	34000	Montpellier	89100	Sens
66200	Dieppe	24700	Montpon-	34200	Sète
21000	Dijon		Ménestérol	02200	Soissons
22100	Dinan	149730	Montsoreau	22000	St. Brieuc
39100	Dôle	50116	Mont-St. Michel	33220	Ste. Foy-la-
51200	Épernay		(le)		Grande
24620	Éyzies (les)	29210	Morlaix	15100	St. Flour
76400	Fécamp	68100	Mulhouse	78100	St. Germain-en-
51230	Fère-	41210	Neung-sur-		Laye
	Champenoise		Beuvon	62500	St. Omer
48400	Florac	30000	Nîmes	67000	Strasbourg
77300	Fontainebleau	79000	Niort	12380	St. Sernin-sur-
85200	Fontenay-le-	24300	Nontron		Rance
	Comte	60400	Noyon	40500	St. Sever
49590	Fontevrault-l'	84100	Orange	17700	Surgères
	Abbaye	45000	Orléans	31000	Toulouse
35300	Fougères	64360	Orthez	63680	Tour d'Auvergne
45500	Gien	31000	Pamplona		(la)
70100	Gray		(Navarra, ESPAÑA)	37000	Tours
64240	Hasparren	75000	Paris	10000	Troyes
76600	Havre (le)	79200	Parthenay	41100	Vendôme
14600	Honfleur	44640	Pellerin (le)	78000	Versailles
86150	Isle-Jourdain (L')	66000	Perpignan	40480	Vieux-Boucau-
44500	la Baule	86000	Poitiers		les-Bains
43300	Langeac	30210	Pont-du-Gard	12260	Villeneuve
33190	la Réole	50170	Pontorson	47300	Villeneuve-sur-
17000	la Rochelle	11210	Port-la-Nouvelle		Lot
		43000	Puy (le)		

Index

List of Titles Available from Bicycle Books

Title	Author	US Price
The Mountain Bike Book	Rob van der Plas	$9.95
The Bicycle Repair Book	Rob van der Plas	$9.95
The Bicycle Racing Guide	Rob van der Plas	$9.95
The Bicycle Touring Manual	Rob van der Plas	$9.95
Roadside Bicycle Repairs	Rob van der Plas	$4.95
Major Taylor (hardcover)	Andrew Ritchie	$19.95
Bicycling Fuel	Richard Rafoth	$7.95
In High Gear (hardcover)	Samuel Abt	$21.95
In High Gear (paperback)	Samuel Abt	$10.95
Mountain Bike Maintenance	Rob van der Plas	$7.95
The Bicycle Fitness Book	Rob van der Plas	$7.95
The Bicycle Commuting Book	Rob van der Plas	$7.95
The New Bike Book	Jim Langley	$4.95
Tour of the Forest Bike Race	H. E. Thomson	$9.95
Bicycle Technology	Rob van der Plas	$16.95
Tour de France (hardcover)	Samuel Abt	$22.95
Tour de France (paperback)	Samuel Abt	$12.95
All Terrain Biking	Jim Zarka	$7.95
Mountain Bike Magic	Rob van der Plas	$14.95
The High Performance Heart	Maffetone/Mantell	$9.95
Cycling France	Jerry. H. Simpson, Jr.	$12.95
Cycling Kenya	Kathleen Bennett	$12.95
Cycling Europe	Nadine Slavinski	$12.95
Mountain Bike Maint. and Rep.	John Stevenson	$22.50
Mountain Bike Racing	Gould/Burney	$22.50
Cycle Touring International	Kameel Nasr	$18.95

Buy our books at your local book shop or bike shop. Book shops can obtain these titles for you from our book trade distributor (National Book Network for the USA) and from Ingram or Baker & Taylor, bike shops directly from us. If you have difficulty obtaining our books elsewhere, we will be pleased to supply them by mail, but we must add $2.50 postage and handling (as well as California Sales Tax if mailed to a California address). Prepayment by check (or credit card information) must be included with your order.

Bicycle Books, Inc.
PO Box 2038
Mill Valley CA 94941
Toll free tel.: 1-800-468-8233

In Britain: Bicycle Books
463 Ashley Road
Poole, Dorset BH14 0AX
Tel.: (0202) 71 53 49

"THE BEST ROADS ... G ARE IN FRAN
says author Jerry H ... after having
planned, researched, organized and led ... in cycling tours f
American cyclists for 20 years. In this book, he shares his secrets v
the reader, showing just which of the thousands of minor roads to
choose, where and when to go, what to see and how to get the m
of the French experience. Bring your own bike or rent locally!

CYCLING FRANC
THE BEST BIKE TOURS IN ALL OF GAU

- *Accurate and fully researched route description*
- *Cycling-specific cartographic information*
- *Easy, intermediate and challenging rides*
- *All you need to know for planning your tour*
- *Fully illustrated with excellent photos*
- *Twenty years' experience between these covers*

ABOUT THE AUTHOR
*Jerry H. Simpson Jr. is founder and director of Bike To
France, an organization devoted exclusively to
organizing bike tours in France for American cyclists.
An experienced touring cyclist himself, his specialty ha
been France, where he knows every road and every
town described in this book.*

"The best book on cycle touring in France ever published.

Rob van der Pl
author of *The Bicycle Touring Manu*

Bicycle Books, Inc. PO Box 2038, Mill Valley, CA 94941
Distributed to the book trade by:
USA: National Book Network, Lanham, MD
Canada: Raincoast Book Distribution, Vancouver, BC
UK: Chris Lloyd Sales and Marketing, Poole, Dorset

USA: $12.95
Canada: $16.95
UK: £8.95

ISBN 0-933201-47-

9 780933 201477